I dedicate this book to the Potter, my
Lord and Savior,
Jesus Christ.
This book is written to the vessels
who have been cracked in some way.
The Lord is an amazing potter who
never throws away the clay.
He can mold you, rebuild you, and
even fill you with gold.
If we allow Him, He will mold us to be
a vessel for Him.

Broken to Beautiful

The Journey of a Vessel

Before I formed thee in the belly, I knew thee; and before
thou camest forth out of the womb I sanctified thee
- Jeremiah 1:5

Oh, Lord, thou art our father; we are the clay, and thou our
potter; and we are all the work of thy hand
- Isaiah 64:3

I am confident that we are all alike when I say we
can't remember being formed or molded in the womb of
our mothers. The Lord crafted us into a beautiful vessel that
He could use and placed us into this world. I know that He
had great plans for this vessel. The Word tells us in
Jeremiah 29 verse 11 "For I know the thoughts I think
towards you, saith the Lord, thoughts of peace, and not evil,
to give you an expected end." The New International
Version explains it this way, "For I know the plans I have
for you, declares the Lord, plans to prosper you and not to
harm you, plans to give you hope and a future." Although
God had great plans for me, His vessel, we (as humans)
have free will. Vessels are made from clay and can crack
or even break. Sometimes, we crack our own vessel but
other times, people or circumstances can crack us.

Table of Contents

The Beginning

I am sure I was abused younger than I can remember but the first crack that I remember was when I was three or four years of age. My father asked my mother to take my brother and newborn sister to town. I remember that he told me that I was his princess and that I was going to help him with something. He stripped my clothes off and laid me on a very soft brown blanket on his bed. He put me on my stomach and pulled me to the edge of his bed. My little legs hung off the side of the bed. He stood by the bed and dropped his pants. I can still smell the cocoa butter lotion that he put on my bottom. I held on tight to the blanket with my little hands. I felt the burning on my bottom as the blood began to run down. He raped me that day; he sodomized me. I laid screaming and he just laughed at me. He just let me scream the whole time.

After he finished, he gave me a bath, and there was blood in the bathtub. As he washed me, the blood began to fade into the water. He threatened me that if I told my mom that he would kill me. As a young child, I believed him and feared for my life. After that day, I don't remember going more than two days without him making me perform oral sex or him sodomizing me. This was detrimental to the vessel. This crack was one that wrapped all around me. It broke me to my very core. This not only broke me but caused me to build up walls inside of me to survive. I had to hide my emotions and pretend that I was completely whole when I was so broken. I had to tell myself that feeling safe wasn't important. I convinced myself that I must be a "bad girl" to deserve this from a man who was supposed to love and protect me.

I hid the cracks very well for a child. I began to seek love from others in my family. I had two older cousins that I just adored and spent time with as much as possible. When I was around seven, my two cousins spent the summer with us. One of my cousins was about thirteen and the other was fifteen. I was overjoyed to have them at our house. I imagined that this would deter my father from abusing me as much as he was. About the second week that they were at my house, they locked me in my bedroom with them. The oldest one, held me down while the younger one raped me. Then, the oldest took his turn with me. My little sister, who was in the room with us, sat in the corner and cried the whole time. This was just the beginning with them. After that day, they would stay with us a few weeks during the summer every year. Sometimes, my dad would send me to their house for a week. The abuse continued throughout the years and the cracks began to grow deeper and wider. I no longer felt that anyone loved me.

The Lord knew I needed to feel love. I also needed to hear about the love He had for me. My dad had a friend who was a Christian that would bring his vehicles over to be fixed. He was a children's pastor of a small church in our town. He asked my dad if he could start taking my siblings and me with him to his church on Sunday mornings. My dad agreed to allow us to go. I loved going to church because people seemed to love me. They talked about a God who loved me too. I sang in the children's choir and was at church every chance I could get. At the age of 8, I gave my life to Jesus and was baptized. I wanted to live at church and never go home. Church was the only place that I felt like I was safe and loved. Although this didn't heal my cracks, I felt as though God put a seal over me. This "sealant" held all my cracks together to ensure that I didn't completely fall apart. When I felt that I couldn't live another day, this "sealant" would somehow wrap me up, hold me, and tell me that there was a plan for me. This gave me strength for the day.

Other small cracks began to form around the age of nine. My uncle started coming to my house frequently. He would almost always have me sit on his lap with a small blanket or large coat. He would place his hands in my pants and he would put his fingers inside of me. Sometimes, he would take my hands and put them down his pants. He did all of this while sitting in the living room with my parents in there. I can't understand why they didn't say or do something. My father would also send me to his house to spend the night with him. I would sleep in the guest room or the living room on the couch. When my aunt would fall asleep, my uncle would come in the room and crawl into the bed with me. At this point in time, he didn't hurt me. My uncle would just fondle me and then leave. I feel bad that I didn't tell someone about what he was doing to me but I was happy to be at his house. I felt like I had to choose between being touched and being raped; I preferred the lesser of the two evils. I knew that people would say that it was wrong for him to do this to me but at that point in my life, everyone who "loved" me, abused me. This man must have loved me as well. Most of the cracks that were forming at this time in my life were so deep that I couldn't even see them until I was much older. Some cracks are so deep that they are unrecognizable until the potter starts smoothing them out.

The girls at school started to "like" boys. I couldn't understand why girls would want to be with a boy. I wanted to be with other girls. To me, boys were nasty. I wanted a girlfriend; not a boyfriend. I thought maybe I was a mistake because I didn't think like other girls thought. Everyone around me was telling me that girls were supposed to like boys but I didn't. I couldn't help but think, "Did God make a mistake?" Maybe, just maybe, I really was different. As those cracks formed, I believe small shards began to fall. These pieces were many and very tiny. Only God would be able to put them back together in the right places.

It was around this time that my father started videotaping what he did to me. Some of them he sold but others, he made me watch over and over again to "improve" myself. I already felt as though I was a mistake. Now, I was having to better myself in an area of my life that I didn't even understand. There was one video that he made me watch many times. I can still see the Minnie Mouse sweatshirt that I was wearing; it was pink with silver glitter on it. I would take the shirt and bite down on it so that I wouldn't scream so loud. As I watched the videos, I could feel the glitter in my mouth again. He also hid the camera in my room and instructed me one day what he wanted me to do to my sister that evening. I struggled knowing that I was now becoming someone just like my father. He would watch the videos and if he didn't like what he saw, he would take my clothes off and beat me with a leather belt. If he left bruises on me, I was "sick" and couldn't go to school. This would allow him to do more things to me while the others were gone.

The more I learned at church, the more I knew that I had to obey my dad. I knew God was good but why did He say I had to obey my mother and father. A crack began to spread; I thought God didn't care if I went through that pain. I thought God must be okay with what my dad was doing to me because God didn't stop it. I thought God should have helped me but He didn't. He just left me there in that home with those people who hurt me daily.

School days were hard for me because the teachers that I had always wanted me to sit for long periods of time. The damage that I had to my bottom from my father was absolutely terrible. I would make up any excuse to get out of my seat to relieve the pain. Many times, sitting in the chair would cause me to start bleeding again and I would have to find a way to protect myself from people noticing. Sometimes, I would sneak pads from my mother and take them to school in case I started bleeding. Other times, I would go into the bathroom and take several paper towels and fold them and place them in my underwear. They were so rough that it would make the pain even more intense. My teachers never knew that I was hurting. My teachers never noticed the bleeding or asked me why I couldn't sit in my seat. They just assumed that I wanted to be disobedient and not stay seated. All I wanted was to learn but I struggled because of the pain. I couldn't stay focused on my school work and I couldn't sit very long to listen either. I began to think that teachers didn't care about me either. I truly felt as though no one care about me.

Friends

When I was ten years old, I met my best friend, Jamie. Her father and my father were best friends and they introduced us. She was two years older than I was, but we soon were together all the time. We hit it off quickly and became best friends. She was my first best friend. For the first few months, I stayed at her house often but didn't ask her to stay at mine. One night, while at her house, she asked me why I didn't want her to come to my house to stay the night. I told her that I was afraid that my father would molest or rape her because he did it to me. She had never heard of a father doing this to his daughter. The details that I told her made her sit and cry. She and I sat and cried together. She wanted to tell her stepmom but I wouldn't let her. I told that if my father found out that he would kill me. We came up with a plan to run away but I couldn't do it. I thought that he would just hurt my sister. He would probably even be glad that I was gone. She said that I should let her spend the night sometime and maybe he would leave us both alone. She told me that even if it did happen to her that she would rather it happen to her than me because I was younger than her and much smaller. This was the first time anyone had ever wanted to protect me. It felt as though my walls started to fall for a moment. I tried so hard not to feel but this was different. She loved me. She really loved me and wanted what was best for me. She was willing to put herself in danger if it protected me. I told her that I would have to think about it. That decision was a big decision for a 10 year old to have to make.

After a month or so, I decided that since her father and mine were best friends he wouldn't do anything to her. I finally allowed her to stay the night with me. The first couple of times that she stayed at my house, everything went perfect but that soon changed. One day, it was very hot out and we asked our parents to take us swimming but they were all too busy. That night, after the sunset, my father said that if we got our swimming suits that he would take us to the river. Jamie and I were so excited that we didn't stop and think about what could happen to us. I thought that if Jamie was with me that I would be safe and I was, but she wasn't. My father made me walk down to the river and had Jamie stay with him in the truck. He raped her in the truck that night! I heard Jamie screaming. Her screams seemed to last for an eternity. I tried to go help her but the door was locked. I don't think that I will ever forgive myself for that day. I feel like it was my fault. I should have never allowed her stay the night. Deep down inside, I knew that he would hurt her. I hate to admit this but in a weird twisted way, I was relieved because that was one less time that it was happening to me. How can a person feel that way about her best friend getting hurt? Was I so damaged that I could be like him? I was now being molded into someone that I never wanted to be. I had so many cracks that the potter would never use me for His glory. I felt that I was disgusting. I felt that I was a monster just like him.

Jamie didn't stay the night for about a month after that night at the river. She would sit by me on the school bus but she wouldn't talk to me. Her bus stop was right before mine. Every school day, she would hug me tight, look at me with sad eyes, and then get off the bus. I don't think that she knew what to say to me. After about a week or two, she came to my house and told me that she had thought about what had happened to her. She told me that she thought that she could handle it better than I could. She told me that she loved me like a sister and that she wanted to protect me. We were "stuck together like glue" after that day.

Jamie and I were best friends; we did everything together. Soon, we started drinking together. We didn't feel as much when we were drunk. My parents kept all kinds of liquor in the house and my father would allow us to have whatever we wanted. I knew that it was wrong but it sure helped me to forget things that happened to us. When my father would do things to us, we were so drunk that it hurt as much as usual. It also helped us deal with the pain. We thought we were fixing our cracks but actually, we were making more.

When I was in sixth grade, on November 15th, 1996, at the age of eleven, I thought nothing else could happen to me. I believed that I had already experienced more pain and suffering than anyone else in the world. The abuse happened daily at this point. I was cracked in so many places but still being held together somehow. This day changed my life forever. This day, I became not only cracked but I would have missing shards scattered throughout me and huge pieces of me were ripped out of my very being. It all began like a normal day. I was getting ready to go to school like I did most mornings. My father came out of his bedroom and asked me to run across the road and have my friend Jamie come over. He said that he owed her money and wanted to give it back to her. When I arrived at her house, she had another friend there with her. She had the friend walk to my house with us. Jamie told me that she thought that if the girl came with us that we would be safe from my father. My father met us at the door and said that he was mistaken and he didn't have the right bills in his wallet for Jamie. He told Jamie and the other girl to go to the bus stop with my brother and sister. He made me stay inside the house with him. He forced me to stand by the window and watch them at the bus stop. As I stood and watch the bus pulled up, my heart sunk. I knew that they were leaving me there with this man. I knew that there was no way that my father wasn't going to hurt me. I seriously thought that when the bus was out of sight that he was going to kill me. Many times over my lifetime, I have wished that he would have killed me this day. He silently took his video camera out and set it up on the tripod stand. He took a blue fuzzy blanket off of the bed and placed on the floor against the wall. He placed the blanket between two large picture windows in his room. He calmly instructed me to lie down on the blanket with my head against the wall. His voice was firm and he didn't show any emotion this day. I didn't dare say that I didn't want to because I knew that I would just make things worse on myself. He grabbed the cocoa butter lotion off of his dresser and put it on his penis. He got down in the floor on the blanket with me. Next, he grab my ankles and pushed both of my legs up to my head. He forced himself into my vagina. I actually felt myself rip. It felt like fire on the outside of my body but then quickly spread inside. I began screaming. He started yelling at me to calm down. He said that I was tightening up too much and it was hurting him. I couldn't help but tense up. I couldn't relax my body. My father became so angry that he took his fist and beat me in the side of my head. He told me to stop screaming but I couldn't. I felt him cover my mouth with his hand to stop me from yelling. I couldn't breathe because his hand was so big that it covered my nose and my mouth at the same time. I wanted to die. I was sure my wish was about to come true. It hurt much worse than anything else that he had ever done to me before. I closed my eyes and began to pray. I asked God to send someone to knock on the door and stop him, but no one came. I prayed God would pull him off of me but He didn't. I also prayed that God would just make the pain stop but He didn't. After what seemed like an eternity, he stopped and climbed off of my now limp body. In a stern voice, he sent me to the bathroom to clean myself up. He said that I was stupid because I got blood on his favorite blanket. I left a trail of blood from the blanket, down the hall, and all the way to the bathroom. He told me sit on the toilet until the bleeding slowed a little. He had me put a menstrual pad in my underwear so I could go to school. That night when my mother came home from work, he told her that I had started my period before school. He said that I had to shower and I missed the bus. She thanked him for taking care of me and making sure that I got to school. I always wondered why she never said anything when I didn't have my period the following month. Because of the damage to my body, he waited a couple weeks before he did it again. He would still rape me anally while he waited for me to heal. After those couple weeks, he went back to doing it the same as it did on that day on the blanket. I was ripped opened again and again throughout the years because he never let me fully heal. He never cared how bad it hurt me or how many times that I ripped. He would rape almost daily me no matter what it did to my body.

A few months later, I over-heard some girls talking in the bathroom. They were talking about one of their friends who had been molested by their dad. Without thinking, I turned around and said, "I thought that a lot of dads did that." The girls were shocked that I had said that and reported what I had said to the school counselor. The counselor brought me in her office to confront me. I went into her office and I sat down. I was scared out of my wits but I told her my story. She was the first adult that I had ever told. I had only ever told my friend Jamie about the things that he did to me. I was so scared but I wanted to be brave. I thought that if I told her that she would help me. I thought that she would save me from living like that. She asked me where my mother was when these things would happen. I told her that she was usually at work when it happened. Sometimes, because we lived out of town, my father would ask my mother to go to town for something that he wanted. She told me that she believed that no wife would continuously go to town for one thing just because her husband told her to. I assured her that my mother did! She made a hot-line call into child services while I was in the room. I heard her speak to the social worker. She told the worker that she believed that I was just trying to get attention and that they could take their time on investigating my case. I set there speechless. I had poured my heart out to this lady and she didn't believe me. I felt that no one was ever going to help me. I thought I would be dead before someone noticed that I needed help. The things my father did to me made me feel like I was going to die any minute and this woman told the authorities that I was a liar. I set there shocked at what had just happened. I wondered, would anyone ever believe me? I realized that day that there was no reason to ever tell another person what was happening. I knew that I was just going to have to endure this life as it was. I had lost all hope of anyone helping me.

A few days later, the Division of Family Services called my mother. The social worker told her that they had to investigate a phone call that they had received. They told my mother what I said and then set up a time to come over to my house and talk with me in person. My mother told them that anytime was perfectly acceptable. She said that if anyone was hurting her daughter that she wanted to know about it. When the social worker arrived, my father had a butcher knife and he was sharpening it. He had me sit with him on his lap. When she knocked on the door, my father whispered in my ear that if I said anything that he would slit my throat. He threatened to kill me in front of my mother and the social worker. He told me that the only way I could get out of his house was by death! A social worker named Susan came in and questioned me. Susan asked me to tell her what I had said to the counselor at my school. I had to tell her that I had lied. I was so afraid of what my father would do to me that I told the social worker that I made the whole story up. I told her that I was mad at my parents and just wanted to get them in trouble. I assured her that my life was close to perfect and that I was not being abused in any way. She told my parents that she appreciated their time and left. I watched out the front window as she left the driveway. My heart broke that day. Part of me was upset that I couldn't tell her the truth and the other part of me was angry that she even asked me. Why didn't she just take me away that very moment? Why didn't she save me?

Hoping that I would tell her the truth, Susan came to visit me at school every 3 to 4 months. I never told her what I was going through. I was so afraid that my father would kill me. I was also afraid that she would put me into foster care and leave my little sister at home. Every time that she would see me, she would tell me that she knew that I was being molested or maybe even raped. She would tell me that she could not help me if I didn't talk to her. I continued to tell her that she couldn't help me. I constantly told her that I hated her. Deep down inside, I wished every day that she would just show up and take me away with her. I use to pray that I was her daughter. Susan was the only adult who loved me. As I look back, I wish that I would have told her the truth and allowed her to help me. I wish that I could go back in time and tell her everything. I know that if I would have told her, she would have wrapped me her arms and saved me. I wish I would have trusted her and not listened to what my father had said. Susan truly loved me. She loved me even though my own parents didn't. Susan wanted to protect me but my parents only wanted to protect themselves.

Growing Up

Time was moving forward and I was getting older. I was almost a teenager now. My uncle, that was molesting me, became my favorite uncle. He had been molesting me over the years but I didn't mind it anymore. We had many of the same hobbies so I spent a lot of time with him. He taught me how to draw and how to paint. He was very funny and made me laugh all the time. I knew that I never wanted to be with a man but if I had to be with one it would be him. He never hurt me like the other men in my life did. Anything he would try with me, if I asked him to stop, he would. I wanted him to want me because it made me feel good. He never hurt me like my father did. That summer, on the 4th of July weekend, we went to my great aunt's lake house. My uncle was at this celebration with us. We had a huge barbeque down by the lake. My mother asked me to go inside the house and make some more macaroni and cheese. My uncle said that he would go in the house with me and help me. I put the water on to boil and waited. While we were waiting, my uncle asked me to go to the bedroom with him. He began kissing me, holding me, and then he laid me down on the carpeted floor. I remember wanting him to go further. I didn't want him to stop like I did with my father. He took off his pants and then, he slowly took off mine. He began rubbing his penis against me. He started rubbing himself against my legs. Slowly and carefully, he then began rubbing on the outside of my vagina. You would think that I would have been scared but I wasn't. This man had never hurt me. He asked me if he should stop but I said that I didn't want him to. In a weird way, I wanted it. I wanted my uncle to have sex with me. How could a child who was used for sex daily want it? I asked him to have sex with me. He explained to me he was scared to hurt me because he was much older and larger than I was. I assured him that I would be okay. He had no idea what all had already been done to me. What was happening now was better than my average day at home. He went ahead and put himself inside of me. He was very slow and careful. It was so different from all the other men that had forced themselves on me. He didn't hurt me and, in a weird way, I liked it. This was different because it made me feel good about myself. This time, I felt loved. My body responded in a way that I had never experienced. I felt my heart racing and my insides began to pulsate. He held me for a few minutes afterwards to make sure that I was okay. I started crying after he left the room because I couldn't figure out what was wrong with me. Why did I want that? The mental problems that this caused me is beyond words. It was hard for me to understand what had just happened. I had trouble comprehending why my body felt like that. I thought I loved him. Looking back now, I can see that I was just a child, choosing the lesser of two evils. I believe now that I had developed a form of Stockholm syndrome. Now, I see that I was a victim. My uncle was a child molester, not my lover. I think that my body responded because my brain was trying to cope with the situation. I know as an adult that this was not a relationship like I thought, this was child abuse. This same situation was repeated several times throughout the next several years.

**If you are reading this and have had your body and mind tell you that you wanted it, it is NOT true! As I write this, I hate those thoughts. Many times, when you are broken in such a horrible way, you will tell yourself anything to cope. I told myself I wanted it but I didn't. I told myself that I liked it but I didn't. I didn't truly know what I was doing. This was my life. This is what I thought I was supposed to do. Your body is designed to respond to such sensations and sometimes, there is nothing that you can do to stop it. This reaction doesn't mean that you liked what happened to you. Your body responding does not mean that you consented. These lies are Satan's way of tormenting you. Do not allow it! **

My father was not only abusive to me but my mother as well. He would get mad about something small at least once a week and beat on her. I remember that one night, he called her from the bar. My father told her that he wanted her to talk to a friend of his on the phone. She talked to him for just a moment and then hung up the phone. When he came home that night, he was mad because he said that she had been flirting with his friend while talking to him. He was screaming at her and began punching her. I heard each blow to her body and her screams followed. My father said that she had better stop crying because she would wake us children up. She continued crying while he beat her so he pulled her outside on the porch by her hair. I carefully moved back the curtain in my room and looked out the window to see if she was okay. We had a concrete retaining wall about two feet tall around our porch. As I looked, I could see my father hitting my mother's head on that wall. I watched and cried as he then stomped on her over and over again. Afraid that my father would see me, I climbed back in my bed. A few mins went by and the screams and cries stopped. The sound of her wails ended as quickly as they began. I didn't hear her crying anymore after that moment. I slowly got up from my bed and peeked outside the window again and saw that she was unconscious. He was still kicking her as she laid there on that cold porch. I thought for sure that she was dead. I crawled back in bed sobbing. I couldn't imagine what he would do if he caught me watching. Several hours later, after he went to bed, I looked out my window and she was still there. She was laying in odd position with one arm over her face and her legs sprawled out. She look as if someone had thrown her down and she didn't move from that position. I thought to myself again that she had to be dead. I thought for sure that he had finally killed her and that I would be left for the rest of my life with him. I didn't know what to do about the situation so I went back to bed and cried myself to sleep. The next morning, my siblings and I watched him pick her up and place her in his truck. He drove her to the hospital. My father told the doctor that he found her all beat up like she was. My father said that she had been in a car wreck and he had found her in her vehicle. My mother never told the doctors or the nurses what really happened. She never told the doctors or nurses what my father had beat her. My mother was told that she had a concussion, broken back, and broken ribs. She also had to have several stitches on her head. When my mother came home, she told my siblings and me that she had slipped in the bathroom and had landed over the bathtub. All of us knew that she was lying but we never confronted her. That night, as I laid in bed thinking about the night before, I decided that I would never marry a man. I believed that all men were abusive and hurt their wives and children. I couldn't understand how any woman would ever want to be married to someone that acted that way. I decided that night that I wanted to marry a woman and protect her from this world. If I married a woman, I would be her hero and no man would ever hurt her the way my father hurt my mother. She would never have to live the type of life that my mother and I were living.

My father was always making me do more and more disgusting things. It seemed that no matter what I did, he was always trying something new to hurt me. I felt as though his only goal in life was to destroy me. I was almost 13, when I he told me the specific things that he wanted me to do to my sister. He sat up a camera in our room again one night while she was in the bathroom. He told me to ask my sister to sleep on my bed with me. He made me pretend it was my idea. He said that if she found out that it was his idea then he would punish us both. I was made to do many things that I hated. I was made to ask her to perform oral sex on me and then I did it to her. Then, I had to have her put her fingers in me. I was so disgusted. She didn't know why she had to do it and she was little that she just did as I said. Afterwards, she fell asleep crying because she thought she would get into trouble for the things she did. The next morning, he made me tell him how it made me feel. When I didn't say what he wanted to hear, he became very angry. I had to lie to him so, I changed my story and I told him I liked it.

The Teenage Years

On most school days, my father would drive me to school so that he could rape me in the morning. I missed a lot of school because if he left marks on me, he would make me stay home. Sometimes, I would cry so hard that my face would be swollen, therefore; I couldn't go to school then either. So many times, I would stay home from school because I would be in so much pain that I couldn't function. On days that I was able to ride the bus to school, he would pick me up from school or just send my mother to the store that evening with my brother and sister.

One morning, he told me to ride the bus to school, but to wait for him and he would pick me up after school. I did what he said to do, but he forgot to pick me up. I was still sitting in front of the school when the last teacher came out and locked up. The teacher asked my name and took me into the office. She looked up my emergency contact numbers and then called home. When no one answered at home, she called the next on the list, my grandma. I started crying because I knew that my father would be angry with me. My grandma came to the school, picked me up, and drove me home. When I got out of her car, at my house, my father pulled in right behind her. He jumped out of the truck and quickly came over to me. He grabbed me by my hair and then threw me to the ground. He started kicking me in the stomach and screaming at me. He said that I needed to learn how to listen to him. This was his way of punishing me. My mother just stood on the porch and watched; she never said or did anything! My grandma was the one that was screaming at him to stop but he wouldn't. My grandma finally had to get out of her car, put her arms around him, and physically drag him off of me. I couldn't walk very well for weeks after that incident. My legs were severely bruised, along with my back, stomach, and one side of my face. I am sure that my tail bone was broken that day. A few years later, x-rays showed that I had broken it, but it had healed. I know that this is when it happened because I couldn't do anything without pain spreading through my body from my tailbone. I had to stay home from school for several days because of the pain. My father didn't care that I was in pain, he saw it as a way to rape me again and again. With me not in school, he could now do it more than once a day. He told me that every time that I made him hit me like that, I would have to stay home with him and I knew what that meant. From that day forward, I tried to do exactly what he said to do. I knew that if I didn't, I made things worse on myself. I tried my best to make myself who he wanted so that I might survive. I knew that if I wanted to make it out of his house alive, I would have to become what he wanted of me. Obedience became a situation of life and death.

My father had another friend whose daughter was a year older than me. After she came to my house several times with her father, we became good friends. We will refer to her as Dawn for her privacy. Dawn and I were good friends until her dad suggested that she stay the night with me. My father made us watch lesbian porn and then he had us do those things. Dawn stayed a couple nights and then one night she said that she wanted to go home and my father took her home. She didn't talk to me very often after that. I hated him so much for what he did to her. He would brag to me about how she "was" a virgin and he took it away! He would tell me over and over again how good it felt. He would say that he wished I felt that way still and that I wasn't as good as she was. It makes me sick to think about the manipulation that he was trying to do. It was like he thought the things he told me would make me try to please him more. It just made me hate him even more. I began to see the world through my cracked and damaged eyes. The only thing that I could see was pain and fear in every direction.

During the summers, I had to spend most of my time inside because he "needed" me. He would send my brother and sister outside to play while he did things to me. My friend Jamie still came over quite often. I would spend the night with her, but only once in a while she would spend the night with me. One day, Jamie came over and spent all day with me. My dad was in a good mood so I asked her to spend the night. After Jamie and I went to bed, I heard my father tell my mother to fold out the hide-a-bed, so that one of us girls could sleep on it. Jamie and I were both in my twin size bed. I thought that it was his plan to get one of us in there so he could rape us. I told Jamie that it was my father and my life and that I would deal with it. I went into the living room and crawled into the bed. My father gave me this weird look and then he and my mother went into their bedroom. My mother came out and told me that my father wanted a soda. She hadn't been spending any time with me so she said that she wanted me to go with her. My father walked into the living room and told me to get my shoes on and go with my mom. My father wanted my mother and me to go to the gas station and get him a soda. I tried to stay there by telling them that I was too tired to get dress. My mother told me that it was okay that I was tired and carried me to her car. I waited in the car while she ran into the gas station to get the soda then, we drove back to the house. We pulled into the driveway and she just sat there. She turned the car off and just sat in silence. I asked her what was wrong and she said that she didn't know why the lights were off in the living room of our house. She then said that my father must have gone to bed. She started the car again and told me that she wanted to show me something. She took me to the graveyard where my friend, who died in a car accident when I was five, was buried. After about ten minutes, we drove back home. We pulled in and she looked at the house, the lights were still off. She then suggested that we go get her a soda also. As we started to back out again, the lights in the living room came back on. She stopped, pulled back in, and said that maybe we should just go in because it was getting so late. She was acting so weird. When I walked in the house, the hide-a-bed was messed up and my father told me to just go to bed. I went to my bed and Jamie was crying. She told me that she was okay and that she was glad that it happened to her and not me. I got in the bed with her and then I just held her. We both held each other tight and cried ourselves to sleep. I couldn't believe that I couldn't help her. Anyone who tried to help me was hurt as well.

My mother started referring to Jamie as a slut and a whore after that night. She would say that Jamie was a prostitute and that she would sleep with anyone. My mother had to have known what happened that night! I think that she helped set it up. They had a plan that night to allow him to rape Jamie. There is nothing else to describe the lights except that it was a sign, telling her when he was finished! What kind of woman allows their husband to rape little girls! If she knew about those girls, she knew about me too. The woman that God chose to be my mother and protect me was in on the abuse. She didn't care what happened to me or my friends. Why didn't she love me? Was I such a terrible person that the woman who is designed to love me with her whole heart couldn't love me? What did I do to deserve this? After all these years, I still don't understand why she didn't try to protect us.

There are no words that can express what knowing this did to me. The bond between a child and their parents is created to resemble the bond between the Lord and us, His creation. As a child, we are molded by our parents into the person that we will be as adult. Childhood is meant to form a person into a loving and trusting adult. The mental and physical abuse was forming me into someone who never wanted to be loved. I now never wanted anyone to hold me or even hug me. I thought that if my parents didn't want to hug me and truly love me the way that God intended, then I never wanted love. I built walls around my heart so that the little bit of me that I had left wouldn't collapse. This vessel needed to be thrown into the trash and the potter should have started over but He didn't. Anyone who works with clay will tell you that a piece of clay is never trash. With just a little work and moisture, the potter can fix any piece of clay and allow it to be molded again. I felt as though I was the one piece that was never going to be salvageable. I wish I had an amazing story from this point forward but I don't. My life continued to be worse and the vessel became even more unrecognizable.

Living in the Ozarks of Missouri, my parents took us to the river often. My father would make me walk down the river with him and then he would rape me on the river bank. I hated it when he did this because I knew that my mother must have heard my cries. She never acted like she heard anything. Once, my brother heard me and asked me why I was crying. My father told him that I had been given a spanking because I wasn't listening to him. My mother never said a word! She never even questioned him on the response that he gave. He would also take my siblings and me to the river while my mother was at work. Most of the time, he would rape me behind the truck while my brother and sister were playing in the river. He would have me hold on to the tail gate while he raped me. Sometimes he made me put my hands on the driver's seat while he stood outside the truck and rape me. He always parked the truck where my brother and sister couldn't see what was happening. He would tell them if they got out of the water he would beat them with his belt. If I made any noise while he raped me, he would make it rougher on me until I stopped crying. He would tell me that I needed it to be rougher because I hadn't learned how to take it like I was supposed to. He always made me feel as though the pain that I experienced was my fault. I was so mentally abused that I believed him. I sincerely thought that everything that happened to me was my fault because of something that I had done. I thought that if I was a better daughter then those things wouldn't have happened to me. I look back and see how sad it is that I believed all of his lies.

I wanted to be a better daughter. I wanted to be the best me that I could be. I prayed daily that God would help me but I never became better. No matter how hard I tried, my father was never happy with me. I wondered if God had thrown me away. I wondered if God even existed. I attended church weekly but only to get out of my house. I wanted so desperately to know that God was who the Bible said He was. I would sit in church and hear songs about how God could change anything but He wasn't doing anything in my life. I was being raped daily and on top of that, I was closet lesbian. Church was becoming very hard to attend. God was so silent to me. He helped others but I felt like he wasn't helping me. He created me to be an abomination to Him and stuck me in a family where everyone hated me. God was in control but He wanted me to be where I was being raped every day! I needed Him to reveal himself. I was no longer the little kid who wanted to serve Him because He loved me. I needed more. I didn't want anything to do with "love". I just needed to know that He cared about me. I needed to know that He didn't want me to be hurt all the time. I needed Him to heal me. I needed some cracks filled in. I needed something that I couldn't explain.

When I thought I had lost all faith, my father drove my siblings and me down to the river to his favorite secluded place. He had my brother and sister play in the water and took me on the other side of his truck. He sat me in the driver seat with me facing the door. He stood beside the truck and he was the "perfect" height to rape me. I started praying as he took my swimming suit off. I told God that if he loved me, the way the Bible said, I needed him to prove it! My father bent me over and began to rape me. Just as my dad pushed himself inside of me, a truck started pulling down the hill onto the bank! Not very many people knew where this spot was! I quickly saw that it was a close friend to my dad. I will never forget that day. That is the only time that when I asked God to intervene, he did it that very second! I could never figure out how his friend didn't notice that something was happening when he drove up, but I was so grateful that he was there. Just when I couldn't take life, God showed me that He was right there. He really did love me. He really was with me the whole time. God answered my prayers that day. He showed me that He did care about me. He saved me that day.

At the end of that summer, I told Jamie that I never wanted to see her again. I called her every name I could think of until she hated me. She was crying as she walked away from me. I felt terrible for hurting her feelings but I felt as though I had to do it. I had to treat her so poorly that she would never come back around me again. I had to do this because she had been hurt too many times. I couldn't allow my father to hurt her anymore. I had to love her the way she loved me. I had to put her above myself. I had to protect her the way that she had protected me so many times. My heart ached but I had to push her out of my life. I miss her so much. She was the best friend that I ever had. The last time I saw her, was the beginning of 7th grade.

Moving On

When God begins to give you hope, the devil will always work harder to tear you down. My family moved about 20 miles out of town halfway through 7th grade. We moved into a two bedroom trailer in the middle of nowhere. This new place didn't have running water so we hauled water to use for drinking and cooking. Hauling water was just another reason that my dad had for my mother to leave me with him and to go to town. We lived so far out that it would take her a long time just to go get the water. We also lived so far out of town that no one wanted to give me a ride to church, so I was stuck at home except when I went to school. There was an old trailer behind our trailer that was empty. The trailers were so close that the two trailers actually touched in some places. If my mother or siblings were home, my father would take me into the other trailer to help him "clean it up." This trailer reminded me of a haunted house in a scary movie. It was rusted out, had cobwebs everywhere, and smelled like a moldy cave. He had a mattress on the floor in there along with his favorite sex toys, his camera, cocoa butter lotion, and other things that he chose to use on me. This was around the time that he started getting turned on by my molesting me with objects. He would put many different things inside me: tools, bottles, sticks, sex toys, vegetables, his fingers or anything else that he could find. He would always use the lotion on me or Vaseline for a lubricant. He almost always would let me scream in that trailer. He would tell me that we lived so far out in the country that no one would hear me and even if they did, they wouldn't care. He said that sex was the only reasons that I was on the earth. I would scream the loudest when my mom was home. I would try so hard to get her attention but she never seemed to hear me. She never questioned him on anything.

Even though things were hard, I knew that God heard me when I cried. I would remind myself of that day at the river. I would sit and tell my siblings the stories that I had heard at church. I tried so hard to remember them. I thought that if I kept my mind occupied that I wouldn't focus on how terrible life was. I had to tell myself daily that God was not the enemy. I had to convince myself over and over again that my life was not God's fault. I had to hold on. I had to hold to the hope that God was with me. I had to get through this mess. I had to take every piece of my broken self and keep them together like a jigsaw puzzle in a little tin box. I didn't know how, but I had to believe that one day God would put me back together. I knew there were missing pieces of my heart and some parts of me were battered and torn. Although I was so broken, I prayed that I wasn't too much for God to fix. Someday, I didn't know when, God might be able to create something out of this mess that I called life.

One night, I was laying in my bed wide awake. I was in so much pain that I couldn't sleep. I spent many nights awake during the night. Like most nights, I heard my parents arguing about something. I heard her repeatedly saying "no" then, I heard my mother screaming. The next day, I found out what he had done to her. He had a pump action pellet gun that shot lead pellets. He had stripped her clothes off, stood her against the wall, and started shooting her with the gun. She showed me the next day and she had them all over her back, belly, and legs. The pellets were just underneath the surface of the skin. It looked disgusting. The next night, he came home drunk and took a knife and began to cut the pellets out of her. He removed them one by one. I heard her screaming for hours. I laid in my bed cringing but now I had a new perspective towards my mother. I was living a nightmare in that house but so was she. I somehow couldn't shake the feeling that maybe she didn't save me because she couldn't save herself. I wondered if she felt the way I did that night at the river with Jamie. I wondered if the abuse that I was experiencing was giving her some form of relief. I wondered if she felt terrible for what was happening to me but also felt a sense of relief too. Maybe, just maybe, she felt like she was becoming a monster like him too. I knew that I was young but I still felt as though I had to endure the pain each day to protect her. Each time I was raped, it was one less time that she was...

He bought some pills that said that they would increase a woman's sex drive. The box said to take two pills so, he gave me four. He said that he wanted me to desire him the way he thought that I should. He said that I should enjoy having sex with him and desire it because that's what I was made for. He explained that he thought that the medicine would help me. It actually made me very sick and all I did was vomit for a few hours. He waited a few days and started giving me two every other morning for a while. They made me nauseous but that was it. I told him that the pills were made for adults but he said that they should work better for me then. After a few weeks, he finally let me stop taking them.

My father became friends with the neighbor that lived up the road from us. This neighbor had a daughter that still lived at home. The daughter was a sweet girl around 17 or 18. The girl became friends with my mother as well. For her privacy, I will refer to her as Maggie. One night, my mother called Maggie and asked her to drive my father to get some beer, because my mother was too tired and had to get to bed so that she could work the next morning. The sweet girl didn't think twice and came right over. My dad insisted that he was driving so, Maggie said she would ride along. Maggie could tell that my father had been drinking and she wanted to make sure that he was going to get back home safely. An hour later, a woman and her mother-in-law picked the sweet girl up. Maggie was found screaming and running down the road. She told them that a man was trying to rape her. The two women who picked her up took her to the sheriff's office. There was a trial but my father was found not guilty. There were no witnesses that placed my dad at the scene except the girl. My mother testified that he was home all night on the night the girl was almost raped. After the trial was over, I overheard him bragging to a friend that he couldn't believe that he got away with it. He was so happy that he did it and no one believed he could do such a thing. He was so happy to have them all fooled.

My birthday that year was the worst ever. He sent my mother and my siblings into town to get me a present. He raped me over and over again until they pulled into the driveway. He said that it was his present to me and he was doing it to help me. He said that the more he had sex with me, the sooner that it wouldn't hurt anymore. I had never heard of anything so stupid. I hated it! It hurt more than usual because it lasted longer. Birthdays were supposed to be a celebration but not mine. All I got from my father was pain and agony. I already hated birthdays but this year truly was the year I decided never to celebrate it again.

Once again, before 8th grade started, we moved. Since we lived so close to town now, my dad's friend started giving us a ride to church again. I began working in the children's puppet ministry, and I loved doing so! I was also able to start working with the tent ministry as well. As long as I did what my father asked of me, I could participate in church activities. The only time that I remember being truly happy, was when I was at church or helping in the ministry. I would stay at the altar for a long time after each service. There was something there that connected me to God. It was like the presence of God would meet me there. With me on my knees, and ignoring the whole world, I was face to face with the Lord. No matter how bad life was, while on my knees, I felt love and peace. It was almost as if going to the altar put me in another universe. It was my way of coping. It was my way of going to the potter and allowing him to put another layer of sealant on me. I became almost addicted to this presence. It strengthened me. He strengthened me.

My father started leaving money under my pillow or he would hand it to me when he would drop me off at school. At first, I would always give it back, but he would give it to my mother and she would give it back to me. When I would tell him that I didn't want his money, he would say that I was his prostitute and that he needed to pay me. I think that the money made me hate him even more. I felt like I was a piece of trash. I not only hated him, I hated myself. This self-hatred cut deep. It took this vessel and cracked it down to the foundation. The entire vessel would be built on a base that was uneven and broken. If the potter doesn't fix that, the vessel would never be able to be used. It would never stand up straight. It would never stay where it was placed. This vessel would never be able to hold anything. A cracked foundation would devastate the whole vessel. This hatred would continue to build and cause problems until somehow fixed.

Someone, Save Me

My grandpa (mother's father) came to stay with us for a while. My mother had him sleep in my room. I had a set of bunkbeds so he slept on the bottom bed. One night, I woke up to my grandpa putting his fingers inside of me. I started to yell but he covered my mouth and then stopped. He said that he just wanted to touch me. The next day, I asked my mother to make him leave but she didn't. Every once and a while I would wake up and he would have his hands in my pants or up my shirt. I wondered if I had a blinking red light on my forehead that said, "Abuse me". It seemed that everyone around me had only one thing on their mind, hurting me. With my grandpa around though, my father had a harder time getting me alone with him. Most of the time he would have me go for a ride with him. We would go down an old dirt road in the middle of nowhere. One day, my grandpa was outside playing with my brother, so my dad told my sister to go out there as well. My dad made me stay inside the house. He called me into his room and he told me to perform oral sex on him. When I refused to do what he said, he punched me in the face. I fell sideways and hit my eye on the bed post at the end of his bed. I had an instant black eye. He became very angry with me after he saw my eye. He told me to walk through my brother's room, fall on the floor by his bed, and say that I hit my eye on his bed. I went into my brother's room and fell down about five feet from the bed. When my grandpa came in he saw me crying on the floor. I told him "I tripped and hit that bed way over there." I thought for sure that Grandpa would notice that there was no way I was telling the truth and questioned my dad but he didn't. Everything that I expected to happen, in this situation, was wrong. Grandpa just picked me up and took me to my dad's bedroom and laid me on his bed. He went outside and shut the front door behind him. My father then raped me. He was very rough this time. Resisting him earlier had made it worse on myself.

The school called my house one day and asked why I was missing so much school. They also said that they were concerned that I was being abused by someone, but they didn't know for sure. As I heard the secretary on the phone, my heart seemed to stop beating. The day had finally come where someone would help me. This would be the day that people were able to help me get out. He told them that he was unaware that I had been skipping school and that he would take me to a doctor to get checked out. My mother made me a doctor's appointment and he volunteered to take me. The morning of the appointment he raped me as usual but then, he did something different. He made me get into the shower and sit down. He took a half empty shampoo bottle, filled it up to the top with water, and shook it up. He took off the lid and forced the top of it into my vagina. After he got it about two inches inside of me, he began to squeeze the liquid out inside of me until it was empty. It hurt very badly and stung like fire inside of me. He said that he wanted to make sure that there was no evidence of him left inside of me. After he handed me a towel to get out, the phone started ringing and it was the doctor's office. They said that the doctor had an emergency and that we needed to reschedule. He never did reschedule though. I felt like I was never going to get anyone to help me. I knew then that I shouldn't have gotten my hopes up. Even if the authorities did check me out, there would have been no evidence. He knew how to clean me up from what he had done. Even I they found evidence, he would somehow get out of the charges like he did with Maggie. I was hopeless.

My mom was laid off work for a while. I was happy at first, but he soon found new ways to get me alone with him. He would have my mother go to town for things and make me stay there. He would need special food, soda, or a tool from a friend's house. He would also have her go to town and do the laundry while he was home with me. My siblings went with my mother whether they liked it or not. Sometimes they would want to stay home, but my dad would insist on them going. My brother and sister thought that Dad liked me more, because he always wanted me with him. What they didn't know was that he hated me and that's why I was forced to stay there.

The "special" treatment that my father gave me caused issues between my brother, my sister, and I. I already felt like an outcast but now they began to hate me. They would call me "Daddy's Pet" or "Daddy's girl". If they only knew that I hated being left alone with him, maybe they wouldn't have said those things. I wished sometimes that they knew how good they really had it. They were so blessed and didn't even have a clue. They didn't want to be Dad's "favorite" like they thought. It took everything I had to take the verbal abuse they dished out and not tell them who their father really was. He wasn't a great dad and I wasn't his favorite. He was a monster and I was his sex slave.

My father began switching every few days the way he would rape me again. He told me that this was for my own good. He said that he had to make sure that I didn't get too tight in one specific area. He would tell me that he had to keep me use to it so that it didn't hurt me as bad. One day, he switched places in the middle of what he was doing to me. He started by putting himself in my anus but then after about 20 minutes he switched and put himself into my vagina. After about 5 minutes, he started hitting me in the back of my head. I had had a bowel movement on him and I didn't even know it. He made me wipe off with a towel and then he was much rougher than usual. He said he had to teach me a lesson. He assumed I did it on purpose to make him stop so he raped me for over an hour to prove to me that nothing would stop him.

I started to believe even more that I was just a piece of property. I lived and breathed abuse. It was my only reason to be alive. I thought that feelings were bad and pain was normal. I was always waiting for the "next time". I couldn't even sleep because he would come into my room and I would wake up to him hurting me. I could not use the bathroom when he was home because he would come in there with me and make me perform oral sex on him while I was sitting on the toilet. Showers were avoided at all cost if he was home or expected to be home anytime soon. I became known at school for being the "skanky" girl because I was so afraid to be in the bathroom very long. I also developed severe bowel issues from only allowing myself to have a bowel movement at school if I had time. By the time I was an adult, I could only "go" once every 3 or 4 weeks. Years of "training" did this to me without me knowing it. These were just more "grooves" cut into the vessel that should have never been there. These were all "errors" in His creation that the potter would have to eventually smooth out.

My father started getting bored with me, so we got pets. He would make me hold down our cat so that he could have sex with it. After several cats died, we got dogs. The dogs seemed to stay alive longer with the abuse they were taking. They would die after about 6 months. He would take the dogs into the field next to our house and let them rot there. He didn't even bury them. When one would die, we would get another. Soon after this started, he began making me watch animal pornography. We watched them over and over again. He would make me touch the dog's privates. He would tell me to say how much I liked it and how I wished I could have sex with it. He made me hold down the dog while he had sex with it as well. While thinking back, I can almost still hear the dog whimpering. When the dog cried, I cried too. He would tell me, "Do you want it to be you or the dog?" I know that this sounds bad but when it came down to it, I would rather hold the dog. I would tell him how much I hated it after he was done. My father would always tell me that it was my fault because I wasn't good enough. It made me feel like I wasn't good for anything. In a weird sense, I wanted to be good at it because I felt that was what I was made for. I wanted to be good at something. I wanted to have some form of purpose in life.

Our landlord had some horses that he needed fed for the week while he was on vacation, so my father agreed to feed them. He put them in a pen that was just big enough that they could stand in it. He stood behind the pen and had sex with one of the horses. The horse didn't seem to notice. He made me stand beside him and watch. He did this a few times that week. These moments with the animals engraved images into my head that I couldn't stop seeing and gave me nightmares. I hated animals for a long time. I never wanted to touch dogs, cats, or even horses. The sight of them would cause a feeling of disgust to rise up in me. I would become nauseous and dizzy. Sometimes, these feelings would cause me to have and anxiety attack. It would make me feel like I had done something wrong or that I was going to be punished for something. Animals and/or pets are still hard to deal with sometimes.

Love is Confusing

I didn't have many friends at school, so I would often sit alone but then I met Amie. I just happened to sit by her at lunch one day. From the moment I met her, I thought I was in love. Everyone has their "high school sweetheart" and she was mine. She was the most beautiful girl that I had ever met. I am sure that she didn't even noticed me for a long while. I would sit and watch her laugh and smile. She was so kind to everyone around her. Her hair seemed to be flawless. I sat across the table from her at lunch everyday trying to explain to my head why I couldn't be with her. She had a boyfriend and I kept telling myself that there was no way she would ever be interested in me. As a 14 year old girl, sexually abused by all the men in her life, I wanted a girlfriend. Every dream I had about marriage and children had Amie in it. She was my dream girl. Many times, I would wake up from a dream about her and my body would respond the way it had that one time with my uncle. I was involved in church and knew it was wrong. I couldn't understand why I felt the way I did. My mind and body were lying to me. I had to keep these thoughts to myself. I was gay. Well, actually, I was a lesbian. I was a "closet" lesbian. She was the one that I wanted to be with. I wanted to spend my life with her. Everyone around me told me that I was wrong and that it was not acceptable to be with other girls. I knew that I had to hide these emotions and feelings from everyone. I decided that we had to be just friends and in my heart she would always be my secret love. We became friends but only at school.

One morning, after my mother went to work, my father sent my brother and sister to school and kept me home. He took me into the room and made me lay sideways on the bed. I was crying when I heard the bedroom door open. I looked and saw that it was my mother. My father never even stopped. My mother walked over to the side of the bed, kissed my forehead, told me she loved me, and then left. She just left me there!! She left me there with him. She saw him on top of me, raping me and she still left! The next day she came to my room and asked me if my father was doing anything to me that I didn't want him to. I just stared at her. She said, "I didn't think so!" then, left the room. I don't know why she didn't help me. She didn't even care what was happening to me. Why didn't she love me? What did I ever do that would make her hate me? Do you remember being a young child and playing with Play-Doh? You created something so "beautiful" and then an adult came and "helped" put it away. Without thinking, they picked up your creation, that you were so proud of, and smashed it down to fit into the container. I felt as though I was holding myself together and I was so proud of the life I was surviving. I was taking everything that was going on with me and molding me into a creation that I could be proud of. I thought that I was doing a great job and maybe one day my mother would at least like me. I spend years sculpting myself into exactly what they wanted. I tried not to complain. I cleaned, cooked, and slaved for them. I focused on being the daughter they wanted. This moment, she smashed me down and stuffed me into the container. She didn't care about me or what I was going through. She wanted to take the Play-Doh "mess" and put it away so that she never had to think about it again. She destroyed me and every dream that I had. I was never going to be able to be anything of value to her.

My dad went to the bar most evenings and he would send my mother out when he got back. He started having me use sex toys and vegetables on him. His favorite choices were cucumbers and carrots. He would have me insert them into his anus. I can't understand why but this would arouse him. He would also use them on me. After this, he would have me perform oral sex on him and he would sodomize me. I hated smelling the liquor on his breath. When he was drunk, he would kiss on me more than usual. He would make me kiss him over and over again. I hated the taste of the beer. He would tell me to tell him how much I was enjoying it. He would tell me what to say. If he didn't think that I sounded like I was really enjoying it, he would choke me or slap me until I said that I would do what he wanted me to say. He often didn't remember what he did to me by the next day, because he was so drunk. He would sit me down and ask me tell him everything that he did to me the night prior. He seemed to enjoy hearing what he did to me. I would always tell him just a little bit without details because it made me sick to sit and talk about it.

As I got older, I began getting a little pubic hair. About once a week, he would make me lay on his bed and he would shave me. He said that it made it smoother for him. One time, after he shaved me, he did something that he had never done. He began kissing my thighs and my stomach. He had never been gentle with me. I had never been touched in anyway by him that wasn't painful and aggressive. He told me that I was becoming a woman and that there was something that all women liked. He started kissing me. I hated it. He started slowly moving his way down my body until he got to my private area. He then started licking me and kissing me there. I tried so hard to hate it but it actually felt good. I couldn't believe that I was allowing my body to feel this. I couldn't help but enjoy it. It only lasted for a few minutes then he stopped. He turned me over and leaned me over the bed. He then tried to put himself inside me. He had to tell me to calm down because I was so tight it hurt him to try to get inside me. He told me that he knows that I liked what he just did and that if I ever told that he would tell everyone that I liked the things that he did to me. He told me to tell him how much I enjoyed him. When I wouldn't say what he wanted, he held my head into the bed and pushed himself inside me. I felt like I was going to suffocate. Just as I felt like I was going to pass out, he finished and let my head up. He told me that I was just like any other women, only wanting to please myself. I hated that anything he did felt remotely enjoyable. After this time, he was never gentle again. That day must have been another sick fantasy that he had and he forced me to bring it to pass.

As I went to bed that night, I "knew" who I was. I should have liked men inside of me but I didn't. The one thing that I did like proved that I was different. I truly was a lesbian. I started dreaming of the day that I could move out of the house, run away, and marry Amie. Maybe I was born this way, I thought, or maybe I was just a mess of a person. The one thing I did know was this was who I was. I had finally found myself. The scary thing was, I couldn't tell anyone yet. I couldn't tell anyone who I was. I knew that no one would understand the desires that I had.

Before too long, he started asking me why I hadn't started my period. He said that he wanted me to get pregnant so that he could do whatever he wanted to the baby. I started praying that I wouldn't start because I did not want a baby to be his "toy". He started asking all the time. I asked him why he wanted a baby so bad. He told me that he started making me perform oral sex on him and doing other things to me before I could walk. He said that if I lived through it, then the baby would live also. He said that sex was the only reason that God put girls on the earth. He said that I was made for sex and to please him. A baby would grow up to be his sex slave like I was.

My father never said that he loved me or anything nice about me. He made me be his maid. I had to fetch his clothes and bring them to him in the bathroom. I had to put his shoes and socks on for him; I also had to take them off. I have never even seen my father take his own shoes off! I felt like I was a slave instead of a child. I was also in charge of most of the housework. If things weren't done the way that he wanted, he would beat me, rape me more, and ground me from school and/or church.

Getting Out

On October 24, 2000, my father came home from the bar as usual; he was drunk. He told my mother to take my sister to get her some ice cream. My brother was already asleep. My mother didn't ask any questions, she just did what he said. I begged her to take me with her, but she said that I needed to stay there and help my dad with whatever he needed. After they left, he made me lay down while he performed oral sex on me. I kept telling him to stop but he said that I was supposed to enjoy it. He said that I deserved it for all the times that he hurt me. He was acting really weird. When he finally stopped, he had me perform oral sex on him. He then raped me. While I was getting dressed, he told me that he would not hurt me very many more times. He said that he would start using my little sister soon because she would turn twelve the next month. He said I cried too much and I was too loose for him now. He said I was too worn out down there and he wanted something new. He also said I was to "miss" the bus the next morning and that he would take me to school. I was told if I didn't wake him up that I would pay for it when I returned home from school. I went to bed after I got dressed; I didn't even wait up for my mother.

The next morning, I got my brother and sister ready for school and walked them to the bus stop. I told them I forgot to get a paper signed for school, so I had to run back in. They got on the bus and went to school. I woke my father up, just as he had told me too. He was mad at first because he didn't remember telling me to wake him up. He had me sit down and tell him everything he said and done the night before. I told him everything except what he had said about my sister. He then made me watch pornography with him. I still remember the video that we watched. It was about a couple little girls about 9 years old. These girls were going door to door to sell Girl Scout cookies. They were wearing green and brown costumes. The man told them he would buy their cookies for favors. He then had sex with both of the little girls. I hated him for making me watching that movie. I hate that I still remember the details of it too. Next, he made me perform oral sex and then he raped me. He drove me to school after he finished. He repeated the things he said the night prior. He assured me that soon it would be my sister instead of me. He said I wasn't good enough anymore because I was "too loose for him". I went through the day praying that God would somehow save me. When I got home, I went to my room and sat there until I heard the church bus. I ran down the stairs and told my sister she had to go to church with me. She didn't want to go so I actually drug her out the door and on the bus.

When we got to church, I sat in silence. I was so devastated I didn't know how to tell someone. During the praise and worship, a woman walked up and grabbed the microphone and motioned for the leader to stop singing. I will never forget the words she spoke that evening. She said, "God has a message for someone here. Sisters stick up for each other. They do whatever it takes to protect one another. God has heard your prayers. You need to do whatever you need to do to protect her." I began to cry. A small girl sitting beside asked me why I was crying. I blurted out, "My father is raping me and he is going to do it to my sister." I was so scared because I said it out loud that I ran to the bathroom. The girl I told, then told an adult named Liz. After I came out of the bathroom, Liz grabbed my arm and took me back to the fellowship hall. I will never forget the words she said to me, "You will never go back to that hell hole again!" For the first time in my life, I felt safe. After talking to the pastor, he called the hotline for abused children. I sat there in front of the pastor while he made the call. Liz sat beside me and held me close. He placed the phone on speaker phone while he waited for them to answer. As the lady on the other end said "Hello", I recognized her voice. The pastor explained what I had told the little girl beside me in the church during service. He told her I had admitted to him that I was telling the truth. The phone went silent except a quiet sniffle on the other end. After a moment, the lady replied, "Please tell me her name is Donna". The social worker that answered that hotline call was none other than the great and wonderful Susan. I knew after this point God had answered my prayers. I knew God had organized this night to save me. She said to meet her at the police station. Liz agreed to drive me to the police station to press charges. I gave my story to the sheriff's office and told them I refused to tell it again unless my sister was protected too. The deputy called my mother and informed her that she and my sister needed to come to the sheriff's office. I was in the next room when they told her why she was there. I heard her say that I was a slut and a liar. She defended him and said that he would NEVER hurt me. They took me to the hospital and had a safe sex exam done on me. I had so many scars on and around my private area that they actually measured it with a ruler. The doctor who did the exam actually cried while performing the exam. There was more than enough proof that my story was true. I also found out that I had an S.T.D. (chlamydia). The doctor said that they believed that I had the S.T.D. for around 12 years and because of having it so long that I would never be able to conceive a child. The doctor told the social worker there was severe scaring internally. Her estimate for when the rape started was around 1 year of age.

After the exam, Susan (the social worker) and the officer told my mother she had two choices: she could place a restraining order against my father and she could take us home or she could choose him and they would place us into foster care. My mother started crying and hugging my sister. Then my mother stood up, took a step away from us, and said, "You can have them." My mother did not even say "good-bye" to me. She just walked away and left us standing there crying for her to come back. Susan slowly put her arms around me and told me that everything would be okay now. My mother never turned around. She got in her vehicle that day and drove away. As she left the parking lot, I felt my walls build quickly. I did not allow it to hurt me. Instead of allowing the pain of her leaving to be unbearable, I shut down and felt nothing at all. My mother left my sister and me with complete strangers. She had no idea what would happen to us and she still left. Unbeknownst to the both of us at the time, she finally made the best choice she could for me. When she gave me up that day, she gave me the best possible chance for a life. What Satan meant for evil, God would use it to benefit me. God was there with me. He was answering my innermost prayers in a way I never dreamed could happen. He was saving me. He was taking His creation, His vessel, out of the hands of the people who had broken her down in every way possible and placing her where she could be safe. The Lord orchestrated the entire day to place me where no one could ever hurt me again. This place would revive me. This place could take me and mold me into a beautiful vessel for Him. Although it was the worse pain I had ever experienced, that night was the best night of my whole life.

My New Life

The foster home that they placed us in, was the home of an older lady that we all called G.G. She was about the age of my grandma and seemed absolutely terrifying at first. G.G. wasn't mean though. She was a wise old woman that have very tactful approaches to teenagers. I will tell you this, I always felt safe and loved with G.G. I never had to worry about anything. From the very beginning, G.G. did everything in her power to give me a good life.

They brought my father in for questioning a few days later where he admitted to "having a relationship with me". He said that I seduced him and that it was my fault. He told them that we were just fooling around one day and "one thing led to another" and we started having sex. He also said that he was a paying customer. At the arraignment, he plead "not guilty" and bail was set at $10,000. My mother quickly had a bail bondsmen get him released. He was sent home to await trials. Within a few months, the court process began. My mother would sit on my father's side of the courtroom each time. She never asked me how I was doing or seemed concerned with the mental stress that it was putting on me. During the trials, I had a very difficult time sleeping. The nightmares were so intense that I couldn't rest. They seemed so real to me. I would wake up sweating and sick to my stomach. I would dream that I woke up and that being saved was the dream and that I was back in my house with my parents. It was so real that I couldn't distinguish the dream from reality. I also had flash backs during the day as well. Words that someone said to me, places we would go, or even smells would cause me to feel as though I was back in the situation again. Many times, during the flash backs, I would feel the pain as if it was happening all over again. My body would ache and burn just as it did when the he would rape me.

I had to take the stand and testify about the abuse. From the witness stand, I could see him. He sat calmly and smiled at me. I took the stand as a scared child but walked off the stand as a victor. I was so proud that I was able to tell the truth and I didn't allow him to intimidate me. For the first time in my whole life, I had stood in front of him and was bold. Although most people might not understand, testifying in front of him proved my strength. He had spent the last 15 years telling me that I wasn't good enough but this day, I proved him wrong! I grew up that day. I was no longer a child, I was a woman with purpose! I had so many cracks but as I left the courthouse, those cracks didn't seem so deep anymore. After several trials, he finally plead guilty and was sentenced to 19 years.

I was diagnosed around this time with PTSD, ADHD, Depression, RAD, and Bi-polar. I saw a counselor once a week who tried to help me cope. Almost the whole session was just me sitting in silence. She did her best to get me to open up but I refused to talk to her about the past. At the time of writing this book, only a handful of people know what I went through. As I look back, I can understand the love and compassion the counselor had for me. I am sure that each day I wouldn't share with her, broke her heart. If I had it to do over, I would utilize her. If I could change the past, I would tell her every detail of every event. Talking about it wouldn't make me weaker, it would have made me so much stronger. I wish I could hug her neck and thank her for encouraging me to not be afraid of my past. I needed her even though I didn't understand it at the time.

On September 11, as the world was in turmoil, I met a man named Chris. We were doing a crusade for children in a small town in Missouri and he happened to come with his mom to bring his much younger sister. Chris and I hit it off from the beginning. I was never sexually attracted to him but he became my best friend. Chris and I spent every weekend together. He was several years older than me but I didn't mind. I knew that I could spend the rest of my life with this man and be happy. He was a good man. He loved the Lord, and he loved me. After a few months, Chris asked me to marry him and I quickly said, "Yes". We were engaged for a couple months and then something happened. Chris and I were driving on the backroads of our little town. We were passing time before the Sunday night service at my church. Chris put his hand on my thigh and slowly moved up my leg. He looked at me and said, "You want to pull over? No one will ever see us or hear us way out here." Most girls would have been okay but I wasn't. I didn't hear Chris, I heard my father. I quickly became very scared and panicked. I took off my seatbelt and jerked the door open as he was driving. I couldn't stop myself. Chris slammed the brakes and with his arms stretched over me he grabbed the door and held it tight. This sent me into full blown manic behavior. I became very irrational and uncontrollable. He tried to calm me down but I kept screaming at him to let me out and that I didn't want him to touch me. After a little bit, I was able to calm down. I realized what had happened. I quietly asked Chris to take me to the church. He asked me many times to tell him what had happened but I couldn't. As we drove to the church, it became very clear what I must do. I loved him as a friend and he was so good to me but he didn't deserve to have to spend the rest of his life with me. I knew that I was so broken that I may never be able to be the wife that he needed. I knew that I may never get over the pain and memories of the past. I would have been selfish to marry him. He would never know when he could touch me. He may never know if the words he would say would trigger my PTSD or not. We sat at the church parking lot in silence for a long time. After a while, people began flooding the parking lot. Church members stared at us as they walked inside. Finally, he got out of his jeep and came to my side. He opened my door for me and asked me to go in to the church with him for service. I got out and took my engagement ring off. With tears in both our eyes, I handed him the engagement ring. I told him that I couldn't marry him and that he needed to leave. I went into church with a broken heart and he left crushed inside. For the next two weeks, he called several times a day. I am not sure what kept me from talking to him. Partly, it was embarrassment but partly it was love. G.G. would answer the phone and hand it to be but, I would hung it up. She begged me to talk to Chris but I wouldn't do it. One night, I told G.G. that if he called again that I would talk to him, but he never called. The night I decided to tell him what happen, was the night he stopped calling. God knew neither of us were ready for that part of our lives. God intervened on our behalf that night. Sometimes, God's greatest gifts really are "unanswered" prayers.

God Gave Me a Good Man

October 25, 2002, I was at a kid's crusade helping with the music and games when I had to walk out. I was dealing with the emotions of the day being the anniversary of the day I was placed into foster care. I went to the vehicle and sat and cried. A man that was Liz's nephew came out and sat with me. I had never really paid much attention to him before then. He was so sweet to me. He (Billy) sat and listened to me talk about my life and never judged me. He was just who I needed. Not knowing what the future would bring, I sat and poured my heart out to him. I thought he was there just for the moment but he never left my side after that night. That night was the beginning of forever for us. Billy and I became close friends and spent every moment together. I thought he was a great friend but he fell in love with me and was planning our future together. Little did I know that God would begin using Billy to fill the cracks within me; His vessel. The potter would use him as a tool to sculpt me.

In November of 2002, my sister and I began to spend the weekends with my mother. When I arrived at her house, she lived in the same house from when I was taken away. I went upstairs to my same room, to my same bed, with my same bed set on it. I had so many flashbacks hit me at once that I called Billy and he came right over. He would lay beside me while I slept. I would cry every night. As I cried Billy would tell me, "No one will hurt you. I promise." He was so good to me. We didn't do anything sexual together. He just held me while I slept and when he wasn't at work he would spend the day with me. He helped me through that part of my life.

December 6, 2002, was the first time Billy asked me on a date. I was a little nervous about going with him alone. He told me he wanted to go to a fancy restaurant. I was just a young redneck girl so I asked him to take me to Subway. He was very reluctant but gave in and took me where I wanted to go. Much to my surprise, he proposed to me. This was our very first date, I knew I was gay, and I only wanted to be friends but this man asked me to marry him. To say that I was dumbfounded is an understatement. I told him "No". He kept asking me over and over again. After a few hours, I finally told him that if he would shut up that I would marry him. I was thinking that maybe I could get out of care faster by marrying him. He was such a good friend so at least that was a good start. We didn't set a date that night and honestly I didn't even know if I would follow through with it.

In April of 2003, I was sent home on a 6 month trial to live with my real mom. As soon as we got into her house, she looked at me and said, "You don't really think you are going to live here, do you?" Those words still ring in my head. She still didn't want me. She only wanted my little sister to live there. I still couldn't get over the night that she left me at the hospital and now she was abandoning me again. This time though, I was standing there with no options and she still didn't want me. I called Liz and within 15 minutes her husband, J.D., was at my house to get me. He had me bring everything that I owned with me. J.D. came to my mother's door and said, "Come on, Hun, let's go home." As I walked into Liz's house, she hugged me and asked me if I was hungry. She had me sleep on the couch and the next day I had my own bed in my bedroom. I shared a room with her foster daughter that was my sister's age. Liz never asked me to buy anything. I never had to worry about needs or wants; Liz took care of everything. Liz and J.D. became my "parents". From that moment on, "Mom and Dad" took care of me. I would never have to worry if I was loved again. I was their daughter and that was all that mattered.

After several months, the court system realized I was not completing my 6 month home trial correctly. The court system didn't want to give my parental rights back to my mother. I heard from a friend that if a person got pregnant in foster care, there was a possibility of getting married. I was told that if the father of the child could take care of the mom and the baby, that the court would sign for a marriage license. After this, I decided that I must get pregnant and married to escape foster care.

Getting pregnant was much harder than I thought it would be. I thought that all men wanted to have sex. Billy was different. No matter what I tried, he would not have sex with me. I felt so unloved because he wouldn't have sex with me. He finally informed me that he was a virgin. He was 28 years old and had saved himself for marriage. What kind of man was this? I couldn't believe what he was telling me. He told me that he loved me so much he wanted to wait for me. I didn't understand that. I thought sex meant love. I thought those two things were connected and without sex there was no love. I didn't want to have sex with him but he was supposed to want it. He was a man. I knew I was damaged and no one wanted me but I seriously thought he was different. Would he ever want me? Would anyone ever want me? Was I such a broken mess that I was useless?

After several months, Billy and I were alone. I realized that he was half asleep. I basically raped him. I climbed on top of him and wouldn't move when he asked me to. He tried to convince me to stop but I didn't listen to him. I knew what men wanted and I had to get pregnant. He told me to stop several times but after a moment he gave up. I kept begging him have sex with me every day until I got pregnant with our first child. After I was pregnant, I asked the social worker to have a court hearing to get me out of foster care. Billy wrote a letter to the judge that explained his intentions and his plan for caring for me and his baby. Although I didn't really want to be married, I didn't want to be under the control of the state any longer. Billy seemed to be in love me. He never hurt me, never yelled at me, and never stopped me from doing what I wanted. I thought the best thing for me was to be willing to give this "marriage" thing a try.

On August 22, 2003, the judge released me from the states custody. I went straight to the County Clerk and filled out the paperwork for our marriage license. We had to wait 3 days to for the application to be accepted. Those three days were the most stressful days of my life. Everyone I knew tried to talk me out of marrying Billy. Everyone knew he was a good man but they also knew I didn't love him. They all thought I would one day love him but I just wasn't ready yet. I knew I cared about him but I would never want to be married to anyone but Amie. I was told I could take things slow and Billy's family would help me with the baby. I couldn't let my baby be born without her daddy with her every day. I wanted my baby to have a daddy and mommy that would be there for her. I wanted he/she to have what I never had; a normal family. If being married made my baby happy, I wanted it. This baby would have parents who would love them and put them first; and that is exactly what I did.

Married Life

On August 25th, 2003, in front of very few people, I married Billy. As we went up to the front, Billy looked at me and said, "You don't love me, do you?" I had to tell him the truth so I whispered, "No". I will never forget the words he spoke to me in love. He looked at me with a smile and said, "I will spend the rest of my life trying". I said our vows as fast as I could. I just wanted the day to end. I moved in with him that night and I began to pretend that we had the perfect marriage. My sister also moved in with us. She stayed part time with us and part time with my mother.

We quickly found a way to live together but still separate. He went to work and I would spend time working in the ministry or being with my sister. Billy would try to spend time with me but I wasn't interested. He put so much effort into our marriage but I just couldn't. Every time that he wanted to be intimate, I would cry. I felt like I was a terrible wife. I knew the scriptures and I wanted to be a good wife but I did not want to be with a man. I was already pregnant and saw no need to be with him. This was the way life continued for the next several years.

I tried so hard to hide all the cracks in me. I felt that the more I tried to be normal, the more I fell apart. If I allowed Billy to be intimate with me, I felt gross and would have flashbacks. If I didn't, I felt useless and thought he didn't love me. I struggled with knowing how to get my mind to function. I had constant thoughts that I wasn't good enough, Billy only wanted me for sex, and that God made a mistake when He made me. I would try to stay around upbeat people and keep busy but nothing helped me. I was so broken and gay and none of this was okay.

I gave birth to a beautiful little girl in March of 2004. I began trying to be the best mother I could be. We named her Jayde. I didn't have much of a childhood so Jayde and I learned many things together. I didn't know nursery rhymes so I would sit and read them to her. I didn't even mind reading the stories over and over because I was learning them too. I remember wanting to watch all the Disney movies I could because I had never seen them. I held her every moment I could. She even slept with me. I was so scared to let her out of my sight. I wanted to protect her from what my brain told me happened to little girls. I took her with me everywhere because I was so afraid to leave her. I wouldn't even leave her with her dad.

When Jayde was about six months old, she was taking a nap and I had an appointment to go to. Billy was home and offered to keep her. I didn't want to leave her but I felt like I was letting my past dictate my life. After many instructions on how to care for her, I left her asleep in her crib in our bedroom and went to the appointment. I was scared the whole time I was gone. What if he hurt her? What if he treated her the way that my dad treated me? What if he touched her? The overwhelming thoughts made me physically sick. I started feeling dizzy. The world was spinning and I was worried I would to pass out. I got through the appointment as fast as possible and hurried home. As I walked up to the door, I heard Jayde screaming. I jerked the door open to find that the crying was coming from the bedroom and the door was shut. I tried to get the door open but I couldn't get in. I began screaming at Billy to open the door but he didn't. I finally got the door opened to see the back side of Billy and he was bent over the bed with Jayde screaming underneath him. I ran over to them to find Billy putting cream on the creases of Jayde's legs where she had a diaper rash. She was crying because she didn't want to stay still and he was crying because he thought he was hurting her. I immediately started crying with them. He was a great daddy and I had nothing to worry about. I took her and put the diaper on her and told him what I thought he was doing. He just held me and Jayde and calmed both of us down. He told me that he would never do those things and the thought had never crossed his mind. Billy also explained that the door was never locked but I wasn't turning the door the right way. I was in such panic that I couldn't even open the door correctly. I realized at that moment, I had picked the perfect daddy for my baby. I was so glad I married him and didn't even care if I ever fell in love with him. Jayde was happy and loved and that was all that mattered. God had given Jayde the perfect Daddy.

I felt like I needed God to hold me together more than ever now. I was a shattered piece of pottery held together with Elmer's glue. I put all of my focus on Jayde and the children's ministry. I was married to a man I didn't love but had given up on ever falling in love with him. I hated when he touched me but he was so good to me and Jayde that I felt sorry for him. I faked my love for him. I tried to be what I thought a good wife should be. I still cried all the time during any intimacy but wanted to be the wife that I was supposed to be.

I was thrilled when I found out I was pregnant with my second child. I loved Jayde so much and couldn't imagine loving two babies that way. I had a very long and hard pregnancy. I was on bedrest most of the pregnancy. Billy got a very well-paying job in another state. Billy moved to be able to work and I had to stay in Missouri. Due to being on bedrest, I stayed with my Mother-in-law and Billy would come home to us on the weekends for the last couple months of the pregnancy. Most couples would have struggled with being apart but I enjoyed it. Billy missed Jayde and me but this arrangement made marriage bearable.

In August of 2005, I gave birth to a handsome baby boy. He was perfect in every way. Within just a few weeks, I began having nightmares. These dreams were a daily reminder of how badly I needed healed from my past. These dreams would be of my baby, Jeremyah, screaming and Billy rushing in to find me saying that I didn't know why I did "It". In the dreams, I had hurt my son. I never actually dreamt the details but I knew what it meant. I couldn't figure out why I was having such dreams that I was sexually abusing my own baby. I would wake up sick to my stomach, sweaty, and very angry. This was the start of a very terrible time in my life. My sister moved in with us permanently and began helping me with my amazing babies. I began having anxiety when I would change his diaper. The room would begin spinning, I would sweat, and I would get sick to my stomach. I felt as though I was failing my baby. I breastfed him and that was about the only time I would hold him. Jayde would lay with him and give him what he needed throughout the day. I would limit me touching him as much as possible. My sister would hold him when she was home and Billy would take him when he wasn't at work. I felt terrible that I couldn't spend time with him like I did Jayde. I don't really remember much about him other than a few things until he was almost a year old. It took that long for me to "snap out of it" and accept the fact that I wouldn't hurt him.

When Jeremyah was almost 2 months old, I met a woman in the grocery store in the small town we were living. She and I were shopping with our new baby boys at the same time. She stopped me and asked when he was born and told me her son was just 2 weeks younger than Jeremyah. She invited me over for dinner to allow Jayde to meet her 2 older girls. She hoped they could get to know each other. For the sake of her privacy, I will call her Marie. Both of our families had just moved to this little town and didn't really know many people. There was something about her that I just had to know. I went to her place for dinner at the end of that week. She and I became friends quickly. We both shared interests and hobbies and both of our husbands worked a lot. I quickly became intrigued with her. I wasn't sure how she felt about women but I was falling for her. I still talked to Amie once in a while but was really trying to ignore my attraction to women. Marie made this task almost impossible. I did just about everything I could without crossing the line. I would lay in bed watching movies with her and I even cuddled her on the couch. I loved her. She thought I was a great friend and I kept trying to hide my feelings for her.

We both became pregnant at the same time. I was just about 6 weeks along when she found out she was pregnant too. This made us closer and my mind harder to keep control of. I knew what the Bible said and I knew it was wrong so I simply refrained. About half way through our pregnancies, she had a miscarriage and couldn't take the fact that I was still pregnant. She distanced herself. I didn't see her for the next several months.

In February of 2007, Jaymie (named after my childhood best friend) was born. Weighing 8 pounds 1 ounce, she was the cutest ball of chunk I had ever seen. I had 3 babies under the age of 3. Bringing a new baby home added to my triggers again. I had to work through the dreams, the fears, and anxiety again. It was all I could do to hold myself together. I was attending First Baptist Church and helping with their youth on Wednesday nights. I knew that God could heal me from my past but I just couldn't let go. Every time I would try to open up to the Lord, I would feel love, get scared, and shut down.

Marie showed up to Jayde's 3rd birthday party and met Jaymie for the first time. I began pouring my heart out to her about my past, the triggers, and the anxiety. She began letting me talk through a few things and trying to help me to heal. Although she was just being loving to me as a friend, I thought there was only one way to show love. I began struggling more with who I was and why I was that way. I would lay awake at night begging God to let me love my husband. To help me want him the way I seemed to want my women friends. I would cry out to God and ask him why He made me the way he did. Why did I feel this way? Why couldn't I desire Billy? I would sit and cry out to God after getting off the phone with her. I was gay and not okay in anyway with it.

Jaymie was a very sick baby for the first couple months of her life. By May, we knew something was wrong because she wasn't getting any better. Marie called me and told me that Jaymie's symptoms could be caused from black mold in the house and asked me if I had seen any. I told her that I hadn't seen any in our home. She sent her husband over to check in the basement, the ceiling, and in crawl spaces. He found black mold in many places in our home. We packed up what I could carry and he took me to his house until my husband got home. He and Billy packed the rest of the house up and put it in storage until we could find a new house. Marie and her husband invited us to stay with them so we moved in.

One night, we were watching a movie. Our husbands were both at work and the kids were laying down for bed. She was getting hot and took off her hoodie and bra and just left a tank on and I did the same. I snuggled up against her, put the blanket over us, and felt normal. For the first time, in a long time I felt perfect. I couldn't take it anymore and was about to give in so I prayed, "God, I feel like this is normal, but I know it's not. Help me." She looked at me and asked if I was okay. As she was looking at me, I leaned over to kiss her. I got very close to her and then just paused. As I did, her oldest daughter knocked on the door and she jerked back. She said she needed Marie for something and couldn't open the door because it was locked. We both could not figure out why it was locked. I knew God had saved me from messing up my friendship. I asked for help, and He gave it. The next day, we were making lunch for our babies and she said she had something to tell me. She told me she hoped that I didn't judge her but she had been with a woman before. That's all she said before our children came into the room. I know now that God was stopping me and her from making a terrible mistake. He protected us.

We moved into the first house we could find. After that night, I had to get out of there. We only stayed at their house a couple weeks but that was almost too long. I couldn't control my thoughts. Several times, that night would come up in conversation when we were alone but it always got interrupted by our kids coming into the room. It was never talked about. I started distancing myself from her. I had to because I was afraid of what might happen if I didn't. We stayed very close friends though through phone calls and meeting each other in public places and God protected our friendship.

Every year since I was 15, I have went to church camp. Even after I became too old to be a camper, I still went and helped out. I loved taking my children to camp as well. My children grew up through the years at this same camp. When my children were too little to run around and play, I would just carry them with me as I worked throughout the campground. One day I was walking across the campground and it began to rain. Jaymie was only 4 months old and it was a cold rain hitting us. I began running across the campground to get us out of the rain. As I ran down the hill, I twisted my ankle and fell to the ground. I held Jaymie up to keep her from hitting the ground as we fell. I heard a loud pop in my ankle and I couldn't move it. As a teenager ran pass me, I yelled for help. I asked that they take Jaymie in out of the rain quickly. A few other teenage boys ran to me to help me up. I tried to walk but the pain was too much. I had to have someone help me to the nurse. With my boot removed, I could see that my ankle was severely injured. The nurse said that I needed to get an x-ray because she believed it was broken. In the short time it had taken me to get to the nurse, my ankle was very bruised and swollen. I refused to leave camp because of the ankle. I took some ibuprofen and iced my foot often. The nurse told me that she was pretty certain that she could feel a break in my ankle. She explained to me that waiting to get medical attention may result in it healing back wrong and needing it to be re-broke to heal properly. I was very determined to stay at camp.

The next day after a service, I needed to leave the chapel and go to the snack shack to work. My little sister helped me out the door. I was hopping on my foot and holding on to her to get outside. As I stepped off the porch, I heard a voice within me say, "RUN!" I turned to my sister and told her what I thought I heard. My sister told me that if I couldn't walk then I surely couldn't run. She also told me she believed I was crazy. Within a few seconds, I heard it again. I laughed aloud at the thoughts I was having. I few moments later, I heard a loud stern, "RUN". I told my sister that I may be crazy but I have to listen. I began to run. It was the most pain that I had ever felt in my body. At first, I thought that I would fall but I didn't. I finally reached the snack shack and I realized something. I quickly realized that I was not in any pain at all! I ran back to the chapel and went to the nurse. I told her what happened and she looked at my foot. The swelling was gone out of my ankle and the bruising was very minimal. God healed my ankle that day. After camp ended, I was driving home and the kids were asleep. I began thanking God for what He did for me. As I was driving, the Lord spoke to my heart. I heard this, "If you will trust me and obey me, just like your ankle, it may hurt at first but I will heal every part of you." I really didn't understand what God was saying to me. I wish that I would have fully trusted God to heal me that day.

In the spring of 2008, I found out that I was pregnant again. This was number 4 for us. In April, we moved back to Missouri. I loved being around Billy's family again and adored the church there but being back in my hometown made life hard. I hated the memories that came with that town. I couldn't go anywhere without running into an old friend of my parents. Missouri also brought me closer to Amie. I was pregnant with my 4th and she had just had her 5th. We didn't really hang out together but the thoughts were much stronger knowing how close she was. We would spend hours on the phone together and text as much as possible. The more this happened, the more that I hated my marriage. I felt as though my whole life was one giant lie.

I made a huge decision. I would simply decide not to be a lesbian. I also declared that I would be happily married and work in ministry the rest of my life. I felt if I just decided to do something, it would happen. I began doing everything I could for God. I thought that if I was good enough than God would heal me. If I was good enough, God would fix me.

Around the fifth month of pregnancy, I had a doctor's appointment. I was so excited to find out if we were expecting a boy or girl. As the nurse performed the ultrasound, she had a puzzled look on her face. She kept asking me how many weeks along I was and the heart rates of the baby at each visit. After about an hour, she excused herself from the room. I laid there alone and tried to understand what was going on. The nurse came back into my room with my doctor. My doctor sat down with me and began the ultrasound again. He looked over at the nurse and told her that he had been seeing me regularly and that he knew for sure that I was indeed almost five months pregnant. As he performed the procedure he was very quiet. He then wiped off my stomach with a warm cloth and asked me to come into his office. Another nurse escorted me, and sat with me while I waited. My doctor came in with my charts and he was shaking his head. I was so nervous. What was wrong with my baby? What was wrong with me? Was he/she okay?

His first words to me were scary. He looked at me with a weird look and said, "I think it might be a girl but I am really unsure. I can't tell a whole lot about it." I was dumb-founded. Why couldn't he tell? What was going on? He sat in his chair and began a very long and drawn out explanation. Although the heart rate had been normal each time, she was not growing. He said that her size was that of a fetus that was around 4-6 weeks along. She was very under developed. His advice for me was an abortion. He said that he was a Christian man of 7 children and fully understood how hard a decision like this would be. He told me that aborting the "fetus" was the best thing I could do. According to his expert opinion, if she were born, she would never live a normal life. He said that odds were that if my body didn't abort her, she would die moments after birth. He said if by chance she lived past the first day of life, she would need constant care for the rest of her life. He explained she would never walk, talk, or even eat on her own. She would basically be in a vegetative state the rest of her life. He also told me that allowing her to live a life like that would be selfish and ungodly. Without even thinking about what he was saying, I simply said, "No. I am carrying this baby with or without your help." I asked him to run blood test to see what could be causing the issue. I wanted to know what I could do to help her. He thought I was crazy but drew blood before I could leave.

Leaving the office that day, I knew what I had to do. I had to carry a healthy baby. As I walked to the car, I placed my hands on my stomach and said a silent prayer, "Lord, this baby is yours and I will do whatever I need to keep her safe. Please heal my baby." I explained to Billy what the doctor had said and the extreme state our baby was in. I prayed over her daily and tried my best to eat well and exert as less energy as possible. I wanted my body to focus on the baby. We were determined she would make it. Jynna Danielle would be her sweet name. Danielle for Daniel who never backed down from a challenge. Daniel was brave and this baby girl would have to be brave and courageous too.

After about a week, the test results were back and the doctor's nurse called me on the phone. They found that I had 2 blood disorders that were causing blood clots throughout the umbilical cord and also in the placenta. Jynna wasn't growing because she wasn't receiving blood that carried oxygen and nutrients to her. He said that carrying her to full term would most likely result in me having a massive stroke and/or a heart attack from all the blood clots that were in my body. He recommended that for the sake of my life, that I abort the pregnancy and that I start on blood thinner injections immediately. I told him that aborting my baby was not an option but that I would do the injections. He recommended that I also go on light duty or a bed rest. He was concerned that as the blood clots broke up that I or the baby would have adverse effects. I started the injections that very day.

The months passed very slowly. I had to have someone give me a shot in my abdomen every few hours. I was placed on strict bed rest towards the end so being a mother of 3 was complicated. Billy's family stepped right up and helped me through it. I prayed over her every single day and thanked God for such an amazing baby girl.

In November of 2008, Jynna made her grand appearance. Jynna came so fast that the doctor did not have time to get to my room. A nurse that had only been working there a few days was the only one that was in the room. Without pushing at all, Jynna was born. They nurse quickly handed her to me and as she proceeded to cut the cord. I grabbed her and covered her up with the sheet I had. She was so quiet and calm. As the nurse was getting the placenta, the doctor came in. He said that he needed the nurse to prep her for flight because she only had a chance at life if they flew her to St. Louis immediately. Another nurse, took Jynna and Billy followed her out. The doctor showed the placenta to the nurses and to me. It looked like it had small dark bouncy balls attached to it. You could see all the blood clots. The doctor said that if the baby lived it would be a miracle. Within about 10 minutes, Billy and the nurse returned pushing Jynna in the rolling hospital crib. The nurse took her out and went to hand her to Billy. Billy told her to give Jynna to her momma. As I held her, the doctor said that she was 100% healthy. They couldn't find anything wrong with her. I told them that God healed her. My baby was a miracle from the Lord.

Jynna grew up but was not normal. Jynna talked and walked early. By the time she was a year old, she knew her colors and could count to 10. She was completely potty-trained by 16 months. Doctors could not believe how smart she was. When God heals, He goes over and beyond what we could ever want or even dream. I knew that God was the healer. I had proof now. I had not just heard about such healing, I experienced it. He was no longer the God of the old times; He was the God of now! I realized that the miracles in the Bible were for today. I knew that no matter how unworthy or sinful I was that God still loved me. He loved me so much that he answered my prayers. He loved me so much that he healed my precious baby. He was my healer! My God was a healer!

I intensely began seeking God for my healing after this. I knew that God was a healer and I wanted to be healed. I would lay in bed and beg God to fix me. I wanted to be a vessel for Him. I was so damaged and I wanted Him to step in and heal me. I still struggled with being with Billy and would silently cry during intercourse. I tried my best to not think about Amie. I tried to not watch any movies or listen to music that would make me think of her. I would pray that God would give me a love for Billy. I wanted so bad to be a good wife for him. The more I prayed for it, the worse life got!

Within a few months after giving birth to Jynna, I was admitted to the hospital with kidney stones. They were so large that I had to have lithotripsy and stents placed in as well. The pain was so severe that they had me rotating pain medications. During this time, I received a notice that my father was going up for parole. The physical pain combine with the emotional mess was too much. I began taking the medication whether I needed it or not. I had to seal these cracks. I had to do something to fill in the cracks within me. I was so out of it that Billy's family would stay with me while Billy was working. I couldn't keep up with what Jynna or the other babies needed. I was such a mess. At the time, I didn't even realize what I was getting myself into. I didn't notice what I was doing or why. Our human brains are sometimes smarter than we know. Without knowing, I was trying to fix myself. I was taking something that only God can do and tried to do it myself. I knew that I was broken. I knew that I could not function with such pain and I was unconsciously covering it up.

Because of my surgery, I had to put Jynna of formula. She broke out in a rash daily. We found that she was allergic to gluten, eggs, pineapple, nuts, and milk protein. We had to have special formula for her and watch her very carefully. She was completely normal in every way but struggled with food allergies. I was so excited that she made it through the pregnancy that I didn't care how hard it was to feed her.

The parole hearing came and I felt that I had to go. My pastor's wife drove me there. I worked on what I would say if given the opportunity to speak. I knew that I had to go and I needed to be brave. I knew that if I allowed him to intimidate me, he would think he was winning. Everything in life was a game to him. As I walked in, I saw my mother sitting beside my father. She was right there for him to show him her moral support. She wanted the parole board to know that she stood behind him and that he had a place to live if released. I struggled but I didn't let them know that. He was given permission to speak first. He told the court how he was a model prisoner and how he had found god in prison and was going through classes to be ordained. When they asked him if he had anything to say regarding the crimes that he had committed, he had no remorse. He said. "Well, I guess that I'm sorry." After he left the room, I was able to tell the parole board what he had done to me and why I thought he should remain in prison.

I found out a few weeks later that his parole was denied. I was so thankful but the whole process set me back. I began having more flashbacks. I began to feel angry yet couldn't really find the source. Nothing I did was able to make me feel anything, I was angry yet numb. It was a feeling that only someone who experienced it could understand. I tried to reach out to a few people about the things that I was experiencing but they all told me the same thing. All of them said that I needed to give it all to God and walk away. I tried so hard to give all my pain to God but it didn't help. I would go to the altar and cry and beg God to take it. I would tell Him that I didn't want it anymore. I wanted Him to relieve the pain and heal me but nothing really happened. I would feel better at the church but when I walked out, I was back to the pain. People would tell me that I wasn't letting it go but I didn't know how. I finally decided that the best way to get through this was to pretend that everything was okay. If I didn't acknowledge that I was cracked and damaged, maybe no one would notice. Sad thing is, it worked. Billy talks about what a great wife I was at that time and how he thought our marriage was perfect. It was all an act. I became a lie. My whole life became a huge stage and I was the main actress. I look back and think, I could have won a Grammy. I wasn't good at it, I was great. I knew all the right things to say and how to act. I played the part of the good Christian, great mom, loving wife, and healed survivor. I went through each day going through the motions and suppressing any thoughts or feelings that might complicate the lie that I was living. Amie wanted to get together more often but I couldn't do it. If she was around, I knew in my heart that I was an imposter. Her presence was like a light inside my vessel. It would shine and show every crack that I was so desperately trying to hide.

When Jynna was almost two years old, I decided to go to college. I would homeschool my older ones and take care of the younger ones during the day and attend college classes at night. Four months after I started, I received the best Christmas gift ever, my 5th positive pregnancy test. I called my doctor and he put me on medication. I immediately went on blood thinners a couple times a day. Even with my pregnancy, I continued to take my college courses.

Three weeks into my sophomore year in college, I gave birth to my fifth blessing. Joyanna Grace was born completely healthy and cute as ever. All of my children were so happy to have another little sister. I took a week off school and then got back to work on my degree. Billy worked days so he was able to keep the children while I attended evening classes. I still homeschooled and took care of the house during the day and pumped and stored breast milk for Billy to use while I was away. I tried to keep myself focused on becoming a better me.

When Joyanna was 5 months old, Billy and I felt God wanted us to travel. I started praying about it. I wanted to do what God wanted but I still knew that I wasn't spiritually where I should be. I was living life right but my heart still wasn't what it appeared to be. One night, I woke up to use the restroom. As I walked in the bathroom, the cabinet doors were open. I didn't think anything about it at first but then, it got weird. After using the restroom, I went to the kitchen to get a drink. Every cabinet door was open in there as well. I began to shut them and walk through the house. I checked every room to find all doors to the closets were open too. I quickly shut all of them and then went back to my bed. I won't lie, it scared me a bit. I woke up Billy by running to my bedroom when I was done. He asked me what was going on. I told him the whole story. I asked him if he thought that there could have been an earthquake or something but he said that others would have been reporting it on Facebook. We checked but nothing indicated any such events. Billy told me that I needed to just go back to sleep. As I lay in my bed, I heard something. This "voice" didn't sound like a human's voice but wasn't scary either. I heard, "I will close doors that no man can open and open doors that no man can shut." I was not a very "spiritual" person. Although I attended church, I wasn't what you would consider for a person who just heard from God. I thought at first I was crazy but something within me knew that it was real. I woke up Billy again and told him what I had heard. I told him that I wanted to travel and that God would open doors. Within the next few weeks, we bought a Suburban and a travel trailer and began selling everything we had. Looking back, I think that God meant that for the future and not right away but I took it has the present word from the Lord.

We moved into the travel trailer and began seeking God for where we were to go. While waiting for God to lead us, we tried to help others in ministry. We decided to park at the church camp and help clean it for a few days. As I was cleaning in the kitchen, Joyanna became very sleepy and cranky. She was 8 months old so I put her in a back pack carrier and proceeded to wash the dishes. Liz was in the room with us and could see her face at all times. After just a few minutes, Joyanna fell asleep. Liz told me she could see her face and that she was sound asleep. I began to feel very uncomfortable after about 10 minutes. I asked Liz if Joyanna was visible and if she looked okay. She assured me that my precious baby was fine. Approximately 45 minutes went by and I could not shake the feeling that something was wrong. When you spend your whole life living in fear, it is hard to distinguish between fear and God trying to warn you. I asked Liz about every five minutes up to this point and she annoyingly told me she was okay. I knew that I had to do something to make the fear go away so I reached back and patted her little leg. Much to my surprise, she didn't move. I then proceeded to pinch her leg but that didn't affect her either. I yelled for Liz to help me get her out. She came over to me and was telling me she was okay but then Liz became silent. Liz started frantically grabbing Joyanna. She yelled her name, shook her a little, and then began trying to get her to breathe. We both tried for a while to get her to take a breath. We were so far out of town that 911 wasn't really going to help. After giving up, Liz handed her to me and said that she didn't know what else to do. I took her and laid her down. I knew that I didn't deserve a miracle. I took my hand and laid it on her small lifeless chest. I silently prayed, "Lord, I know that I gave you this child the day she was born. No matter what happens I will serve you the rest of my life and not be angry. Thank you for the last 8 months with her. I know that you can also give her back. God, I will only ask once. Can I please have my baby back?" The next few seconds seemed to go by in slow motion. In that moment, I was calm, I knew that if it was God's will that He could give her life back. I also knew though that if He didn't I had to figure out what I would say at the funeral. I had to let people know that God was still good and that she was in a better place. My thoughts were interrupted when her eyes opened. Next, she smiled the biggest smile ever followed by the deepest breath she can take. She looked over and saw Liz and put her arms up to be picked up. My baby was alive! God had given her back to me. I collapsed on the floor and Liz laid her on my chest.

All those years, I wondered if God loved me and yet He made it a point to heal two of my children. I didn't deserve His help. I was a wretch and yet the Lord of Lords and the King of the Kings was right there to answer me. I had this idea in my head that I was so damaged that God didn't want me. I thought that I was such a mess that there was no way that the God of the universe would hear my prayers. Matthew 21:22 says that whatsoever ask in prayer, believing, you shall receive. I had asked, and believed, and He answered. When you are abused by your father and then you approach God, you feel as though He will treat you the same way. Sometimes, we forget that God is NOTHING like our earthly father. God loves us. His love is unconditional and He will ALWAYS do what is best for us. This day, God saw past the broken, bruised, and sinful girl and gave me grace; literally. That day He gave me back Joyanna Grace.

We soon parked at a church and helped some friends build up a congregation. I was in the children's ministry and Billy helped me. I also sat on the board of the church and dug into living the "right" lifestyle. Amie began coming over more and more. I tried to keep it on an "acquaintance" level. I loved her so much but had to put walls up so that I didn't "feel" anything. I wouldn't talk to her about much and just keep conversation about our children. I thought that if I didn't do anything with women, I wasn't a homosexual. I didn't realize that it was still lingering in my heart. We are who we are in our hearts.

The pastor's wife and I became very close friends. God knew that I needed a good Godly friend that could love me and not complicate life with sexual issues so, He sent me Terra. When I would struggle with flashbacks, she was always there for me. I had never told people of the triggers that I had. She would allow me to tell her what triggered me and then ask me why that bothered me. She is the one that helped me identify many of my triggers. I had many triggers that most people would have laughed at. Glitter, lotion, smell of coconut, loud screams, taking a shower, knocks on a door, a slammed door, bathrooms, and being alone terrified me. She helped me to understand that it was okay not to be over that. She showed me it is okay not to be okay. She taught me that we need to treat ourselves the way that we would treat others who have been through it. Many times, we give others time to heal but expect ourselves to "get over it". God used this amazing woman to take clay and fill the deep cuts. As I look back, I see that God used her arms to hug me. He used her words to build me up. She was a tool in the potter's hands. Not very many people can touch me and do it in a loving Godly way but Terra did. On days where I felt so unloved, she was there. I could share my dreams and failures with her without judgement. Terra was the first person to ever kiss me on my forehead. It was almost like a secret kiss from the Lord. I could feel the love of God through her. She taught me what it was like to be a friend. She was a true friend. The Lord will send good Godly people to help mold you. The Word says in Proverbs 17:17 that a friend loves at all times. The Lord will send a friend that can help you by loving you through all your issues. She is also the one who taught me what true prayer was. She showed me that prayer isn't just talking, it is communication. She molded me with the Word. She always knew verses that I needed to get me through situations. God will send someone to mold you with His Word. Proverbs 27:17 says, "As iron sharpens iron, so a man sharpens the countenance of his friend." Although I was broken, God used Terra to begin molding me into the right direction. I can't imagine who I would be without her.

Life Changes

My life seemed perfect from the outside looking in. Although I was a mess on the inside, God was using me. I was hired on as a teacher for a private Christian school. I put all my children into the private school. I began attending the church that owned the school. I taught at the school during the day and went to college in the evening. Life began to finally look up for me. I had everything that I could possibly want as long as I didn't allow myself to feel. I had to always have walls up so that my thoughts were focused on what was right in front of me.

Amie had completed the police academy and found a job a few hours north of us. I didn't see her often but when I did, I felt as though I was a different person. I could be myself around her. I could be true to me. I didn't have to pretend with her. I could let my walls down. Life with Billy was so complicated after seeing Amie though. I couldn't understand why I hated him for a while after seeing her. It was almost like God was tearing down walls slowly and then when I would see her, I would build them back up again. I hadn't done anything sexual with her but that was all I could think of while with Billy. I felt as though I was betraying him but I couldn't fix it. I had tried all these years and yet nothing worked. I tried to find ways to be with him and not hate him.

Pottery is something so precious. Many times we can't help the damage that has caused the cracks. Accidents happen, life is out of our control, and we can't prevent things from happening. Sometimes though, the cracks we get are our own fault. We open doors with good intentions, and fall into a trap. No one plans on destroying their lives. No one wants to break themselves but we often do it without realizing it.

I joined a support group for abused women. I met a woman who was very kind. We became very close online friends. I was talking to her about my difficulty with showering and being with my husband. She would have me video chat with her while I showered and she would talk to me through it. At first, it was completely innocent. She would chat with me or sing to me while I showered. She mentioned to me that she got use to letting someone touch her after touching herself and being comfortable with that. She asked me if I wanted to do that while texting. I thought it might help so I was willing to give it a try. Satan has a way of trapping us into things that we don't even realize. Before too long, we were "texting" and I was dreaming more and more of Amie. My relationship with Billy was getting so much better. I thought that this was really helping. During anything physical with Billy, I would imagine Amie and I was able to do it without so many flashbacks. I didn't realize that I was breaking myself. Things with Billy was perfect. Church was going well, teaching was amazing, and I was passing all my classes. I had a 4.0 and was on the Dean's List. I thought God was finally fixing me. I thought life was as close to perfect as it would ever be. I have never been more wrong than I was at this point in my life. I wasn't being healed, I was breaking more.

In January of 2014, I had to attend another parole hearing for my father. Amie went with me this time. I sat there terrified of this man and he sat there so calm. My mother was at the first hearing but didn't attend this one. I sat there and expected the same thing that happened last time; little or no remorse. The parole board asked him what he was in prison for. He said in a meek voice, "Well Sir, I am here for raping my daughter." This was the very first time that he had ever taken responsibility for what he did. Hearing this froze me. His words cut me to my very core. It reached inside of me and pierced a part of me that I didn't even know existed. I had never experienced this much emotional pain at one time. I am not even sure if I was breathing. I just stared at Amie's leg and didn't move. His response shocked the parole board too. They asked him why he did those things to me. He sat still for a moment and cleared his throat. You could hear that he was fighting back tears as he answered, "Sir, I think I did it because I thought my daughter was my personal property. I forced her to do what I wanted." They asked him why someone would hurt their own child. He looked down at the floor and very quietly and sincerely spoke, "I was molested as a child. I did to her what was done to me and I shouldn't have." He was serious and completely open and honest. I had no idea that he had gone through that. My heart sank. I couldn't speak or even swallow. The whole board was silent for a moment. The main speaker searched through paperwork for a little while then, put the papers down and folded his hands. He asked my father why he had never told the counselors this information. My father replied with tears running down his face, "I didn't tell because I was embarrassed and ashamed of myself. I put her through exactly what I went through and I hate that." Next, they asked him if he could say anything to me, what it would be. He stared at the floor, thought for a minute and said, "I am sorry for not being a good dad and treating you the way a daughter should be treated. I understand if you hate me for the rest of your life. I would if I were you." After this, I was asked to speak. I shook my head and refused to speak. They escorted my father out of the room and then, I fell to pieces.

Most people would be happy that he apologized but I wasn't. I hated him even more now. He knew how I felt and the pain I was going through and he did it anyway. The crazy part was that I felt sorry for him at the same time. After he left the room, the board asked me if I had anything to say or a recommendation for them. I told them that I couldn't say anything because I would be betraying myself. I felt that if I said he should be released then I was somehow diminishing the pain that I went through. I also felt that if I asked them to deny his parole, I was not considering forgiveness. Anything I could say seemed like a terrible idea to me. Amie spoke up and asked to speak on my behalf. She spoke about the flashbacks I had my whole life and how the abuse had impacted every aspect of my being. She told them that she believed that my father was playing them to get out of prison. They took notes and then thanked us for coming.

As we drove home, I kept telling myself that he manipulated me. He manipulated me just like he did as a child. He had convinced me not to tell anyone. He had convinced me that everything was my fault. Now, he was convincing me that he was sorry for what he did to me. I couldn't believe that I fell for that act. I had to be tough. I had to build more walls around my heart. I hated that I actually cared about him during that hearing. I was determined, no more "feelings".

One night, while lying in my bed with Billy and texting with Amie, one of my daughters came into the room. She said that she had a question for us. I was already a mess but this added to it. She crawled in our bed and began to cry. Billy and I held her and waited for her to tell us what was wrong. She wanted to know why God had a made a mistake when He created her. I asked her what she meant by that. She began to explain that she was a boy and that God must have made a mistake when making her body. She said that in her head she felt like a boy but her body was a girl. Billy and I were shocked. I had never spoke anything to my children about how I felt. Billy didn't even really understand me and now we had a daughter struggling too. I knew that she was raised to believe girls didn't "like" other girls and being gay was wrong. I knew she wanted to be a boy because she was struggling with being gay. I couldn't explain it but I just knew. We told her that God doesn't make mistakes. I told her the things that I had told myself for years but I didn't really believe it. She asks us to change her name to "Chase" and let her be a boy. I explained to her that sometimes our minds lie to us and we have to trust God. I sent her to bed with the thought she was perfectly made and would feel different one day. After she was in bed, Billy and decided that maybe we should let her dress the way she wanted and not make a big deal out of it. We would allow her to be herself and love her for who she was. We would deal with whatever happened in the future but for now, love was all she needed. The next day, I told her that she couldn't talk to anyone except me about the way she felt. I was not going to allow someone to insult her or make her feel as though she was wrong. I knew that I had tried my whole life to change and felt terrible that I couldn't. I would not allow her to go through the torment that I went through. She was perfect, absolutely perfect and God NEVER made mistakes.

I finished the school year teaching at the Christian school but life was different. I completely shut down. I had no idea how to get through what I had experienced as a child, let alone the parole hearing. I received a phone call that his parole was indeed granted. He was going to be released. They set his release date for October 25, 2014. The day that was the hardest day of my life would now be even harder. I was already in "shut down mode" but this kicked me into overdrive. I could no longer hold my vessel together. I was too damaged. I couldn't feel anything yet I hated everything. I felt as though my vessel fell and shattered into a million pieces. I was now a large pile of tiny pieces that would never be put back together. The nightmares increased greatly. I didn't want to be touched in anyway. I hated Billy because he always wanted to hold me. I couldn't sleep or eat much. I felt as though I was dying. Every part of me had finally fell apart. I did what my children needed and then I would lay in bed. From the outside looking in, I would say I was depressed but I wasn't sad at all. I didn't feel sadness, I didn't feel anything.

Amie would text me often to see if I was okay. I tried so hard not to want to be with her instead of Billy but I couldn't help it. Men hurt me and Billy only wanted to touch me. I thought he was like all other men and just wanted one thing. I didn't know how to hide stuff anymore. I didn't know how to stuff it all back in so, I didn't. This vessel had no idea how to fix anything. I began spending the weekends with Amie. The kids and I would drive up and spend the weekend and sometimes the week with her.

I found a T.V. series that I became obsessed with. It was called "The Fosters". It was a show about a lesbian couple who did foster care. One of the moms was a police officer and the other was a principle of a school. I began thinking that this would easily work in life. I would think about the possibilities that I was wrong on my "traditional" thinking and that it really was okay. What could possibly be wrong with loving someone? Love is love, right?

My Life Flipped Upside Down

Church camp came around and no one knew that I had fallen apart. I would lead worship and then go to my cabin and beg God to help me feel. I prayed that God would allow the kids to get something out of the services because I knew I was faking life. I was pretending I was okay but I wasn't. Towards the end of camp, Billy came to a service. I begged God to allow me to want him. I begged God to help me be a good wife. I thought that if I could let Billy hold me, and make love to me, maybe my pieces would somehow go back together. I thought he might be able to help me feel. I asked Billy to stay the night with me but he wouldn't. He said he didn't want to be there. I told him that he didn't understand that I needed him but he wouldn't listen. I prayed all day for that moment and he wouldn't even stay with me. I finished the camp and planned on walking away. I couldn't fake my way through life anymore. The last day of camp, I prayed and told God I was sorry. I loved him but just couldn't lie to myself any longer. I had to be where I felt loved. I remember packing my suburban and telling God, "I quit." I called Amie and told her I was done. We never talked about our feelings. She never told me she wanted to be with me. We both just knew. She said two simple words, "Come home."

Looking back I see that I was at a fork in the road. I could go home to my husband and let God heal me or I could take the easy road for the moment. I chose wrong that day. I left camp and drove to her house. I stayed with her for the weekend and then drove home to allow Billy to see the kids and to switch clothes for the next camp. This camp only lasted five nights and then I went back to Amie. On the drive there, I told myself that I needed to be true to myself. I needed to accept me for who I was. Although I had never been with a woman, I was a lesbian and in love with my best friend. It was about time I was just "me". So, with me broken in a million pieces and walking down the wrong path, I decided it was time I told her how I felt about her.

I tried to tell her for five days. I contemplated right and wrong. In my head, I went through all I knew about the Bible. Everything I ever heard said that the greatest thing was love. It also said that being gay was an abomination to God. I was so confused. Why couldn't I just be me? The thought of me being someone God hated pushed me to my limits. I decided that if I couldn't figure it out that I would drown the thoughts with alcohol. Amie and I were at Wal-Mart, I picked up some wine coolers. I hadn't drank in so long that I thought I had better take it easy. As we walked to the front of the store, I placed my hand on hers as she was pushing the cart. She didn't move her hand. She simply smiled at me. I didn't need to tell her what I felt; she already knew.

That night, our children and her husband had went to bed leaving us alone. We were watching a movie and snuggled up on the couch. Deep down inside, I knew what I wanted was wrong but honestly, I didn't care. I had wanted this my whole life. It was who I was. It was who I was meant to be. I needed to be true to myself. I had been through so much in my life and had never done anything for myself. I deserved more than what I had. She made the first move and I didn't stop her. She started to kiss me. She put her lips right up to mine and then paused. I knew she was waiting for permission so, I just closed my eyes. I gave up everything I knew to be true and did what I always dreamt about. I began a sexual relationship with a woman. A few minutes into this, I thought of her family. I didn't want to mess up her life. I told her that we should probably stop. She simply laughed and told me to shut up and enjoy myself. In that moment, I knew that she had already been contemplating this for a while now and she was just like me. We had both waited for a long time for this day. Afterwards, she asked me if I was okay. She wanted to make sure that I didn't feel like she had forced me. She didn't force me. She had no idea that made my dreams come true. I told her for the first time in my life, I was okay. Actually, I was more than okay, I was great. For the first time in my life, sex wasn't gross. It finally felt right. I finally knew what it was supposed to feel like. I had been living life wrong. Until this day, I had no idea what it meant to be intimate with someone. It wasn't just sex. It was a connection on a whole new level. I had only heard of such a connection. I had finally found out why the world made such a big deal about true love. I now understood why it was important to have this connection with someone. This was what I needed to hold me together. I needed love. All I needed was love.

I want to say that I felt terrible after that night but I didn't. I want to tell you that I regretted it that very moment but that wouldn't be true. For the first time in my whole life, I felt normal. This gave me the feeling of all my pieces being put back together. I thought that I had finally found how to be happy. This couldn't be bad because it made me feel so much better. After a few weeks, she told her husband but he didn't care. He loved us and wanted us to be happy. We kept our relationship from everyone else including our children. We would hold hands in front of them and that was all. They knew what close friends we were so they never thought anything of it. We spent every moment that we could together. During the day we tried to pretend that we were just friends but then when the kids were in bed, we could be ourselves. We also would go for walks together or just go for a ride so that we could be together. I was so happy not to have to hide the feelings that I had.

Most people have a moment as they become a teenager when sex isn't "gross" anymore. I didn't have that moment until I was with Amie. This was the very first time in my life that I actually felt as though sex was a natural and wonderful thing. I was no longer embarrassed to be seen naked by a person and I finally wanted to be touched. Every time I was with her, my body would respond the way it had only done once in my life; with my uncle. I had never felt that since that day at the lake. I felt as though God was finally rewarding me for all the struggles that I had gone through. I felt that He had finally shown me the way that love was supposed to be. Love was supposed to feel amazing. I should get butterflies in my stomach as her hand touched mine. Love meant that we were completely safe with one another. Love was okay. I was designed to feel love. I needed to let someone love me. I needed to feel safe. I needed to allow her to love me the right way. Life made sense when I was with her. Her arms around me made the whole world fall into place. I was happy, loved, and peaceful.

The end of the summer brought Amie's birthday. As I asked her what she wanted, she didn't seem to have to think about it. She knew what she wanted. She wanted the two people that she loved to be together for her. At first, I was devastated. I didn't even want her married to the guy. I definitely didn't want to share her with him sexually. I thought about it for a while. Her husband was my closest guy friend. I loved him as a friend. He was such a good guy and I already felt bad for being with his wife. It wasn't that I felt that being gay was wrong but we were married so we were committing adultery. As I thought about the situation, I realized something. She was the love of my life and he was my other best friend. He allowed us to be together and loved us through it. I decided that I would give her what she wanted.

Words can't express the chaos that sin will bring. I was now not only confusing my mind but theirs as well. I have done many things wrong in my lifetime but this was one of my biggest mistakes. Her husband and I began having sex and then we allowed her to join as her birthday present. Being with him wasn't awkward. I just thought of him like a friend and tried not to think of anything else but her. With her there, I felt safe and didn't have flashbacks. It was easy to be there if I had her with me. I wanted to please her. I would do anything for that woman. I did whatever it took to make her happy.

Amie and I would often walk to the park to allow the children to play. We would allow them to walk in front of us and we would talk about our future. One day, while walking, Amie and I were walking and holding hands. As we looked ahead at the children walking, we noticed something Amie thought was "cute". My daughter and hers were also holding hands. Her daughter didn't know what I knew. My daughter wanted to be a boy and liked her in a different way than just friends. The other children thought they were adorable but my heart broke. My daughter had her first "crush" and was starting to follow in my footsteps. I always had kept my "sexual preferences" to myself yet my daughter was feeling the same thing. How could this happen? Why would God make her that way too?

This didn't seem fair to her. She was so young and so confused. After that weekend was over, my daughter told me that she was in love with Amie's daughter. Her daughter thought they were best friends but mine wanted more.

As August came, I had to start back at college. I would spend the week at home and then drive on the weekends to be with Amie. I finally got the courage to tell a few of my friends about our relationship. The ones that I told were very supportive. They were so glad I was finally happy. This gave me even more "confirmation" that I wasn't making a bad choice. I was just following my heart. I was being true to myself. Being happy couldn't be a bad thing.

Being with Billy intimately was harder than ever now. I hated it. I knew how I should feel about him because I felt that for Amie. He tried everything to get me to want him. Finally, he found something that help me a little. We would watch lesbian porn throughout the whole thing. I felt bad but it made it a little easier on me. I would think of Amie and me and focus on that while Billy and I were together. I think that he knew what I was thinking but he tried to dismiss it. He truly loved me and tried to ignore what my thoughts were. He didn't know what to do to help me except just love me.

Jynna started acting different. She would get tired very easy and she began getting sick very often. With just a little cold, she wouldn't get out of bed. She went from a very active child to one that would barely move. She also started complaining a lot that she didn't feel good. Doctors said that she was a normal heathy child. She cried often from her legs hurting but doctors assured me that it was just growing pains. Most of us just assumed that Jynna wanted attention and tried to ignore her.

Because October 25, 2014 was on a Saturday, the prison released my father a day early. I was called on that Thursday to let me know he would be out on parole. I drove to Amie's house that very night. I did NOT want to be anywhere near home when he was released. I was sure that he would come after me. To cope with the emotional side of the situation, I began drinking the night that he was released and slowly worked my way up to drinking daily.

I tried to cope with all the emotions and flashbacks. I felt as though the only way to get over the abuse was to do the things that hurt me. Amie and I would have sex every chance we got. We would be "together" every single night and almost every single morning. I would have flash backs during it and she would walk me through it. She would tell me how much she loved me and when I needed to she would stop whatever we were doing and just hold me. She would tell me that I never had to do anything with her, she would tell me that true love was more than sex. True love was something much more than that. True love was how we had felt our whole lives toward one another. It was the power and safety that it brought. Love was the only thing that mattered. Even with feeling safe there, I had nightmares that would wake me up. I would often wake up to Amie shaking me and telling me that I was safe. I couldn't let my children out of my sight either. I spend several weeks there. I used every allotted day from college without effecting my grades but soon I had to go back home.

Being home brought more problems. I had anxiety so bad that just walking out the door of my house would trigger a panic attack. I would have Billy walk me to the truck, talk to me on the phone all the way to school and on the way back. I would have him wait outside the house to walk me in after each class. I was failing at holding things together. I thought for sure that I would run into my father.

He lived 45 minutes away but my brain thought he was closer. I felt like he was always there. I saw him everywhere I looked. I would her him call my name in public but he wasn't really there. I was a complete mess. My children would literally have to hold my hand and talk me through stores to get groceries. I remember my son saying, "You are okay, Mommy. You can do it. Just a few more things and we can leave. You are doing a great job." He was nine! He was nine years old and had to walk me through the store while my oldest daughter picked out what we needed. I was supposed to take care of them but I couldn't. I was supposed to take care of them but they took care of me instead.

I couldn't sleep while I was at home. I would stay up for days with only a small nap here and there. If I tried to fall asleep, I would see my dad at the foot of my bed. I would also have nightmares that my father would be hurting my children and I couldn't stop him. I knew that it wasn't real but I couldn't make myself overcome it. On Billy's day off, he would sit with the kids and watch a movie and I would sleep. I would lay where I could see them when I would open my eyes. I would sleep through the movie and try to catch up on sleep. If I opened my eyes and couldn't see my children, I would immediately begin to panic. I would also sleep when I got to Amie's house on the weekend and she would take care of our children. Many times, Amie would just hold me while I slept in the living room and our children would play quietly. The anxiety seemed to rule my life. Between Billy, Amie, and God I made it through.

I began feeling like the reason I was falling apart was because I wasn't allowing God to lead my life. I thought that maybe I needed to get my focus back on Him. Amie called me and told me that she also felt that we might need to stop seeing each other and focus on God. We had went to the Joyce Meyer Women's conference before we had started the relationship and thought maybe we should do that again. We needed a fresh start with the Lord. We booked a room that slept 4 people and decided to go as friends. The week prior to the conference, Amie and I did life as friends. We still loved each other but was trying to "martyr" ourselves for the Lord. We felt that we could just stop and not be gay anymore. The first night of the conference was amazing. We felt the Lord as we worshiped together. We thought that since we decided that we weren't gay that God was with us again. That night at the hotel, I woke up kissing her. I couldn't help it. We broke the "rules" again and quickly realized that nothing had changed. Abstaining did NOT change anything. I loved her. I was in love with her. Whether we were sexual or not, I was STILL a lesbian. I couldn't change it; I had tried. I wanted her. Our souls seemed to be knitted together. We felt as though we were truly soulmates and that we could never be separated. We spent that weekend worshipping God, learning about Him, and being together. These things were the answer to the perfect life, or so it seemed.

When you live life, knowing the truth, but not listening to it, life gets complicated. I loved being with Amie and prayed that somehow I could leave Billy and be with her permanently. But when I was with Billy, I prayed God would forgive me and heal me. While with her, I was happy but couldn't feel the Lord. At home, I begged God to fix me and make me want to be with my husband. I felt as though I was living complete separate lives. I thought as two separate people. I couldn't function this way. I had to find a way to cope. I began drinking from the time I got up until I went to bed. Many times, I would get somewhere and have to have Susan, the social worker who saved me, come drive me home. She always told me that she would be there for me and she was. Several times, I had to call her. I was so drunk I couldn't get myself home. I would even drink in my van or in a car with a friend on breaks during my college classes. I couldn't deal with life.

My vessel stayed carefully together, I thought, until my father got released. I thought he caused this but looking back, I was falling apart because I told God "I quit". He, God, was the only thing that had held me together. Without Him, I not only was cracked, I was not even together. Without Him, I wasn't even a vessel any more. Being with Amie only seemed to put me back together for that moment but it was a lie. It was a fake sense of security. Sin always gives that.

Amie told me that she couldn't have a relationship with me anymore. She said she was trying to work on her marriage and that she didn't want me to lose my marriage or my ministry. I was devastated. She was the one person that brought me joy. She was the only person that I ever wanted to be with. I had finally wanted to be with someone and now I had to go back to faking life.

Cracked and Looking for Healing

I went back to focusing on my kids and trying to survive the anxiety. I drank as often as I could and hid my problems from everyone around me. I went to college and took the kids to a homeschool co-op and decided to be miserable for the rest of my life. I became so good at living the lie that no one even suspected there was a problem with me. I figured that I would never be put back together and the best option was for me to raise my children to be the best they could be. I still attended church and played the part of a perfect wife.

A few weeks after we started attending a Christian co-op, I began noticing a pretty woman. In worldly words, my "gaydar" was going off. I thought she was the smartest, prettiest, funniest woman in the world. I knew all the struggles I had with being a lesbian and didn't want to suck her into it. I knew that my heart was still broken from Amie and I needed to be cautious. The more that I got to know her, the more that I wanted to "save" her. She talked often about her marriage and how terrible it was. I hated that for her.

In March 2015, about 8 months after starting attending the co-op, she had a wedding to attend. She really didn't want to go to it. I volunteered to go with her and guaranteed her that we would have fun. After the wedding, the two of us went out for a drink and to just have a good time. Before the end of the night, I had started my second relationship with a woman. I couldn't help myself. She made me feel safe, beautiful, and loved. Her touch brought back all the feelings that I had been without since Amie ended the relationship. I had missed being held. I had missed being kissed in such a way that the entire world seemed to fade away. We snuck away to a place where we could be alone. This time, I made the first move, and she didn't stop me. I had fallen into the trap again and found myself in bed with another woman. This time was different. I was tired of hiding. I felt like I was born gay and I should be okay with it. This time, I was confident in my relationship. As I got home that night, Billy found out something was going on. When I came home drunk, and with hickeys all over me, he knew that I had been with someone. I just went to bed and tried not to talk to him about it until I had a plan.

I began missing college classes to be with her. For the sake of privacy, we will call her "Laney". I would skip classes and be with her and then go home to Billy after class was over. I would meet her and hang out for a while and it usually ended with us having sex again. After about a week, she looked at me and said, "What are we doing? What do you want out of this? Is this just for fun? What do you want?" I didn't really have to think about it. I knew what I wanted. I wanted to be hers. I wanted to be her girlfriend and one day, her wife. As I left that night, she said, "I guess it is set, I officially have a girlfriend."

A few weeks later, I took my kids to her house for a play date. Billy called me very upset that I was staying there too long. He began screaming at me over the phone and Laney heard it. She told me to just go over and get clothes and stay the night with her to let him calm down. We ran to my house to get an overnight bag. Billy flipped out and started screaming at me and chased me to the van. It freaked me out. I left with him beating on the van and screaming at me to stop. On the way to her house that night, we decided that I would stay with her and that I wanted a divorce. I had finally found someone that was worth "coming out" for. I wasn't going to go back to being miserable. I wanted to be happy. I deserved to be with someone who made me happy. I had gone through enough in life, it was time for a change.

I filed for a divorce and soon so did she. We were living together with my five children and her three and sometimes her two step-children. This relationship was not a secret. We posted it on Facebook and practically screamed it from the rooftops. We were happy with the life we had. With Amie, I was worried I was wrong, but with Laney, I didn't care about anything. I deserved to be "happy". I posted pictures of us kissing on Facebook. I wanted the whole world to know that I had found love. We didn't care what others thought. We wanted to be with each other. We were going to be together and the difficulty was worth it.

We both were in ministry and had never lived "openly" before. The people around us did not take it very well. Our family didn't want to talk to us anymore. Most of our friends didn't want anything to do with us either. I was so confused. I was the same person as I had always been but just because I came out, no one wanted to be around me. It was so hard to function. I loved her but people didn't understand. I was already such a mess and now everyone was abandoning me. I know that this is crazy but I thought they had to be wrong. I thought of all the examples in the Bible: Ruth and Naomi were almost "too" close, David loved Jonathon more than his wives, and John laid his head on Jesus' chest. Maybe I knew something that "religious" people didn't. God would NEVER create something to be an abomination to Him. I had seen that He loved me. He answered my prayers when He knew who I "was". My God couldn't possibly hate me.

I was happier than ever but the battle between my mind and my heart were unbearable. Everything made sense yet, nothing did. I was finally able to let walls down but, everyone around me said I was failing. I was on top of the world but people said I was drowning. I knew who I was but, I didn't know how to be that person. Before too long, I went from drinking to drugs. This girl who had never wanted anything to do with drugs was now smoking Marijuana daily. In case this wasn't enough, I began taking Adderall that was not prescribed. I would do the highest form of Adderall, smoke pot, and drink almost daily. (We did not do these around the kids.) I thought that I was living the greatest life ever but I know now that I was trying to cover up any conviction that I was feeling.

Because it wasn't legal for homosexuals to be married, we said our vows and got matching rings and didn't tell anyone. We thought that we would be married once it was legalized. I was so excited and proud to show off our rings. Life was more perfect than I ever thought it could be, or so I thought.

I stopped talking to Amie. I blocked her on Facebook and changed my phone number. I knew that if I was going to make my relationship work, I had to let go of her. She was the one person that I had always held on too. She was the only one that could jeopardize my marriage with Laney. I knew that if I didn't let go, she would be the one that I would run to when things got complicated. I hated to hurt her but I knew that the only way to do it was to just walk away. It didn't mean I didn't love her, it just had to be done. This would save my new marriage and help Amie with hers.

Drugs cost money, something we didn't have much of. We would sell anything that we could do without in order to buy more. We got to the point where we were debating making a run to get marijuana for our dealer in California. He would pay us good money and all expenses to get us there and back. All we had to do was bring back a couple coolers full of "green". We were so close to doing this but was unsure about what to do with our children and didn't want them to be with us if we got caught. I can't believe the things you will change and give up when you are mixed up in something like that. We were willing to give up so much just for what we wanted. Drugs make people very selfish.

Laney had a degree in counseling and used it to walk me through flashbacks and triggers. Many nights, we would sit in the bathtub and I would tell her all the things that had happened to me. She would walk me through why she thought I had the flashbacks and ways to overcome them. For an example, as I shared my story about the Minnie Mouse, Laney saw my problem. I was so scared of glitter because of that shirt that I would shove into my mouth to bite on so that I would not scream. I hadn't realized that the things that triggered me were actually the past hurting me over and over again in my mind. The Lord used her to help me. No matter what you are doing, God will always try to help you. I began being able to sleep through the night without nightmares. Laney started giving me things with glitter on it and slowly, I began to love it instead of freaking out. I even was able to touch lotions and Vaseline without triggers. I realized why I was scared and then forced myself to use them in situations where I felt safe. The Lord was trying to help His vessel even though I wasn't living for Him. God used this situation to help me heal and to teach me coping skills.

One night, as I went to bed, I felt like something was staring at me. I believed that maybe I was just overreacting and being paranoid. As I fell asleep, I felt something heavy on my chest. I opened my eyes to find a large black blob on me. It was almost like a dark shadow. It had part of itself wrapped around my neck. As the moon light shown in, I could see that this "shadow" was not see-through in anyway. It was like a solid mass. It was so heavy and I felt as though it was choking me. I had known that the name of Jesus had power so I tried to speak. I could hear it in my head but the words would not form. I began screaming it but still no sounds exited my mouth. I tried to move but I was paralyzed. I kept struggling to speak until it slowly came out of my mouth. The first "Jesus" came out at almost a whisper. The more I tried to speak the louder it got until a loud "Jesus" rang out. At that moment, that "shadow" was gone. This happened several times over the next several weeks. This was terrifying. I knew that this evil presence was out to destroy me but all I had to say was the name of "Jesus" and it was gone. That name has so much power that even the demons are subject to it.

One day while alone in the bedroom, my daughter and Laney's daughter were experimenting. They were caught kissing. They were also seen under the covers together a few times. Our girls were so confused. They really didn't understand what could be wrong with being together since their moms were doing the same things. We will refer to her as Brittany. My daughter began writing "Chase loves Brittany" on everything. Her school work even had "Chase" written in as her name. She was so sure that God had made a mistake and that she should be a boy. I knew that she could not be with Laney's daughter but I thought one day she would follow my footsteps. I hated that she would have to endure the same struggles I did. I hated that she would have to decide to live life to be happy or fake life and marry a man. I prayed that God gave her strength to be herself; whatever that was. She would have to be tough to get through this life. She would have to also be courageous if she was a lesbian too.

Laney and I started focusing on our sexual relationship more and more. I was so excited about the things that I could do without flashbacks now. I began wanting to try everything everywhere. I hate to say this but we became obsessed with sex. It was like the one thing that I had always struggled with was the only thing that I wanted. We would have sex in public, in our vehicle in a parking lot, or anywhere we were at. The thrill of possibly being caught was exciting to us. We also would have sex where are friends could hear us. We were proud to be gay. We loved watching porn as well. We would watch porn several times a week. It was almost like it was taking more and more to satisfy us. When porn wasn't enough, we would make our own porn videos and watch them later. We would literally spend hours, daily, just having sex. We would ignore our responsibilities, our children, and friends/family to be with one another. I began wrapping my entire world around the same things my father did. God took me out of a family deep in sexual sin and I placed myself back into the same junk. I thought that since we were consenting adults that it wasn't wrong. I believed that it wasn't hurting anyone. I was wrong.

Jynna began struggling even more. She would have days where she would just lay around and not get out of bed. She complained of chest pains, leg cramps, and that her lungs hurt when she would breathe. She would have days at a time that she would have us carry her around. She never had a diagnosis because doctors simply said that it may have been gluten that she had eaten or more growing pains. We did our best to just keep her comfortable and take care of her on her difficult days.

Although we were happy, our children struggled. She had always been with her children and me with mine. We both didn't like our marriages so we put almost our entire focus on them. They were not use to us wanting to spend time with anyone but them. They all loved each other and were best friends even though they all fought for our attention. We wanted to be with one another and have our children happy. The struggle broke our hearts daily. We would go back and forth on being together or not simply because of the children. She was my best friend and we tried to go back to that but it didn't last. We couldn't just be friends. We had waited too long to find each other and was too wrapped up in the sexual relationship to stop.

We would try to raise our children in church but most churches acted like we had the plague. No one who was a strong Christian reached out to us. Christians either supported us or ignored us and there wasn't any in between. This was so hard for the kids. We would sing praise and worship together and teach them about God at our home. Teaching the Bible and living a homosexual lifestyle didn't really go together. Before long, all our children were worried that we were going to hell because we were gay. We talked about seeking a relationship with God and began praying before bed with our kids.

The beginning of February was very rough. Laney struggled with the people around us criticizing us. She felt like a terrible mother for sharing her home and time with me and my children. She wanted to be with me but just struggled with the life that revolved around us. She told me that she needed some time to think. I took that as that she didn't want me anymore. I felt rejected and alone. She wanted me to give her some space to think about things but

I had nowhere to go. She thought that I would just go to Billy's house but I couldn't force myself to do that. I didn't have a family to stay with or any friends that would want me either. I felt so scared and worthless. I called the one person that I knew would always love me, Amie. She had her husband come and get me and my children. We went to her house and spent a few days.

I spent the several days talking about Laney. I was so broken. Amie and I were not intimate. She was just a great friend and wanted to be there for me. She truly just wanted to do whatever I needed. When I would get overwhelmed, I would lay my head on her lap and cry. She would run her hands through my hair, kiss my forehead, and tell me that I would be okay. I sat and told her all the things that I had done. She was shocked when I told her about the drugs that were a huge part of our lives. She said that she didn't even know this new person that I had become. This lifestyle had changed me. I wasn't even close to the same person that I once was. I was so ashamed of myself because I had disappointed her. She knew me so well and never thought I would do the things that I had done. She said that I was unrecognizable and that she loved a different me. Before I left to come home, as we were alone, I leaned over and kissed her. I had to know that there wasn't anything between us. I had to know that I loved Laney. As I kissed her, she seemed shocked. She just looked at me and said, "I love you but we can't do this." This kiss felt different than before, almost like she didn't want it. She loved me but didn't want me anymore. She didn't want the lifestyle that I wanted. I knew then that I wanted to be with Laney the rest of my life. I wanted to be with a woman that was not ashamed of her love for me. I had Amie's husband drive me home after that. I had to find a way to make things work at home. I wanted a life with Laney.

As I got home, Laney told me that she never wanted me to leave again. I hated spending time away from her. We decided that no matter how hard it was, we wanted our lives together. Life didn't seem to make sense without each other. We would continue to work through the struggles. I knew that we just had to find ways to focus more on God together and allow him to help us. Love truly was the greatest thing and we were too stubborn to give up.

The following week, Laney asked me to marry her legally. The "Gay Marriage" law had passed and we wanted to be legal in God's cycs. We were both so tired of society and rules that the churches wanted us to follow. We knew that we loved each other more than we knew how to describe. Although life was difficult, we didn't want to do life without each other. We wanted our children to know that love was love and that true love did exist. We wanted to teach them that although life is hard, love was worth fighting for. We decided to be married in November. That would give us plenty of time to plan.

Missing the Potter

Towards the end of February, my kids were with Billy and we just had her kids. She went to read them a story and then pray with them. I sat down on the couch for a moment to wait for her. As I sat there, I began to wonder when the last time was that I felt God. I felt Him slightly tug on my heart when Laney and I would sing praises with the kids. I was trying to teach our kids about God and I couldn't even remember the last time that I knew He was real. It had been a really long time since I had felt Him. I missed the feeling of His presence. I knelt down beside the couch and began to pray. I just wanted to feel Him. I wanted to know that He was there. I didn't know if it was even possible to still feel Him, but I had to try. I had a hunger for Him. As I was on my knees, Laney came in and laid her hands on my back. She knelt down and began praying for me. She prayed over me for a moment and then something happened that had never happened before. Laney began praying in tongues over me. I had been living with this woman for a year and I had never heard this before. As she prayed, her voice changed and became stern and had authority. I heard her speaking but knew God was speaking through her. As she spoke, I crumbled in reverence to the spirit that was present. The Lord was in our home speaking through this woman. For the first time in my life, I could understand the tongues and I knew what she was saying. God was laying on my heart the interpretation of what He was saying through her. As she spoke, I heard these words, "I know the desires of your heart. Call upon me and I will make your paths straight. I have called you for such a time as this. Step out of the ankle deep water and come out into the deep. I will take you from religion into a relationship with me. You will have a Saul turned Paul experience." As she finished, we both started crying. She asked me if I knew what she said. I told her that I knew what God was saying. She told me that she understood it as well. She explain to me a very similar outline of what I heard. God had showed Himself in our house that night.

I sat and cried for what seemed like hours. God had not only showed himself, He had given me a gift. Romans 11:29 says that the gifts and callings of God are without repentance. Here I was, a sinner. I was no longer a vessel but a pile of debris that no one believed could be put back together. Yet, Jesus Christ, holy and pure, came into our home to speak to us. He, of course, didn't come in human form but His presence was there. I knew how Saul felt that day on the way to Damascus. This changed my life forever. I knew I would never be the same again. It was almost as though, in that moment, His words to me were picking me up and putting me together.

I envisioned a man, in all white, using a broom and sweeping all my pieces into a solid gold dust pan. I would think He would take it and throw it away but He didn't. He poured them into a beautiful glass pan. This pan was like one I had seen on T.V. in a rich woman's mansion. It was crafted so perfectly. It was the purest of glass. He then began sorting out pieces and putting them back together again like a jig-saw puzzle. He knew where every piece needed to go. This was the beginning of a vessel. This vessel was so unrecognizable to the human eye but not to the creator of the universe, my potter. This moment, this very moment, I began being held in the potter's hands again. He was now focused on me and I wanted to let Him do whatever He wanted. I was ready to submit to Him in every way.

After a while, Laney looked at me and said, "We need to fast." I had NEVER fasted in my life. I told her I wanted a deeper relationship with God so I was willing to do whatever it took. She told me that she had fasted several times before and would help me. We decided that we would do a 40 day fast. She chose a liquid only fast and I decided on the traditional Daniel fast. The very next day, we started fasting.

We set our children down and told them that we were going to start a fast. We started each day with prayer and praise and worship. We spent every moment of our free time in the Word. I tried my best to journal every few days so that I could remember the journey that God was taking me on. Every day from this moment forward, I didn't leave the potter's wheel. I wanted him to mold me.

The Lord quickly led us to a verse. 2 Chronicles 7:14 says, "If my people, which are called by my name, shall humble themselves, and pray, and seek my face, and turn from their wicked ways; then I will hear from heaven, and will forgive their sin, and will heal their land". The Strong's Concordance defines the word "humble" as to bring down into subjection. I would say that the best way to humble yourself is to fast. This will bring your flesh into subjection to the Lord. This verse goes further than fasting though. This verse gives a few things to do:

- Humble yourselves
- Pray

- Seek His face
- Turn from your wicked ways

This meant that we had to do more than fasting. We took this verse and made it the verse that we would stand on for the next 40 days. 1 Thessalonians 5:17 says that we are to pray without ceasing so we made prayer, a fellowship with God, every moment of our day. We also started each day and ended each day with intimate quiet time with the Lord. We would spend time in our Word each day and would seek Him and who He was. We also completed Bible studies and listened to sermons as well. We decided that we would do our very best to abstain from sin or even what the world called sin. Kissing was allowed but no sexual relations. We decided that no matter what we felt like or thought that we would try our very best to follow the "rules" until the fast was over. If we finished the fast and still felt no conviction from God, we would get our marriage license the day after we finished. The verse stated that if we did these things, He would heal us. If we ended the fast, and were still gay, God must be okay with it.

I would get up early and spend time with God. I would study His Word, pray, sing to Him, and sometimes just sit in silence. His presence seemed to stay in our house. Our children became calm and loving. We all became the very best of friends. We became more and more like a family. The whole atmosphere in the house changed. It was almost like we were all new people experiencing a new "normal".

Most people want to seek God for healings, blessings, answers, and/or other things but we didn't. We really just wanted a relationship with God. I wanted to know Him. I wanted to hear His voice. I wanted to spend time with Him. I just missed Him. The more time I spent in

His presence, the less I wanted drugs or alcohol. The more time I spent with Him, the more I realized that I had missed it. Serving God wasn't about miracles or blessings. It wasn't about following a book of rules or even how you should look or act. Serving the Lord was about Him. It was about worshipping Him. It was about a relationship with Him. I had made it about all the wrong things. I began begging God to draw me closer to him. I craved Him. I would wake up and He was there. I would feel him right next to me. We would go on walks with the kids and He was there too. I felt Him touching me all the time.

Day 10 came and life was already very different. It was so hard to abstain but we did our best. With trying, we still messed up 2 times and ended up being sexual with one another. Afterwards, we felt terrible. We didn't feel like it was wrong because we were lesbians but because we had made a commitment to abstain. Conviction was strictly from having sex while fasting. We decided that since we were struggling that we would smoke a joint. The assumption was since marijuana was natural that it really couldn't be a sin. After smoking behind our house one day, we went inside. I don't remember which one of the 8 kids asked but one of them asks us to play a song. Laney began playing praise and worship music on the piano. Before we really knew what was going on, we were all in the living room praying. Laney and I were high and praising God. All of a sudden, Laney began speaking in tongues like she did that night by the couch. This was a stern and powerful voice though. The magnitude of this power bowed our kids to their knees. After she finished, she said in a voice that didn't sound like her own, "Everything must submit to me! Everything must submit to me!" I knew that was the interpretation. I know this next part is crazy but it is the truth. I was no longer high. I was more sober than I had ever been. I knew that God was angry. I had often heard of the wrath of God and I knew that we were about to see it if we didn't change. The scripture that says, "The fear of the Lord is the beginning of wisdom" was on my mind at that moment. I had been through so much in my lifetime but I had never been that scared. I was positive if I didn't surrender everything that God was going to change my life in a way that I couldn't imagine. All 8 children, Laney, and myself all prayed and repented of everything that we could think of.

After praying, Laney and I decided that we had to do more. Without ending the fast, we decided to restart the 40 days and give our best. This would make the fast actually a 50 day fast when completed. Laney switched to water only and I gave up all food for a liquid only fast. I knew that God had a huge plan for us. I wanted to be like Paul not Saul. I was ready to give my all and see what God could do.

One night, while laying and cuddling Laney, I had a flashback. Something she said triggered me. I was so angry with myself to have to deal with the past again. As I thought about, I couldn't help but get angry. I was allowing my dad to impact my life again. I hated what he had done to me but I hated even more that I let it rule over me and my life. I told Laney that I was going to take a shower and pray. We were trying to let God lead our life and I needed to hear from Him. I needed God to help me. As I stood in the shower, I began crying out to God. Why did my father do that to me? Why was he like that? What did I do to deserve that? I have heard the voice of God before. I heard it when He told me to run at camp. I heard it in the translated tongues that came forth. I had even heard Him by reading the Bible. This was different. Sometimes, God speaks in other ways. As I laid my head against the side of the shower, I begged God to help me. I closed my eyes and focused on the water hitting me. After a few minutes, I had a random thought in my mind. It caught me off guard. I knew I wasn't really thinking what I heard. I knew it had to be the Lord. The "thought" was this, "Do you love Laney?" At first, I thought that this couldn't be God. Why would He ask me this? I heard it within myself again. It was almost as if my heart had another voice hidden within. It must have been a voice and not a thought I thought. Then, I "heard" it again. "Do you love Laney?" I quietly whispered, "Yes, I do, with all of my heart. I love her with all that is within me. I can't change it. God, you know I have tried. I can't fix this. If I am wrong, then there is something wrong with me."

**What happened next is hard to comprehend. Please pray before continuing reading this. If I had not been seeking God and fasting, I think that this would have pulled me further away. This next part hurt me yet, helped me more than anything else. **

I stood there with my head against the shower wall. I was devastated. I had asked God to change me my whole life and He didn't. I had begged God for answers day after day. I heard this "voice" again coming from deep within my being. "You can't change you and your father couldn't change himself. You love the way you know and he does too." I collapsed into the shower floor. Why would God say this to me? I loved Laney because I was made that way. We were two consenting adults and I was tired of fighting it. If I were wrong, I could not help it. Now, I am not saying that what my father did was okay. I am not excusing what he did in any way but something happened. All of a sudden, with me on my knees and water running over me, I had peace. I had lived my whole life with the desire to be with a woman. I couldn't change my desires. I could not change what aroused me. I did have the choice whether to act on my feelings or not but after a while, I gave up. My father was weaker than I was. He wanted something and gave into it. What if my father had dealt with the same feelings I had for women but towards children. He couldn't change what aroused him. He needed God to heal him. Deep down inside, I knew I was wrong too and I couldn't change it. I needed God to fix me. We both were wrong and had given in. We both "loved" wrong. God would be the only one that could set us free. After I got out of the shower, I realized that I had done a lot of wrong things in my life because of what I felt. I had sinned in so many ways yet God wanted to know me. God wanted to know my father also. God wanted to help him as well. God wanted to heal my father like he was healing me. What my father did was terrible and disgusting but God loved him too. This knowledge was very helpful but very painful at the same time. You see, when God is molding you and sculpting you, it won't always feel pleasant. Clay sometimes has to be kneaded, cut, and molded several times to get to the finished beautiful vessel. Although this was painful, I had to let the potter shape me. I had to understand that the only thing that unforgiveness did was damage me more. If God loved my dad, and his soul, I should love him too. I chose that very day to forgive.

Now, let me make something very clear. Forgiving someone does help you heal but it is not a magic potion that immediately fixes every crack in us. Forgiveness does not make the pain leave immediately and it doesn't give you amnesia. You will still have pain and memories to deal with. Overtime, God can heal the pain though and the memories seem to fade. Forgiveness does allow you not to feel as though you get to be the judge. It takes the punishing out of your hands and places it into the hands of God. It helps you understand that every sin has consequences and that God can and will handle it. I once heard a woman speaking about forgiveness. She said that when we go to the altar and give our lives to Christ, we walk away with the same fat on our stomachs as we did when we approached the altar. Forgiveness of our sins did not give us the perfect body. Forgiveness is not something tangible. It will, however; change and heal us emotionally so that we can heal physically. Sometimes, when people get saved, emotionally healed, and forgiven, they want to get healthy as well. This is because the spiritual side of us will change the physical side of us. Many believe that forgiveness means that we are to forget. I believe that we will always remember the things that were done to us but forgiveness slowly erases the pain attached. You may have to wake up every morning and forgive a person. You may have to do it several times in one day but the day will come when it will change your heart. I decided that day to ask God to take my unforgiveness. I told God that I would no longer hold a grudge against my father. Instead of hating him, I began daily asking God to help him. I prayed for his finances, his friends, and his family. I also started praying for my parents' relationship. I asked God to help him be a good husband. I truly wanted God to help him. I know that my father did terrible things but nothing deserves burning in hell for eternity so I began praying that God would send someone to lead my father to the Lord. I wanted him to have a true relationship with the Lord. Every prayer seemed to smooth out more cracks in my heart. Every sincere prayer was a tool that God was using to form me.

The pain from my past was not gone but the hatred began to ease. I began to understand that my dad had been used by the enemy. Satan was the responsible one for what had happened to me. The enemy wanted to destroy me through my father. For several days, every time that I would think of my father, I had to forgive. I would have to make the decision not think about the things that he did to me. At first, I had to "forgive" about a hundred times a day. When you decide to forgive, it doesn't change how you feel about the situation right away. Many times, it takes hours of praying and allowing God to heal you from the pain and give you sincere love for that person. This was part of the process of the potter forming me though. He knew I had to slowly allow His love to trump the pain from my dad. I had to sincerely want to forgive.

Laney's children came come from a weekend visit with their father. Her son was acting very strange and not moving his arm much. We asked him what happened to his arm. He told us that he was sliding down the stairs and accidently fell down them and injured himself. Laney looked him over to find his collar bone abnormal. We both could see the break in the bone. It was as though it broke and then slightly overlapped itself. Laney immediately said we should get him to the emergency room. I explained to her that we had been fasting and praying and the Word says we should be able to lay hands on him and healing would take place. I placed my hand on the broken spot and she put hers on top of mine. Our children came over and placed their hands on top of ours as well. We prayed over him and demanded that the bone go back in place in Jesus' name. After we moved our hands, there was huge noticeable difference. Her son moved his arm around and said that it was much better and he barely could feel any pain. I refused to believe that God would heal halfway so we prayed again. When finished, he had full range of motion with no pain! God healed that bone right in front of us. We saw that bone be healed! God was not just healing us, he was healing those in our home. The potter was literally reconstructing those around me at the same time as He was molding me. It is amazing how the Lord will use you even when you are still broken. The Lord knew our hearts and had a relationship with us and He used us to heal.

The more we were in the presence of the Lord, the more the enemy fought us. We struggled with fighting the demons within us. Sometimes, during intense prayer, Laney would get very sick. She would begin vomiting. It was the craziest color that I had ever saw. It was a grayish color. I would pray over her and more and more would come out. If I stopped praying, it would begin to choke her. It was almost like it was holding on with every part of its being and praying over it was the only thing that made it release. At times, I would get scared and stop praying. Other times, I was crying too hard to pray. As I stopped, she would begin to turn blue. She would barely be able to whisper, "pray". I know God was digging everything out of us. The more we allowed God to mold in us, the more often these things happened. After about a week of this, it stopped but then, there were other struggles.

After a few weeks, Laney began to have moments of uncontrollable rage. She would hit things, throw things, and bang her head on the floor. I would practically hold her down and speak life over her. While holding her down, I would pray over her. I would rebuke the demons that I knew were within. After a little while, she would calm down. I can't even remember how many times this happened. We never gave up though. We were so stubborn that the resistance of our flesh pushed us to go further. I wanted to see what God would do if we gave our all.

Laney wasn't the only one that struggled. The rage would also come up in me. One night, we were sitting on our bed and I leaned over and kissed Laney. Without even thinking, we immediately began making out. It was almost like something took over and we lost control for about 5 minutes. All of a sudden, Laney stops me. She told me we had to wait until the fast was over and that we had to keep our vow to God. Something took over me. I stood up on the bed and screamed. This scream was a sound that did not sound like my own. Out of nowhere, with all that was within me, I punched the wall. It felt like I released some anger that was exploding inside of me. Before I could stop myself, I did it again. I punched it so hard that it went through to the outside wall. Seeing the holes in the wall and knowing the anger within me scared me. I began thinking the best thing I could do was to die before I hurt someone. I quickly made a plan. I would walk to Wal-Mart, buy a couple bottles of sleep aid and end my life. Billy had my children so I knew they were safe. As I walked out the door, Laney begged me to stop. I couldn't stop myself though, I kept on walking. I walked to the end of the street and I began hearing Laney cry. In my mind, I was doing what was best for her. I had to stop this constant struggle in me. I was a monster and one day I wouldn't be able to control it anymore. I walked about half way there and then Laney called. I didn't even answer her call. About 5 minutes later, I received a voice clip from her. I clicked it to hear it. The clip was her singing in tongues. It melted me. I could feel the Lord's presence in her voice. The struggled seemed worth it after this. I had to press on. I kept replaying the 1 minute clip over and over as I walked home. The walk home was more terrifying than when I left. As I walk back towards our house, I saw things following me. I saw shadows that didn't make sense on the road and sidewalk. I saw eyes peering out from behind houses and from behind tress. I had peace when I wanted to kill myself but the moment that I decided to turn around, the demons were there. It was very spooky. I got home and laid down. Laney sang and prayed over me until I could fall asleep. As I woke the next morning, the evil feeling was gone and God's presence filled the house again.

The next couple of days were calm. Then one night, after Bible study, Laney wanted to go to bed so I laid down with her. As I lay there, thoughts began to flood my mind. I kept hearing things that upset me. My thoughts were completely irrational. I began feeling abandoned and unwanted. I ask Laney to talk to me but she was so tired that she began falling asleep. Anger rose up in me again. I felt pain that I had not felt in a long time. I began missing my family. I missed my mother and father. I began wondering why they didn't love me. I got so angry that I ran to the bathroom and slammed the door. I had to find a way to relieve the pain that was inside. I locked the door and got out a razor blade. I set in Indian style against the wall behind the door. I blocked the door so that no one could come in. I began slicing my left leg right on my calf muscle. Cut after cut felt like I was touching someone else's leg. It was almost as though I wasn't even me. It felt as though this body belonged to someone else. As the blood started to drip down my leg, the blood felt as though it was a symbol of the pain releasing. Within a few moments, Laney was at the door. She ended up pushing in the door and finding me. I felt so ashamed. The Lord had given this body to me yet I was destroying it. I felt conviction for not allowing God to console me. I felt conviction that I would hurt myself after all that the Lord had done in me. Laney wrapped my leg and we went to bed. I hated myself for what I did. I made a vow to the Lord that I would not ever do that again; I couldn't. He was so gracious to me and I had to let him take care of me. I had to continuously go to God for healing. I knew that I had forgiven my father and my family but the emotional scars were there. The cuts on my leg would now remind me that I had scars no one could see. These were on my legs but I had scars on my heart that no one could ever begin to see.

The next morning, I did Bible study as usual and then got on my knees to pray. As I was praying, I saw a vision. My eyes were closed but I saw it like it was a movie playing inside of my head. I saw a little girl about 5 years of age walking towards me. She had a light pink old fashion lace dress on. The dress was very dirty. The little girl had dirt on her legs and on her face. I knew by the way that she walked that she was so ashamed of who she was. I could tell that she had been crying because of the clean streaks down her face amongst the dirt. Her hair was a huge mess and looked as though she hadn't been cared for in a while. For a moment, I didn't know who she was. Then, she began walking closer to me. My heart sank. I began to cry uncontrollably. That sweet little girl was me. I could see the pain in her eyes. She was so innocent yet had endured such terrible punishments. She had received punishments that she never deserved. A voice from behind her began to come forth. I heard a sweet and soft man's voice. He said, "If you don't let her go, she will be in pain forever. Allow her to come with me. I will make sure she is taken care of. Please, set her free." I knew what this meant. I had somehow began holding her captive. Long ago, I locked her inside of me and didn't ever want her out. It was too painful to feel her. It was easier to pretend that it didn't happen. It was so much easier to believe this happened to someone that deserved it. Beyond that though, I wanted to pretend that little girl never existed. Life was easier with her locked away. I knew I had to let her go. I knew I had to give her up. It wasn't fair to her after all that she had been through to be treated the way she was. As I laid there on the floor, my eyes still closed, I began to speak aloud. I said, "God, take her and make her whole. She needs to be taken care of." I heard the words come out of me and the power it held was incredible. I saw a man in all white come down and pick the little girl up. She was looking over His shoulder as they walk off into the distance. She looked back at me with the sweetest smile. I noticed as they faded away that her dress was clean. Her body was now clean too. Her hair had been brushed and was now pretty with a bow in it. She was completely clean and happy. Jesus Christ came and made her new. Jesus had delivered her from captivity, wiped away her pain and shame, and made her clean. She looked totally different. I felt the Lord saying, "You don't need her anymore. I am making you new."

Time seemed to stand still. This vision was exactly what God was trying to do for me. He was taking this broken and destroyed vessel and making it new. I couldn't move on without letting go of that little girl within me. For too many years, my world revolved around what had happened to her but not in the way that it should have. Instead of me acknowledging what had happened to her and helping her heal, I locked her up deep inside and tried not to remember her. I didn't want to see her face. I didn't want to know that it happened. I did everything in my power to keep her memory away from me. The triggers would have brought back the pain she was feeling so I avoided them. I kept walls around my heart so that I couldn't feel her pain and sadness. Many days, I would simply blame her for what had happened. Punishing her made it easier not to be upset with those people who were the actual ones responsible. The Lord was trying to show me that he could mold me into a vessel that was new. This vision is exactly what God wants to do to each of us if we allow it. He wants to make us whole. He wants to take the guilt and shame of the past and give us joy. He wants to make us clean.

I realized that all those years God was trying to heal me. I was the one stopping Him. I didn't want to give up that girl. I wanted to hold her captive and blame everything that went wrong in my life on her and the things she had endured. With her, I didn't have to do the hard things. I would tell myself, "You were abused. You were raped. It is okay to be angry. It is okay to be different. People don't know what you have went through." It was easy not to allow myself to change when I had her. As the Lord removed her, I knew that I could no longer use that has an excuse. Yes, it happened. Yes, it was a horrific life she lived. Yes, some people are evil. These things were true but I could no longer let those things guide my life. I was in charge now. Whatever happened to me from now on was my choice. I had to take charge of my life. I decided that the best thing to do was let God have my life. I was in charge now so I would let the creator lead me. I saw how much He loved that little girl and He loved me too. God loves each of us the way He loved that precious little one. I wanted God to form me into a new creation like He changed her. No matter the pain, I was ready. I was ready for a new journey. I was ready for a journey based upon the future and not the past. I was now ready to be molded into the vessel God wanted. I was ready to be the vessel that He planned from the very beginning. I wanted it more than anything else. Whatever it took, I would let Him mold me.

The Lord will only mold us if we allow it. I was more than ready now. I had to be molded. I asked God that if there was anything in me that displeased Him to please cut it out of me. I didn't want to do or say anything that didn't bring Him glory. I craved His touch. I wanted Him to pull me apart, cut me, push me together, and mold me. God showed me things that displeased Him. He showed me that I had to act like Him. He showed me who He was so that I could be like Him. He began changing me so fast that I couldn't keep up with all the new thought processes and ideas. He truly was renewing my mind daily. I was becoming more and more like love and more and more like Him. He was molding me into a vessel that He could use. I knew one day He was going to use me. One day, I was going to change the world for Him. With all God was teaching me, I still had no convictions about marrying a woman. I couldn't help but to think that I really wasn't wrong and God would use us (a lesbian couple) to change the church.

God began giving me many dreams and visions. Most of these dreams were about the scriptures that I had been studying throughout the day. These were giving me a deep understanding of the scriptures and wisdom that only could come from Him. One night, I had a dream about something that I had not been reading. The dream began with our family hosting a huge BBQ or picnic at our house. Liz and her family was there along with Laney and her extended family. From what I could tell, it was planned for one of my children's birthday. Laney asked me to go into the house and get some tea and lemonade as we were almost out. I ran into the house. As I came in the door, my Bible began flipping pages as if the wind was blowing it. It was flipping quickly and didn't stop as I ran passed it. I began making the drinks and the Bible pages slowed but didn't stop. I stood far away from it and asked God why there was a demon in my house. I felt God say to go pick the book up. I was very hesitant but eventually crept towards it and picked it up. The Bible stopped moving when I placed my hands on it. I looked down to read it but couldn't. It was almost as if I were illiterate. I could see letters on the page but couldn't understand what the words meant. I ran outside and went up to Laney. I pointed to the page and begged her to read it me. She looked at it and said, "Listen. Listen." Then, she looked up at me, calmed her voice and said, "I can't tell you. You have to hear it for yourself. You have to know it for yourself." I was shocked! Why wouldn't she just tell me? I went to Liz and many others to have them read it to me. No one would help me. They all kept telling me the same thing, "Listen. Listen. I can't tell you. You have to hear it for yourself. You have to know it for yourself. You have to listen." After hearing the same thing from each person, I was so frustrated. I walked back into the house and sat down. I looked down at the Bible and finally read the words, "Genesis 8". At that very moment, I woke from the dream.

I seldom wake from a night of sleep with energy but this morning I did. I sat up, jump from the bed, and went to grab my Bible. I had to find out what that dream was about. I didn't understand what it meant but something was important about it. As I began turning to Genesis, Laney called for me. She was in the bathtub praying. She told me she had been praying because she couldn't sleep. She began telling me the scriptures that were on her heart. I told her I would turn to her scriptures but then I had to tell her about my dream. Laney told me to turn my Bible to Matthew 24:36-39. I read it aloud, "But about that day or hour no one knows, not even the angels in heaven, nor the Son, but only the Father. As it was in the days of Noah, so it will be at the coming of the Son of Man. For in the days before the flood, people were eating and drinking, marrying and giving in marriage, up to the day Noah entered the ark; and they knew nothing about what would happen until the flood came and took them all away. That is how it will be at the coming of the Son of Man. Two men will be in the field; one will be taken and the other left. Two women will be grinding with a hand mill; one will be taken and the other left."

I stood in silence for a moment. I was completely shocked. Noah is in Genesis. I wondered I my dream had to do with Noah. I didn't even wait to hear what Laney was praying about that verse. I began blurting out my dream like a mad woman. After I finished, she asked, "What is Genesis 8?" I laughed and replied, "I don't know." I turned to Genesis and as I got to chapter 8, I began seeing that it was indeed about Noah. God had given me a dream and confirmed it. I knew this dream was important. I knew I was doing something wrong but didn't understand what it could be. I also knew that it would have to be a sin revealed by God Himself. I understood from the dream that whatever it was, no one could help me. I had to hear it for myself. I had to let Him, God, explain it to me.

As I type this, I have no idea why I couldn't understand the dream. It was so plain and yet I was spiritually illiterate. I had no understanding of the meaning. Sometimes, God tells us things as plain as He can and we just don't understand it. Maybe it was the enemy that stopped my understanding, or maybe it was my heart. Maybe, just maybe, I didn't really want to know the meaning.

We decided to attend a church close our house. We went occasionally. It was beginning to be warmer outdoors. One day, the spring weather was so nice that we decided to walk to church. That weekend, we just had Laney's children. As we walked to church, I began praying about the dream. I was abstaining from sexual immorality. I was praying and fasting daily and I couldn't understand what else God could be telling me. I prayed the whole way to church as Laney and the kids walked ahead of me. I felt a question from the Lord. It was almost like the time in the shower but not as loud. I "heard" within me, "If you never marry her, will you still serve me?" I kind of laughed at the question. Of course I would still serve God. The last few weeks were hard but I loved how close God was to me. I thought of all the things God had done for me. I could never turn my back on Him. I also thought of all the times God tricked people in the Bible to see if they would truly pick Him. I figured that this was simply a test like Abraham and Isaac. The Lord was testing me to see if I would choose Him over the love of my life. I knew that I had to choose God but I was also hoping that God would never make me choose.

The worship had already started as we entered the church. I felt His presence so strong. It was almost as if I could feel Him right beside me. We quickly found a seat and stood in front of them and began to worship. I felt as though I was standing before the throne of God and just worshiping Him for who He was. I began to praise Him. I raised my hands up and prayed, "Lord, I surrender everything to you. I don't want to do anything or say anything that doesn't glorify you. Please take me and make me what you want me to be. I want to worship you in everything I do." I don't know how to explain this but it was like a sweet feeling of indescribable love that came over me. I didn't care about anything except making sure God knew I loved him. As the worship continued, I stood and sang to the Lord with my hands raised and my eyes closed. All of a sudden, I loud sound came from the platform. It sounded as though someone smacked the pulpit but the music didn't stop. I didn't care what it was. I wanted to stay right where I was and worship the Lord. I didn't open my eyes but I started seeing something. I began seeing a large vessel held by a hand. It reminded me of a water pitcher in older movie that someone would use to pour water into a water basin to wash their hands. It was off white with small pink flowers painted around the top. It had a beautiful handle. It looked as though it was fine porcelain or china. The vessel moved across the church above the heads of the people. I saw it begin to pour oil on each head that it came to. With Laney on my right, I saw it pour on her head too. Then, the vessel came above me. I tilted my head up as though I was seeing it while my eyes were still closed. I saw it start to spill on me so I looked down to the floor as though not to hit my face. The oil poured slowly down my head. I felt the warmth of it run down my cheeks as it splashed on my shoulders. It was very warm yet not oily. If felt as though it made me cleaner. This oil seemed to feel like all the dirt of me spiritually and physically were gone. The vessel then finished pouring over everyone else. As the music faded, I opened my eyes. I looked around to see a man walking up on the platform. He reached down and picked up the bottle of anointing oil and someone handed him a cloth for the spill. The bottle had fallen off the pulpit. That was the loud sound. The oil spilled in that church that day. It did more than spill on the carpet though. That day, the anointing of the Lord spilled on each one of us. I left church that day and was never the same. Something changed in me. I felt free and my thoughts were clear. The anointing that fell changed me.

I didn't know much about the meaning of the oil being pour on the heads of people so I began to research it. Psalm 23:5 says, "You anoint my head with oil." Why would God anoint us with oil? The Lord says in John 10:14 that He (God) is the good shepherd and that He knows us. Several times in the Bible God is referred to as the shepherd and us as the sheep. I knew that God was the shepherd and we were like sheep. Although I didn't understand, I still had to just follow Him.

I began to notice a difference in my life. I began to think more clearly. I studied the Bible daily but it started to become very real to me. I would read and the same stories that I have heard my whole life was meaning something different to me. I was thinking about the words that God spoke to us the very first day of this journey. The night that God came into our living room and flipped my world completely upside down, He gave me a promise. He told me that if I would step out into the deep, I would have a Saul turned Paul experience. I knew the story but I had to read it again. God was giving me more and more understanding of His word and I had to seek this out too. I sat down with a notebook and pencil and turned my Bible to the Book of Acts. I began in chapter 9.

I read it aloud and very slowly, "Then Saul, still breathing threats and murder against the disciples of the

Lord, went to the high priest and asked letters from him to the synagogues of Damascus, so that if he found any who were of the Way, whether men or women, he might bring them bound to Jerusalem. As he journeyed he came near Damascus, and suddenly a light shone around him from heaven. Then he fell to the ground, and heard a voice saying to him, "Saul, Saul, why are you persecuting me?" And he said, "Who are You, Lord?" Then the Lord said, "I am Jesus, whom you are persecuting."

I stopped reading, I was shocked. He said He was Jesus! Jesus! He didn't say that He was the father or the spirit but Jesus. I had always been taught that Jesus was the son of God. He was the human. How was it that Jesus was speaking from the heavens to Saul? Wouldn't God be speaking? Jesus must be God! God must be Jesus! I thought they were separate but they weren't. They had to be one. I had to search this more. How could this be? What had I been missing all these years? Maybe I had His name wrong? I began looking up everything that I could find about the name of God and who He was. I started in the Old Testament and went to the New. I found several scriptures that said the same things so I just chose one for this book. Please study this your for yourself as I did.

- God is the creator. Genesis 1:1- In the beginning, God created the heaven and the earth.
- He is the great I AM. Exodus 3:14- And God said unto Moses, I Am That I Am: and he said, Thus shalt thou say unto the children of Israel, I Am hath sent me unto you.
- God is the redeemer and savior. Isaiah 47:4- As for our redeemer, the Lord of Hosts is

His name, the Holy One of Israel. Isaiah 43:11- Beside me there is no savior.

- God is the king, and the first and the last. Isaiah 44:6- Thus saith the Lord the King of Israel, and his redeemer the Lord of hosts; I am the first, and I am the last; and beside me there is no God.
- God is the rock. Psalm 89:26- He shall cry unto me, Thou art my father, my God, and the rock of my salvation.
- God is coming back for us. Psalm 50:1-6 - The mighty God, even the Lord, hath spoken, and called the earth from the rising of the sun unto the going down thereof. Out of Zion, the perfection of beauty, God hath shined. Our God shall come, and shall not keep silence: a fire shall devour before him, and it shall be very tempestuous round about him. He shall call to the heavens from above, and to the earth, that he may judge his people. Gather my saints together unto me; those that have made a covenant with me by sacrifice. And the heavens shall declare his righteousness
- God is our shepherd. Isaiah 40:11- Behold, the Lord God will come with strong hand, and his arm shall rule for him: behold, his reward is with him, and his work before him. He shall feed his flock like a shepherd: he shall gather the lambs with his arm, and carry them in his bosom, and shall gently lead those that are with young.

After searching through the Old Testament, I began seeking those same names in the New Testament. Below are a few chosen scriptures that I found. Once again, please search the scriptures out yourself. Many times, we believe what we have heard and haven't truly read it for ourselves. This is where many of my theories of who God was came from until I began seeking God for Him to reveal it to me.

- Jesus is the creator. John 1:1-14- In the beginning was the Word, and the Word was with God, and the Word was God. The same was in the beginning with God. All things were made by him; and without him was not anything made that was made. In him was life; and the life was the light of men. And the light shineth in darkness; and the darkness comprehended it not. There was a man sent from God, whose name *was* John. The same came for a witness, to bear witness of the Light, that all *men* through him might believe. He was not that Light, but *was sent* to bear witness of that Light. *That* was the true Light, which lighteth every man that cometh into the world. He was in the world, and the world was made by him, and the world knew him not. He came unto his own, and his own received him not. But as many as received him, to them gave he power to become the sons of God, *even* to them that believe on his name: Which were born, not of blood, nor of the will of the flesh, nor of the will of man, but of God. And the Word was made flesh, and dwelt among us
- Jesus is the I AM. John 18:5-8- They answered him, Jesus of Nazareth. Jesus saith unto them, I am he. And Judas also, which betrayed him, stood with them. As

soon then as he had said unto them, I am he, they went backward, and fell to the ground. Then asked he them again, Whom seek ye? And they said, Jesus of Nazareth. Jesus answered, I have told you that I am he.

- Jesus is the redeemer and savior. Galatians 3:13- Christ hath redeemed us from the curse of the law, being made a curse for us: for it is written, Cursed *is* every one that hangeth on a tree. Luke 2:10-11- And the angel said unto them, Fear not: for, behold, I bring you good tidings of great joy, which shall be to all people. For unto you is born this day in the city of David a Savior, which is Christ the Lord.

- Jesus is king. Luke 23:3- And Pilate asked him, saying, Art thou the King of the Jews? And he answered him and said, Thou sayest *it*.

- Jesus is the First and the Last. Revelation 1:17- And when I saw him, I fell at his feet as dead. And he laid his right hand upon me, saying unto me, Fear not; I am the first and the last.

- Jesus is the rock. 1 Corinthians 10:4- And did all drink the same spiritual drink: for they drank of that spiritual Rock that followed them: and that Rock was Christ.

- Jesus is coming back. John 14:2-3- In my Father's house are many mansions: if *it* *were* not *so,* I would have told you. I go to prepare a place for you. And if I go and prepare a place for you, I will come again, and receive you unto myself; that where I am, *there* ye may be also.

- Jesus is our shepherd. John 10:11- Jesus says, "I am the good shepherd: the good shepherd giveth his life for the sheep."

As I studied the scriptures, everything that God said He was in the Old Testament, Jesus said He was in the New Testament. The Bible never lies and can't contradict itself. If this all is true, Jesus is God. They must be one in the same. I searched the Bible for the word "one". If they are one, then the Bible had to have it in there. I came across Deuteronomy 6:4-9, "Hear, O Israel: The LORD our God is one LORD: And thou shalt love the LORD thy God with all thine heart, and with all thy soul, and with all thy might. And these words, which I command thee this day, shall be in thine heart: And thou shalt teach them diligently unto thy children, and shalt talk of them when thou sittest in thine house, and when thou walkest by the way, and when thou liest down, and when thou risest up. And thou shalt bind them for a sign upon thine hand, and they shall be as frontlets between thine eyes. And thou shalt write them upon the posts of thy house, and on thy gates."

The Lord knew that one day, we might question if the Lord was one God. He put this in the Bible to have us teach our children. The Jewish people put this scripture in boxes and wrapped them around their arms and their heads. They also had it written above their doors so that no one would ever doubt it. Jesus wasn't just the "son of God" like I had always thought. He was God!

1 Timothy 2:16- And without controversy great is the mystery of godliness: God was manifest in the flesh, justified in the Spirit, seen of angels, preached unto the Gentiles, believed on in the world, received up into glory.

God spoke and formed the entire world in Genesis. The Word of God became flesh and dwelt among us as well. He clothed Himself in flesh and came down so we could be saved. Many times, while reading these scriptures, I wondered why the Bible says that He sent His only begotten son. If God came in flesh, then why does that scripture put it that in those words? As the Angel of the Lord is talking to Mary in Luke 1:35, he says something that makes all of this make perfect sense. He says, "The Holy Ghost shall come upon thee, and the power of the Highest shall overshadow thee: therefore also that holy thing which shall be born of thee shall be called the Son of God." This is something that I had never heard. These scriptures were new to me. If God spoke and the Word created the world, and that Word was made flesh, it was the Word of God that was in Mary. When a human has a child, it is either a son or a daughter. The Word of God was placed in Mary and was born a boy therefore; He was called the Son of God.

If "one" was in the Bible pertaining to God, I wondered if trinity was. I couldn't find it anywhere. I did however found something that mentioned the number three. 1 John 5:6-8- This is he that came by water and blood, even Jesus Christ; not by water only, but by water and blood. And it is the Spirit that beareth witness, because the Spirit is truth. For there are three that bear record in heaven, the Father, the Word, and the Holy Ghost: and these three are one.

1 Corinthians 2:10-16- But God hath revealed them unto us by his Spirit: for the Spirit searcheth all things, yea, the deep things of God. For what man knoweth the things of a man, save the spirit of man which is in him? even so the things of God knoweth no man, but the Spirit of God. Now we have received, not the spirit of the world, but the spirit which is of God; that we might know the things that are freely given to us of God. Which things also we speak, not in the words which man's wisdom teacheth, but which

the Holy Ghost teacheth; comparing spiritual things with spiritual. But the natural man receiveth not the things of the Spirit of God: for they are foolishness unto him: neither can he know them, because they are spiritually discerned. But he that is spiritual judgeth all things, yet he himself is judged of no man. For who hath known the mind of the Lord, that he may instruct him? But we have the mind of Christ.

God is one but manifest Himself in three ways. He wasn't three separate. He is one! He is the Father, the Spirit, and the Word that was made flesh. He is the loving father, the spirit which is the mind of Christ, and the Word that was made flesh and His name is Jesus! I can't believe that I didn't know this. No wonder there is power in the name of Jesus! That is the name of God. My God didn't just send someone else to save me. He wrapped himself in flesh and came to die on a cross for me. He was fully God yet fully man and His name is Jesus!

I couldn't get enough studying about Him now. I had to know more. The more I studied, prayed, and worshipped Him, the more the cracks began to heal. The flashbacks and body memories that I use to have daily were there but not very often. I wanted to be with Laney but it wasn't as hard to abstain now. Even the anger that was built up in me seemed to fade away. I felt like the potter was smoothing more and more cracks out each day. I had some scars but they weren't deep cuts like they use to me. I wanted God to keep revealing more and more to me. I realized that had an addictive behavior and I would use it for the Lord. I became addicted to the feeling He gave me. I became addicted to the wisdom and knowledge He gave me about Himself. I would lay in bed at night and pray that God would take anything out of me that wasn't of Him. I loved Laney but if God didn't want me with her, I didn't want it either. I began praying a prayer that I still pray this very day. If you want God's will in every aspect of your life, you can pray this too. The prayer that I began to pray goes like this:

"Lord Jesus, Thank you for who you are. Thank you for loving me. Lord, I give you my life this day. Please take it and use it for your glory. Take anything out of me that doesn't honor you. Please forgive me for the things I do that displeases you. I pray that you take my heart and bind it to your heart. Please take my mind and mind it to your mind. Take my will and emotions and bind them to yours. Lord, bind me so tightly to you that I don't think, desire, feel, or do anything that doesn't glorify you. I pray that you would take me and mold me into the vessel that you can use. Teach me to love and worship you the way you designed me to. Help me crave your Word, your voice, and your will. Help me to hear you constantly. Help me obey you no matter how it feels. I want to fall more and more in love with you. I want to worship you for all of eternity. Teach me, Lord, to give you all the honor, and glory, and praise. Amen."

I can honestly say that I began seeking God for who He was instead of what He could do for me. All those years, I wanted to do the right things and be in ministry for me not Him. The more that I learned about Him, the more I could see that He deserved to be worshiped for who He was. He is Holy, righteous, and pure. He loved me for who I was. He stayed with me my whole life and protected me. My life could have been so much worse. Many people have a past that make mine look like a stroll in the park. I may not have had the perfect life but He gave me strength to come out stronger than I was before. I began falling in love with a savior. I fell in love with a God that knows everything I did, every thought I have ever had, every sin that I have committed, every desire I wanted and loved me anyway. He loved me enough to die on a cross that I might make the choice to spend eternity with Him. I fell in love with the true meaning of the love; the unconditional love of a true father.

Deliver Me

Day 40 came around so slowly yet quicker than I felt it would. This was the 30th day of my liquid only fast and the water only for Laney. We had completed the other fast first and restarted with a deeper fast which put the fast on day 40. This was the day that we had originally set for the decision for our marriage license. At the very beginning, we agreed that at the end of day 40 of the fast, we would get our marriage license and dedicate our marriage to the Lord if we were still feeling that it was acceptable. This day woke me with excitement! I couldn't wait to be her wife. I had a greater love for her than at the beginning. I couldn't imagine life without her. God had revealed so much to me and yet nothing He told me dealt with homosexually. God was love. God loved me just the way I was and I didn't have to change for Him. He would always love me and He would never make me do anything that I didn't want to. I began counting down the hours until I could hold her and kiss her the way I so wanted to.

We wanted to finish that day abstaining for the Lord. We decided to watch a sermon on YouTube to pass the time. Our children were with their dads and would be back late that evening. We knew that day would be the hardest day to keep our vow to God. We were so excited to see what the future held. If you could imagine, sitting there and being "good" was harder than ever. She was the love of my life. The last 40 days, I had fasted with her. I had seen her heart. I watched her as she would pray over our children. I sat and listened to her confess things in her life that no one knew. We knew everything about each other and it only made us love each other more. I had waited my whole life for this moment. She was what I had always wanted in a marriage. She was kind, beautiful, and sweet. She was an amazing mom to all of our children. Since the fast, she also now had a close relationship with God too. I imagined the rest of our life together. I thought about how we would teach the church that they were behind the times. I would show them that God loves everyone. I had proof that God loved me because of the relationship that we now had. The church had taken the Bible and made it a list of rules that we must follow in order to get into the kingdom of God. I had spent 31 years begging God to change me but He never did. He never took the desire away to be with another woman. I sat and thought about how I was created this way. There was no other reason to explain the way my body was responding just by sitting next to her. I was drawn to her. I couldn't help but think that this was God's plan.

I dismissed my thoughts and focused on the video we were watching. If I were to make it through the night, I had to keep my focus on God and Him alone. I watched as a video spoke on many different things about the Lord. It was speaking about a boy's vision of heaven. As he spoke, he said something that grabbed my heart. He said that all of our sins hurt God. All sin was equal and everything from lying to murder was wrong. He never once mentioned homosexuality. This boy explained that it saddened God to have sin in His people. This sin would separate us from Him forever. As I listened, something rose up in me. I had asked my whole life for God to take the desires I had away. I spent many nights praying that God would make me fall in love with Billy. God never changed me though. At that very moment, I closed my eyes and got on my knees in the middle of our bed. I felt Laney move and do the same. I knelt there and prayed, "God, speak to me. I need you." I began seeing a vision. It appeared slowly into my view. I saw Jesus Christ on a cross. The whole world around didn't matter. The only thing that mattered was me. I watched as the soldiers beat Him. As I saw each swing of the whip, I could see sins that I had committed. I saw lies, thoughts, stolen items, disobedience, drugs, alcohol, and then, I saw something that hurt more than anything else. The last thing I saw was Laney and I in bed together. I looked at the face of Christ. He had sweat and blood running off His forehead. The crown of thorns was digging into the top of His head. His skin was torn open and I could see a piece of a rib. I knew that He wasn't stuck there. I knew that all He had to do was get down but He didn't. He looked up at me with love. He was being beaten and still didn't have anything towards me but love. The vision then faded away as it came. All of sudden, I felt shame. This was not the shame of abuse. That kind of shame I was accustom to. I felt a different shame. This shame was like conviction. I thought of everything I had been so proud of. I thought of everything that I had done and how the whole world could see it on me. I felt shame because I was hurting God and the whole world had tried to tell me but I would listen. All those years, I had asked God to change me for me. I didn't want to be a lesbian because it was too hard for me. In the past, I wanted God to change me because people said it was wrong. I wanted to be delivered because I didn't want to be kicked out of the ministry. I want God to make me love Billy so that my life was easier. This was different now. I felt different. Now, I wanted God to change me for Him. I didn't want to hurt Him. I loved Him so much that the thought of sin separating me from Him broke me. In my heart, I knew that I didn't have to change. I knew that God would love me unconditionally. I knew that God would always want to be with me. I didn't have to be changed; this was a choice. I was weeping as I prayed, "God, take this away from me. I don't want to be anything that you didn't create me to me. I never want to do anything that hurts you. I don't care what it takes. Lord, rip everything out of me that displeases you. I want you to have control over this body, mind, and soul. Jesus, I surrender everything I am to you. I am yours! Take me and make me yours. I want to please you not myself anymore. Please forgive me for caring more about myself than you. Please forgive me for putting earthy fleshly desires above you. I will honor your commands. I will honor your will for my life. Here I am Lord, I am yours…"

With tears continuing to fall, I stayed knelt there for a long time. My heart was broken. This whole fast was about getting to know God and I had. He loved me enough to show me what I was doing that hurt Him. Nothing I wanted or desired compared to the love of God towards me. I made my mind up, even if I always wanted to be with another woman, I would never give in. I wanted to please God. Pleasing God was now my number one focus. After 20 minutes or so, I sat up and looked at Laney. She had tears running down her face. We stared at each other for a moment and then I spoke, "We are wrong. Aren't we?" Words can't express the moment that followed. We simultaneously cried out, "I am so sorry! Please forgive me!" We grabbed each other in a hug and there it was; nothing. We pushed each other back. We both looked confused. I tilted my head for a moment and hugged her again. Nothing. There was absolutely nothing there. I wasn't sexually attracted to her at all. I felt as though I was hugging my little sister. She looked at me and said, "Do you feel that?" I nodded at her. We felt the same. I had an overwhelming love for her. This love was greater than before. This love was more than a love that made me want to marry her. This love was like Ruth and Naomi. I knew right then the love that David had for Jonathon. I loved her more than myself. I wanted what was best for her above all else. I didn't think I could love her more but I did. The relationship before wasn't love; it was lust. We knew right then what true love was. We sat crying and holding each other. We were apologizing to one another and promising never to go back to that life again. We found deliverance that night. As we sat there, wrapped in each other's arms, we didn't feel bondage anymore. We felt free. It was the most amazing and pure love that we had ever felt. We were completely free. Time passed and someone had to break the silence, so she did. She looked at me, "Donna" she said, "I can't marry you but I can be your best friend forever." We both smiled. "I am glad because I can't marry you either" I told her.

I reached over and picked up my cell phone and she did the same. Without letting each other know what we were doing, we both made a post to Facebook. We publicly repented and asked the forgiveness of our family and friends. I wanted the whole world to know that I was sorry and that I would serve God for the rest of my life. After we put our phones away, I looked at Laney. I told her there was something I had to do now. I needed to be baptized. I told her I would study out baptism and I wanted to be baptized the last day of the fast. We only had 10 days left of fasting. I vowed to be baptized before I ended the fast.

That night changed my life forever. I knew that the potter was molding me but I didn't quite understand the vessel He was making. I thought He was making me into one thing but His vision of me was something totally different. Many times in life, we think we know what God's plans are for us. We often work towards goals or changes that we believe that God wants for us. I have found through this that only the potter knows the right vessel for us to become. He knows what will make us the happiest and healthiest. He knows what we really need in order to fulfil the plans that we were created for. As I look back, I understand that it was only through complete submission to the potter that He is able to mold me. After this night, I felt like a new person. I had always been the closest lesbian who couldn't stand herself because of the fake life she was leading. This one event changed all of that. Some days, the potter makes small differences but other days, major changes must occur. I finally felt real. Several times I wondered if I had dreamt it all. My thoughts were different. My wants and desires were different. I was different. I had finally completely given myself to the potter and He changed me from the inside out. There was so much left for the potter to do but, this was a big start. This day, I found true salvation. He saved me from a prison I didn't know I was being held in. From this moment on, I was no longer a slave to sin. I knew the God that could break any chain and His name is Jesus.

I had just 10 days left to study out baptism and the fast would end. The first thing I did was read back through the story of Saul/Paul in the Book of Acts. I had to read it all again and see what He did when God changed His life. Then, I began seeking everything I could on baptism. I remember giving my life to God has a child and getting baptized in a nice warm river but I don't think that I fully understood it all. I wanted to study it out. Why should I get baptized? What would it mean? How do I go about it? There were so many questions that I had. I will try to walk you through the scriptures as I journaled them. I learned in this order and if you have questions, it might help you as well.

These are the words of Jesus. Matthew 28:19- "Go therefore and make disciples of all the nations, baptizing them in the name of the Father and of the Son and of the Holy Spirit."

This verse says to use one name. The Father, Son and Holy Spirit must all have one name.

Acts 2:38- Then Peter said to them, "Repent, and let every one of you be baptized in the name of Jesus Christ for the remission of sins; and you shall receive the gift of the Holy Spirit"

One verse says that I should be baptized in the name of the Father, the Son, and the Holy Spirit. The other verse says it should be done in the name of Jesus. The Father, Son, and Holy Spirit are all titles. What is that name? Jesus is His name. Matthew, who wrote Matthew 28:19, was with the other disciples when Peter said this. (Acts 1:13- And when they were come in, they went up into an upper room, where abode both Peter, and James, and John, and Andrew, Philip, and Thomas, Bartholomew, and Matthew, James *the son* of Alphaeus, and Simon Zelotes, and Judas *the brother* of James.) I believe that if Matthew knew that Peter was preaching it wrong, he would have said something. Throughout the book of Acts, I found that they baptized people in Jesus' name. So, the disciples must have understood the name of the Father, Son and Holy Ghost to be Jesus! NOWHERE in scripture did I find anyone being baptized using those three titles. I only found them being baptized in the name of Jesus.

Acts 8:12- But when they believed Philip as he preached the things concerning the kingdom of God and the name of Jesus Christ, both men and women were baptized.

Acts 8:16- For as yet He had fallen upon none of them. They had only been baptized in the name of the Lord Jesus.

Acts 10:48- And he commanded them to be baptized in the name of the Lord.

Acts 19:5- When they heard this, they were baptized in the name of the Lord Jesus.

Acts 22:16- And now why are you waiting? Arise and be baptized, and wash away your sins, calling on the name of the Lord.

I had never heard of this kind of baptism. Everyone, that I knew, always preached in the name of the Father, the Son, and the Holy Spirit. I had to keep digging. I had to be sure that this was right. If God was one, it would make sense though that I would be baptized in one name. I kept searching.

Colossians 3:17- And whatsoever ye do in word or deed, *do* all in the name of the Lord Jesus, giving thanks to God and the Father by him.

Scripture tells us that whatever we do in word or deed should be done in the name of Jesus. Baptism is an act of both word and deed.

John 4:1-2- When therefore the Lord knew how the Pharisees had heard that Jesus made and baptized more disciples than John, (Though Jesus himself baptized not, but his disciples,)

Acts 19:1-5- And it came to pass, that, while Apollos was at Corinth, Paul having passed through the upper coasts came to Ephesus: and finding certain disciples, He said unto them, Have ye received the Holy Ghost since ye believed? And they said unto him, We have not so much as heard whether there be any Holy Ghost. And he said unto them, Unto what then were ye baptized? And they said, Unto John's baptism. Then said Paul, John verily baptized with the baptism of repentance, saying unto the people, that they should believe on him which should come after him, that is, on Christ Jesus. When they heard this, they were baptized in the name of the Lord Jesus.

So Peter, John, and the rest of the disciples baptized everyone in the Jesus' name. Paul even re-baptized the believers in Ephesus in Jesus' name. When Jesus' was on this earth, He baptized His disciples and then commissioned them to go and baptize others in His name, or in His place. When Jesus baptized someone, He didn't have to say "in the name of Jesus" because He was Jesus.

Philippians 2:8-10- And being found in human form, he humbled himself by becoming obedient to the point of death, even death on a cross. Therefore God has highly exalted him and bestowed on him the name that is above every name, so that at the name of Jesus every knee should bow, in heaven and on earth and under the earth.

Ephesians 4:4-6- There is one body and one Spirit—just as you were called to the one hope that belongs to your call—one Lord, one faith, one baptism, one God and Father of all, who is over all and through all and in all.

This means that I needed to be baptized in Jesus' name too. Now that I knew how to be baptized, what exactly was the meaning of the baptism? I had to begin another search. I wanted to understand it to the fullest.

 Romans 6:3-4- Or do you not know that as many of us as were baptized into Christ Jesus were baptized into His death? Therefore we were buried with Him through baptism into death, that just as Christ was raised from the dead by the glory of the Father, even so we also should walk in newness of life.

Colossians 2:11-12- In Him you were also circumcised with the circumcision made without hands, by putting off the body of the sins of the flesh, by the circumcision of Christ, buried with Him in baptism, in which you also were raised with Him through faith in the working of God, who raised Him from the dead.

The reason that we are baptized in Jesus' name is that we are being baptized into Jesus. We do this in the name of Jesus because He is the one who died for us. We are taking on his name. This is like the way a woman takes on her husband's name. We are saying that we belong to Jesus and we are giving our old selves with Him in His death and burial. We are declaring that we have made the choice to follow Christ and we are giving up the former life or name and accepting the life and name of Christ. 2 Corinthians 5:17 says, "Therefore if any man *be* in Christ, *he is* a new creature: old things are passed away; behold, all things are become new."

After all of this studying, I knew I was ready to be washed clean. I wanted my former life to be gone and to take on the name of Christ. I never wanted a name more in my life. I was ready to have the name of Jesus attached to my life. I made a decision that changed the rest of my life; the evening of the last day of the fast, I would go to the river and I would drown the old me. I knew I had to bury that old wretch and be resurrected under the blood of Jesus. I made the decision to become new by being baptized in the mighty name of Jesus Christ!

The last day of my fast, in the early afternoon, we headed to the river. I knew the fast would end at midnight and I refused to start my new life without being baptized. I will never, ever, forget this day. It was a very cold April day. The snow had just melted off a few days prior to this. It was approximately 45 degrees outside. As I walked into the middle of the river, the water was so cold that I could barely move. It took me awhile to get out deep enough to even be submerged under the water. The deeper I went out, the heavier the spirit of God fell. As my hand was put over my nose, I prayed. I quickly, because it was so cold, asked God to let that old woman die and for Him to raise a new woman. Then, according to Acts 2:38, I was baptized in Jesus' name! I went under the water and it was ice cold but when I came up, the water around me was very warm. It was amazing! God took that cold water and changed it just like he changed me. I walked out of the river that day a new woman.

That night, at midnight, Laney and I prayed and then took communion. I had participated in communion many times in my life but never like this. This time, it meant so much more. I finally understood the meaning of it. I knew that it was to remember that Jesus Christ gave His flesh and blood for me. He had given everything for me. As I took the bread, and broke it, I began to cry as I passed it to Laney. This bread was broken like His body. This bread was broken like we were. That piece of bread was the sweetest thing that I had ever tasted. The juice was next. We used grape juice for the wine. This was for His blood. This represented the blood that He shed on the cross so that I could be free. I took in the juice. I can't explain to you the presence that filled that room. 50 days prior to this, I wanted to marry a woman. I was so wrapped up in myself that I only sought God for my own benefit. Most days I had wanted to die. This day, I took communion and broke the fast as a healed and delivered woman. I broke the fast excited to see what God wanted next for this vessel.

As I am writing this book, I can see that there was a change in us daily but the last week or so changed us more than the rest of the fast. I looked back through the events and noticed that the day the oil was poured out made a shift in our lives. Something that day was important. The anointing that fell and the vision I had symbolized something.

As I am writing, the Lord impressed upon me what the oil meant. The Lord is our shepherd. He knows us and takes care of us as the shepherd does His sheep. I grew up around church. I knew that God was my shepherd. I had heard the stories of how sheep would follow anyone and how the shepherd would have to leave the herd to find the one that was lost.

Matthew 18:12-13 How think ye? if a man have an hundred sheep, and one of them be gone astray, doth he not leave the ninety and nine, and goeth into the mountains, and seeketh that which is gone astray? And if so be that he find it, verily I say unto you, he rejoiceth more of that sheep, than of the ninety and nine which went not astray.

John 10:11 I am the good shepherd: the good shepherd giveth his life for the sheep.

John 10:14 I am the good shepherd, and know my sheep, and am known of mine.

At first, I didn't understand what the oil had to do with the sheep. Many times in the Bible, the anointing oil poured on a head would mean that a person were being called by God onto a position. This was to symbol the blessing, protection, and empowerment of God on that particular person. Why did He use oil though? Where did that meaning come from? As I researched the Bible and google, I found that it originated in the sheep farmers. Many times throughout the Bible, God is referred to as the great shepherd. I learned that the shepherd will pour oil on his sheep for several reasons. The first reason is to keep the pest, parasites, and/or insects off the sheep. If allowed, these things will deposit their eggs into the membrane of the sheep's nose. These eggs will eventually drive the sheep crazy. The mother sheep will even stop giving milk and the little lambs will stop growing. These lambs can get so sick that they die from malnourishment. These insects or parasites can also go through the ear canal of the sheep and into the brain. These insects would then eat away at the brain of the sheep and cause intense pain. It is not uncommon for these sheep to beat their heads against a large rock until death to try to escape the pain and torment inside their heads. They will try anything to get relief from the parasites that would eat at the brain. The oil keeps all of this at bay for the innocent sheep.

Shepherds also anoint them with oil for healing. The oil serves as an antibiotic and heals the sheep from any wounds that they have obtained. Sheep like to butt heads and play together which can sometimes result in injuries. The oil will prevent any wounds from infection.

The oil is the physical symbol of the presence of God. The oil represents the anointing of God. When God's anointing comes over us, it has the same effect on us as the oil on the sheep. The anointing of God will take away things in our mind that eat away at us. The sheep believed that they were crazy but in all actuality, it was insects that they could not see that was causing the issues. I believe that God anointed me that day and it removed "insects" or thought processes that I thought we were part of me. The scripture tells us that the anointing breaks the yoke (Isaiah 10:27). The anointing of God will break things off a person if we allow it. I can see how the vision I had at church about the oil was the physical representation of what God was doing in me. He was talking oil and anointing my head. I was trying so hard to serve Him. I was completely surrendering to Him but I had "things" in my head that were literally driving me crazy. As God poured out the anointing oil, my thoughts cleared. I remember walking home and thinking more clearly than ever. That oil also healed parts of my heart. I felt cracks deep in my soul just smooth at. Parts of my heart that I had hid away were feeling the world around me again. Many times in life, we just need to be in the presence of our shepherd and have Him pour His precious oil on our heads. I needed my shepherd to anoint me that day. The oil broke the yoke.

The New "Me"

After we broke the fast with communion, we drove to my sister's house in Kansas and then on to Oklahoma to attend a Joyce Meyer conference. While on the way to Kansas, I had to take the same route that Billy and I use to take to come home to Missouri when we lived there. The trip made me think of all the trips we made together. I thought about how it was so weird without him. I could NOT believe that I was thinking about HIM. Billy and I weren't really on great terms after the divorce. We tried to be friends for the kids. We had joint custody but always allowed them to go between homes freely. During the fast, when he came over to pick up the kids, he would bring me a juice or Gatorade. We were kind to one another for the kid's sake. We wanted them to know that parents could work things out and be friends for the children. I heard many things that he had said about me from his co-workers and couldn't believe that I could even miss him. It wasn't really even that I was missing him but I was missing our family together. I really NEVER thought I would miss that. I tried to stay quiet on the drive. For the most part Laney and our friend that went with us slept so it was easy. I kept telling myself all the problems we had had in our marriage and how I never wanted that life back. I couldn't live that life with him ever again. Even if Billy and I both wanted our family back, I had done too much wrong. I had hurt him and our kids too much. I thought about all that I had put them through. I didn't believe they would ever forgive me. Even if I never was with Billy again, I still hated what I had done. How could I ever get over this? How could I ever fix things between us? Could we ever be friends?

During the 3 day conference, I kept thinking about forgiveness. The conference was amazing but in between the services, all I could think about was forgiving. Scriptures kept coming to my mind and I couldn't understand why. I didn't hold a grudge against my parents. What was I missing? Scripture after scripture flooded my thoughts.

Mark 11:20-26 NKJV Now in the morning, as they passed by, they saw the fig tree dried up from the roots. And Peter, remembering, said to Him, "Rabbi, look! The fig tree which You cursed has withered away." So Jesus answered and said to them, "Have faith in God. For assuredly, I say to you, whoever says to this mountain, 'Be removed and be cast into the sea,' and does not doubt in his heart, but believes that those things he says will be done, he will have whatever he says. Therefore I say to you, whatever things you ask when you pray, believe that you receive them, and you will have them. "And whenever you stand praying, if you have anything against anyone, forgive him, that your Father in heaven may also forgive you your trespasses. But if you do not forgive, neither will your Father in heaven forgive your trespasses." □□□

The Lord showed me that you must forgive to have enough faith to move those mountains. We must have faith and forgive. This goes together in order to expand the kingdom. You can't have faith and not forgiveness. When you can forgive, you have faith about the future, and you understand what the future holds. When you can forgive the hard stuff, you are strengthening your faith. You have to have faith in order to forgive. The more you forgive, the more faith you have.

Hebrews 11:1-40 NKJV "Now faith is the substance of things hoped for, the evidence of things not seen. For by it the elders obtained a good testimony. By faith we understand that the worlds were framed by the word of God, so that the things which are seen were not made of things which are visible. By faith Abel offered to God a more excellent sacrifice than Cain, through which he obtained witness that he was righteous, God testifying of his gifts; and through it he being dead still speaks. By faith Enoch was taken away so that he did not see death, "and was not found, because God had taken him"; for before he was taken he had this testimony, that he pleased God. But without faith it is impossible to please Him, for he who comes to God must believe that He is, and that He is a rewarder of those who diligently seek Him. By faith Noah, being divinely warned of things not yet seen, moved with godly fear, prepared an ark for the saving of his household, by which he condemned the world and became heir of the righteousness which is according to faith. By faith Abraham obeyed when he was called to go out to the place which he would receive as an inheritance. And he went out, not knowing where he was going. By faith he dwelt in the land of promise as in a foreign country, dwelling in tents with Isaac and Jacob, the heirs with him of the same promise; for he waited for the city which has foundations, whose builder and maker is God. By faith Sarah herself also received strength to conceive seed, and she bore a child when she was past the age, because she judged Him faithful who had promised. Therefore from one man, and him as good as dead, were born as many as the stars of the sky in multitude—innumerable as the sand which is by the seashore. These all died in faith, not having received the promises, but having seen them afar off were assured of them, embraced them and confessed that they were strangers and pilgrims on the earth. For those who say such things declare plainly that they seek a homeland. And truly if they had called to mind that country from which they had come out, they would have had opportunity to return. But now they desire a better, that is, a heavenly country. Therefore God is not ashamed to be called their God, for He has prepared a city for them. By faith Abraham, when he was tested, offered up Isaac, and he who had received the promises offered up his only begotten son, of whom it was said, "In Isaac your seed shall be called," concluding that God was able to raise him up, even from the dead, from which he also received him in a figurative sense. By faith Isaac blessed Jacob and Esau concerning things to come. By faith Jacob, when he was dying, blessed each of the sons of Joseph, and worshiped, leaning on the top of his staff. By faith Joseph, when he was dying, made mention of the departure of the children of Israel, and gave instructions concerning his bones. By faith Moses, when he was born, was hidden three months by his parents, because they saw he was a beautiful child; and they were not afraid of the king's command. By faith Moses, when he became of age, refused to be called the son of Pharaoh's daughter, choosing rather to suffer affliction with the people of God than to enjoy the passing pleasures of sin, esteeming the reproach of Christ greater riches than the treasures in Egypt; for he looked to the reward. By faith he forsook Egypt, not fearing the wrath of the king; for he endured as seeing Him who is invisible. By faith he kept the Passover and the sprinkling of blood, lest he who destroyed the firstborn should touch them. By faith they passed through the Red Sea as by dry land, whereas the Egyptians, attempting to do so, were drowned. By faith the walls of Jericho fell down after they were encircled for seven days. By faith the harlot Rahab did not perish with those who did not believe, when she had received the spies with peace. And what more shall I say? For the time would fail me to tell of Gideon and Barak and Samson and Jephthah, also of David and Samuel and the prophets: who through faith subdued kingdoms, worked righteousness, obtained promises, stopped the mouths of lions, quenched the violence of fire, escaped the edge of the sword, out of weakness were made strong, became valiant in battle, turned to flight the armies of the aliens. Women received their dead raised to life again. Others were tortured, not accepting deliverance, that they might obtain a better resurrection. Still others had trial of mockings and scourgings, yes, and of chains and imprisonment. They were stoned, they were sawn in two, were tempted, were slain with the sword. They wandered about in sheepskins and goatskins, being destitute, afflicted, tormented— of whom the world was not worthy. They wandered in deserts and mountains, in dens and caves of the earth. And all these, having obtained a good testimony through faith, did not receive the promise, God having provided something better for us, that they should not be made perfect apart from us."□□□□

   I sat and thought of all those people mentioned in these scriptures. I thought of all they had to forgive. I thought of all the opposition they had against them. They had to forgive and move on to accomplish what God had for them. That forgiveness strengthened their faith. The opposition's strengthened their faith. I had to forgive my parents who abused me. I had to forgive my family who didn't help me. I had to also forgive my old friends who didn't want me when I gave my life to Christ. I even had to forgive those who broke my heart. I knew that I had already prayed and worked to forgive those. I seemed to have forgotten someone. I realized that I had forgotten the most important one, I had to forgive myself. I knew that there was so much to come in the future. I knew that none of this could happen though if I had unforgiveness distracting me. I knew that God couldn't fully use me if I didn't forgive. We can't have faith without forgiveness and opposition. I had the opposition down but the forgiving part was a little harder. If I can't forgive, I have a problem with faith. I couldn't see the future but I knew that there were more important things than the hurt I felt. God's plan is so much greater and more important than what they did to me. God's plan is also more important than what I did to me. I felt God saying that forgiveness will build faith. Then, I thought of Luke 7:47, "Therefore I say to you, her sins, which are many, are forgiven, for she loved much. But to whom little is forgiven, the same loves little." I had already been forgiven of so much and I loved Him for that. This time, I needed to love Him enough to do something new, it was now time for me to forgive myself.

Ephesians 1:7- In Him we have redemption through his blood, the forgiveness of sins, according to the riches of his grace.

We have forgiveness through His blood. I felt as if God was saying to me that when we don't forgive ourselves, it is as if we are telling God that the crucifixion wasn't enough. It is as though the fact that Jesus Christ was whipped and beaten and literally became the sacrificial lamb was not enough. God laid it on my heart that if the sacrifice was enough for God to forgive us, it should be enough for us to forgive ourselves. When we hold unforgiveness in our hearts towards ourselves, we are actually telling Jesus Christ that He isn't enough.

Jesus is enough for me. I knew how Jesus felt when He said, "Forgive them, they know not what they do." I had no idea what I was doing back then. I looked back and saw a person that I didn't even know anymore. I had to forgive myself. I had to forgive the old me for the affairs, the divorce, and the pain I caused my family. I had to forgive myself for choosing what I wanted over what God wanted for my life. The hardest thing though, was letting go of the guilt and shame for the terrible mother I once was. I put my own desires above being a mom to my precious babies. I missed so much of their lives while out with someone else. I also didn't love their daddy like I should have. I had to let that go. I was not that person any longer. I couldn't hold on to that anymore. I asked God to forgive me and then I decided to move forward. I vowed to be the best momma and ex-wife I could. I knew that I had to make it up to them. I asked God to teach me how to be what they needed; I would let Him guide me.

The trip home from the conference was so emotional. I tried so hard to ignore the route but it was more intense this time. As we drove, I remembered the gas stations we had stopped at and the events of the adventures. I thought about Billy playing with the older kids as I was nursing the baby. I thought of diapers changed on the side of the road. I even thought about the small parks that we stopped at to allow the kids to get out and stretch their legs. Billy never complained how many times we stopped on trips. He was such a good daddy. I didn't even realize I was smiling until someone brought it to my attention. I was shocked that the memories were putting a smile on my face. What was I thinking? How could I be so happy thinking of him? I started thinking maybe being friends wouldn't be so hard. Laney and I could live as friends and Billy and I could work together to raise our kids for the Lord. I seemed to have my life figured out. Little did I know that when I asked God to have His perfect will for my life, His will wasn't what I thought it would be.

When you allow the Potter to form you, you have to be submissive to what vessel He wants you to be. I sincerely wanted God to mold me into the vessel that He could use for His glory. God was changing me so fast. It doesn't really take long for an experienced potter to change His creation if He has pliable clay. I never dreamt what God would do next. I am still in awe of Him.

We got back from the conference so late that we met our ex-husbands at church with our children the next morning. I grabbed all five of them in a great big hug. I missed them so much. As Billy walked over to me, I smiled at him. He got to me and hugged me. Over the course of our separation, he always tried to hug me but I told him to stop. This time, I hugged him back. I didn't know why but I didn't mind hugging him. After church, he brought the kids and their overnight bags to my house. As he left, I stared out the window. Laney asked me what was thinking about. She said I had a cute smile on my face. All I was thinking was that he really wasn't quite as annoying as I once thought. I actually had missed him while I was at the conference. God was really changing me.

I had no idea what God was going to do in my life. I began asking God to turn my life around and that He would be able to use me for His glory. All I wanted was to be used by God. I had spent my whole life seeking what I wanted. Now, I just wanted whatever the Lord wanted for my life. Could He even use me now? I began to ask God to show me. I had to know that there was hope for me.

Genesis 50:20-But as for you, ye thought evil against me; but God meant it unto good, to bring to pass, as it is this day, to save much people alive.

Romans 8: 28- And we know that all things work together for good to them that love God, to them who are the called according to his purpose.

2 Corinthians 12:8-10- For this thing I besought the Lord thrice, that it might depart from me. And he said unto me, My grace is sufficient for thee: for my strength is made perfect in weakness. Most gladly therefore will I rather glory in my infirmities, that the power of Christ may rest upon me. Therefore I take pleasure in infirmities, in reproaches, in necessities, in persecutions, in distresses for Christ's sake: for when I am weak, then am I strong.

I thought of the people in the Bible....

Daniel- goes from being thrown into the lion's den to becoming second in command in his nation.

Jonah- goes from being stuck in the belly of a great fish to saving thousands with a Word from the Lord.

Joseph- goes from being sold into slavery and thrown into prison to being second in command and saving his entire family.

Ruth- goes from being a poor widow and gathering leftovers to being rich and being the great- grandmother of David and linage of Jesus.

David- goes from being attacked by a lion and a bear and ignored by his family to being king.

Moses- goes from being sent away as a child from his mother to save his life and then being a murderer to leading the children of Israel out of bondage.

The trials in our lives may look terrible but God always has a plan. What the devil meant for evil, God will make it good. He will turn it around.

Jeremiah 29:11- For I know the thoughts that I think toward you, saith the Lord , thoughts of peace, and not of evil, to give you an expected end.

The Amplified Bible puts it like this: "For I know the plans and thoughts that I have for you,' says the Lord, 'plans for peace and well-being and not for disaster to give you a future and a hope."

So, I have to trust Him!

Proverbs 3: 5-6- Trust in the Lord with all thine heart; and lean not unto thine own understanding. In all thy ways acknowledge him, and he shall direct thy paths.

Lastly, no matter what I am going through, I have to give thanks for this is His will of God for our lives.

1 Thessalonians 5:18- In everything give thanks: for this is the will of God in Christ Jesus concerning you.

I just had to trust God, thank Him for my life, and allow Him to turn my life into what brought Him glory. I had so much to be thankful for. He had brought me through so much. I wanted to be a vessel that He could use. I asked God to put me right where He wanted me.

True Love

Laney and I were best friends and lived together while we tried to figure out what God wanted for us. Billy was coming over very often. The more he came over, the more I felt comfortable around him. I apologized to him for all the things I did to him and our family. I hated the things that I had done and the damage that they had caused. He said that he forgave me and we began spending time together with our kids. I just wanted God to heal his heart and the hearts of our children. Billy began coming over daily and even praying with us and studying the Bible with us. God was taking what Satan meant for evil and making it good. He was fixing our daily lives. We were all becoming friends. Our children were very excited to see their parents getting along. Billy lived in his house and us in ours and we shared the kids like great friends.

After reading the Bible one morning, I was praying about our future. While I was praying, I saw a vision. I saw myself standing on a platform type stage. I was standing there with a woman. I couldn't see in the vision who this lady was. We stood there as friends with my arms around her. Behind us was a dark colored wooden cross. I could see that the walls were white and the cross seemed to stand out from the wall. The platform wasn't very tall but needed a couple steps to get to it. The carpet was a mixture between gray and beige. As I stood there with this woman,

I knew that we had been involved intimately in the past. I knew that we were giving our testimony. As I stood there with my arms around this woman, I began to speak. "We were once lovers," I began, "But now, Jesus is the lover of my soul." I continued my testimony. "God delivered us and now we are head-over heels in love with our husbands." We both pointed to our spouses in the crowd. As I envisioned this, I felt peace. I felt a love that is beyond words rise up in me. It was almost like I could feel the way I would feel if I were actually experiencing what was in the vision. I immediately thought of how God had delivered Laney and I. God didn't tell me but I just thought it would be Laney and I one day. From this day on, I would begin looking for the building that this vision matched. I knew that in the future, this vision would come to pass.

A few days later, while studying the Word before the kids woke up, I happened to turn to the book of Ruth. I began reading this beautiful story about a kinsmen redeemer. I had read this story before but the Lord began revealing something new to me. This story showed me that God was faithful in bringing to pass His perfect plan for our lives. The potter molded and crafted this life for Ruth. Ruth thought that she had lost everything when her husband died. As a widow, with no children, she was an outcast. She would no longer have the intimacy of a family. She would be cut off from protection and provision. A rich man, Boaz, sees Ruth and had compassion on her. She could offer nothing to him but yet he showed her love. Boaz was the closest family to Ruth's late husband so he could marry her. Instead of just marrying her, he builds a relationship first. She falls in love with him because of his kindness and generous heart. They get married and this gives her a family that is the linage of Jesus. God restored her life, her name, and her future. God took her and walked her through the hardest part of her life in order to place her where He could use her the most. She had to work through several things but God saw her through. I wondered how God would redeem me. I put my Bible away and began to complete some chores. Laney came in from a run and told me she needed to talk to me. She had no idea what I had been studying. She didn't even know which part of the Bible that I was in that morning. She told me that God had laid something on her heart and that I needed me to sit down. I sat on the couch as she told me to open the Bible to Ruth. I froze there. I felt as though I couldn't move. She wanted me to open to Ruth but why? I didn't know what she was going to say but I knew but her facial expressions that I didn't want to know. This was serious. She NEVER looked at me like that unless it was serious. I told her that I didn't want to open the Bible. She looked dumbfounded that I didn't want to see what God had to tell me. A part of me was scared my life would change. The other part of me was somehow still surprised that God would tell her the same thing I had been reading. Finally, she began to tell me what she had heard through prayer from the Lord. She began telling me that she was sorry to have to tell me what she heard because I wasn't going to like it. This made me even more scared. Then, with a tear running down her cheek she said, "It's time to find you a husband. The Lord led me to Ruth 3:1." I grabbed her in a hug and screamed, "NO! I don't want to do this. I can't. I just can't"

I cried for a while and then looked up the verse. Ruth 3:1 in the Contemporary English Version says, "One day, Naomi said to Ruth: It's time I found you a husband, who will give you a home and take care of you." I knew what God was going to do but I didn't know how. I decided to do a 3 day water only fast and that on the third day, I would ask God what He wanted me to do.

For 3 days, I only had water. Every moment I was praying to God. It didn't matter what I was doing physically, on the inside I was praying. I begged God to continue to fix me. I knew that He was molding me but I needed more. I wanted more of Him. I wanted to be used in a mighty way for Him. I also began praying for Billy. I wanted Billy to get closer to the Lord. I wanted Billy to have the same relationship with God as I did. I wanted Billy to be healed from our marriage and divorce. I began praying that God would send him the perfect wife. He deserved to have someone to love him. He deserved to have someone that adored him. I wanted God to give him someone to help ease his heart. I truly only wanted the best for him. I prayed for Billy almost more than I did myself. On day 3, God told me that I would marry him again. I told Laney and she agreed that this was what was best for me. Now, I just had to wait for God to mold my heart to Billy's heart.

After 2 days, I felt like God told me to fast again for three days and then ask him to marry me. I started another 3 day water only fast and began interceding for our marriage. The only person who knew was Laney. I poured my heart out to God every moment for 3 whole days. I prayed protection, love, and strength for us. I sincerely prayed that God would give me an overwhelming love for Billy. I prayed that God would help me be the wife he deserved. As Billy came over to the house on those days, I began noticing a spark inside me. At first it was like a spark but by day 3, it was a flame. The smile on his face as he played with our children made my heart melt. His jokes, that I once found annoying, made me laugh so hard my stomach would hurt. Lastly, his laugh made butterflies in my stomach. When he laughed, I felt my insides react. It was almost the "high" I got when I would smoke pot but this was slightly different. This "feeling" wasn't in my head, it was in the pit of my stomach. The crazy thing was, I LOVED it!

Around noon on day 3, I asked Billy if I could borrow his vehicle as mine had some mechanical issues. He sweetly said that I could use it as long as I took him to work first. I had decided that I would prepare a huge dinner and invite him over and then ask him to marry me. I quietly rode with him to his work. When we got there, I got out of the passenger side and walked around and proceeded to sit in the driver's seat. Billy was going to shut the door for me but instead I leaned over and did something incredibly out of the ordinary. Without thinking, without hesitation, I leaned over and kissed him. I couldn't believe it! Why did I do that? I hadn't done that in a very very long time. I don't think I had ever wanted to kiss a man before that day. I was in complete shock! Not only did I kiss him but, I liked it! Billy was just as shocked as I was. He couldn't believe it. He looked at me with a weird look and said, "Can we do that again?" I couldn't believe it! He wanted to kiss me and I wanted him! I quickly responded, "Yes, we can." I had heard how kissing someone felt like seeing fireworks on the 4th of July but this was even better than that. Those two small kisses gave me a feeling that I can't even describe. In those few moments, my cracks were filled in. I felt whole. He completed me. I knew that I still had a long ways to go but I was so excited now! I could not wait to marry him. I loved him! I really loved him! I was staring at him when he finally spoke, "What are we doing?" he said. I smiled and told him to come over for dinner that night and we could talk about it.

I was so excited that I called Laney and told her what happened. She couldn't believe it either. I told Laney but I had to find someone else to tell. I went to Billy's aunt and told her. She was so happy for us that she started crying. She told me that only God could heal our relationship. She also said that she loved the smile on my face. She could tell that I loved him. I had that "in love" glow about me. I quickly went to the store and bought all of his favorite foods. I would cook a feast and ask him to marry me. A part of me knew there was a chance he would say no but the other part of me knew I had to try. I couldn't live my life without that feeling he gave me. I had to be his wife. I had to spend each day seeing his smile, hearing him laugh, and trying to make him the happiest man alive.

I cooked and cleaned while he was at work. I told all of the children to dress up because we were going to have a special evening. I wanted Laney's children to witness the event too. They had no idea what that night would bring. I sat down and prayed about what I would say to him. One of my favorite movies to watch with Billy when we were married was Fireproof. I thought of the ending of that and I came up with the perfect plan.

After Billy arrived, we sat down for dinner. I wanted to pray over the food and then ask him but I was so afraid that I couldn't do it. I began shaking inside and sweating. Finally, I asked Billy to bless the food so that we could eat. After he finished praying, I stood up. I told everyone that I had one thing to say before we ate. I looked at Billy with tears in my eyes. I had in front of me the most handsome man that I had ever saw. I wiped my eyes and began my speech: "If I haven't told you that you are an amazing man, you really are. If I haven't told you that I love you, I do. God has done such an amazing work in my life. He has given me a love for you that I could have never imagined. So, I have a question for you. Is it too late to ask you to spend the rest of your life with me? Will you marry me again?"

If you have read this book much at all you know what he said. This man didn't hesitate. This man didn't even have to think about his answer. He immediately grabbed me, wrapped me into his arms and said, "Of course, I will marry you. It would make me the happiest man alive." He held me so tight the whole world seemed to fade away. All that mattered in that moment was us. This was the beginning of a new life for us. This was the beginning of the fairy tale story that I had always told myself that I didn't want. I would become Mrs. Billy Hudson once again. But this time, I wanted it more than anything in the world.

That night, as I went to sleep on the couch and Laney in what once was "our" bed, I couldn't help but be scared. My life was changing so fast. Everything that I had ever wanted had changed. The things that I didn't want was now my deepest desires and the desires that had had all my life somehow felt like they belonged to some stranger. I had heard in church that if you delight yourself in the Lord that He would give you the desires of your heart. I had completely surrendered every aspect of my life to the Lord and delighted in doing so. God didn't just give me the desires of my heart though. He took me and molded my desires into new desires. He took away all the desires that I had that didn't please Him. He even gave me new desires that would increase my happiness in the future. After He changed me, He then gave me the desires of my heart. These new desires were the complete opposite of who I always thought that I was. God had given me a new heart, new emotions, and new desires to be more like Him. The old me truly had passed away and behold all things were made new. I fell asleep thinking how much God must know me. He was giving me a life that I never knew I wanted; a life that I could be happy with. He was taking care of His daughter. My Daddy knew what I needed. This new life would be scary but in the end, I knew I would love it. My Daddy, the King of Kings and the Lord of Lords, had the best plan in store for me. I could now sleep in peace without fear but with great expectation of the future.

Preparation for Marriage

We set the date of the wedding to be May 7th. It was just 2 weeks away from the night that I proposed to Billy. I felt that God led us to that date because the 7th in the Bible represents completion. God was about to complete something great in my family. We had wondered through a great wilderness for far too long. God was completing a season of our life so that He could begin a new one. I knew that this new season would be for God to establish me as a submissive wife and a selfless mother. I had no idea how He would bring it all to pass but I was still excited to see the outcome. I was aware that there would have to be many more changes in our life. I knew that a new season would bring more struggles but it would also bring growth. I was ready for a new adventure. I was nervous but completely at peace that my God was in control.

As the first week flew by, Laney and I began planning. We picked out colors, dresses, food, decorations and the whole works. She was right there with me through it all. I even asked her to be my Maid of Honor. If anyone knew that I was a new person, it was her. If anyone knew that I wanted to marry Billy because I loved him, it was her. I wanted her to be by my side because she truly knew my heart for God and Billy. I wasn't marrying him because it was "the right thing to do". I wasn't even marrying him to make things right with God. And even though I love my children, I wasn't marrying Billy to make them feel better. I wanted to marry Billy because I loved him and did not want to go through life without him. I wanted to spend the rest of my life with him. I wanted to be his wife and belong to him. I knew that people would gossip and wonder my motives but that didn't bother me. Billy, our children, Laney, and most importantly, God, knew my heart.

As the countdown to the big day continued on, my mind started wonder some things. I had to know before I got married why I was gay. Why did I have those feelings for so long? I began to pray about the reasons behind the feelings I had had my whole life. I asked God to show me the "whys". I didn't want to go into this marriage and not understand who I was. I needed to know if I was "born that way" or maybe it was a "choice". I had to understand before I started the next season in my life. I felt that God had been molding me and I was at a point where I needed Him to speak to me and let me know where some of the cracks came from. I needed to know how to protect not only my vessel but others around me. I needed clarity. I began to seek God for the "why".

I don't know too many people that have been sexually abused that live a normal sexual life after the abused had stopped. I believe that God laid it on my heart that people who have experienced traumatic events early in life, especially those who have been sexually abused, have the greatest chance of being a homosexual. As I prayed about this, I feel that God showed me something. Our brain is wired to learn things every day. If the same feelings happen at a particular event, many times, our brains will learn that feeling is associated with that event. Our brains then believe that those feelings will occur each time the event happens. As a child, we learn to walk based upon this way of learning. As a small toddler, we may try to take a step. If we lean too far to the left, we fall and feel pain. This teaches our brain that leaning too far to the left will cause pain. Then, we try to lean to the right while standing. We soon find that leaning to the right will cause us to fall which also brings us pain. This is repeated several times for the front, back, left, and right until we found what doesn't hurt. We find that keeping our balance and walking while straight up is not painful. We strive for the thing that doesn't bring us pain which in turn teaches us to walk.

When a child is sexually abuse, especially at a young age, their brains find different coping strategies to allow them to get through the trauma. One way that many do this is, like walking, we try to find the way that doesn't hurt. Sometimes, the way that doesn't hurt as much is to justify the abuse in the mind. This is done but convincing the mind that you are enjoying the abuse or that they are attracted to the person. Unconsciously, a male may tell himself that he is gay so that he can justify the abuse from the adult male. Equally so, a girl may tell herself that she is gay so that the woman who is sexually abusing her is looked at as a mutual partner instead of an abuser. Many times, the child has no idea that the brain has tried to fix the thought process behind the abuse.

Another way, that the child may justify it, is as a relationship with the opposite sex. This is the case where you see a young girl who thinks that it is important to have sex with men. Many times, these girls will be promiscuous at a young age. They believe that sex is love. These girls don't understand that they are unconsciously trying to overcome the abuse they experienced. Boys who take this path usually are teens that don't respect women but believe that all that the woman needs is a man to have sex with them. These boys grow up to be womanizers.

The most common way that I have found that people use to relieve pain is simply refrain from the events happening as an adult. These children cope by telling themselves that when they are older they will never have to do those "things" again. They "learn" that what happened to them is painful so it can't possibly be right. Without even knowing it most times, they decide to never take a chance with this painful circumstance again. These children may not even understand that they are "gay" simply to cope with their past experiences. Their brains chose to be gay without the knowledge of the child for safety.

The mind really has a hard time "learning" how to walk the right way when a child is abused by both sexes. This, in my opinion, creates the strongest feelings of homosexuality in women and womanizes in men. Just like learning to walk, our minds try to figure out which way is the right way based upon what doesn't hurt us. The mind takes into consideration the feelings that are associated with the events to find the way to "walk". Boys who are abused by men and women will most of the time follow a specific path. They become aggressive and use women for their pleasure only. They tend to follow the footsteps as the men that abused them. They also struggle with women being in control of anything. They want to be in authority at all times and feel as though they must constantly prove their superiority. They do this to ensure that they will never have to be the victim again.

Little girls who are abused both women and men have the hardest time with their past. You see, just like learning to walk, most of the time when a woman abuses her it is uncomfortable but not painful. When the girl is abused by the man, the pain is almost unbearable. Even after the abuse continues for months or even years, the pain doesn't seem to fade. Even if the physical pain is bearable, the emotional pain and guilt is unimaginable. These events make a "clear" statement to the brain. The brain sees that being with a man causes harm but being with another woman is not that awful. Being with a man can't possibly be what is right for the body of this girl because it is so terrible. The brain often tells the body that the only way is that she is different and is a lesbian. This girl might find that being with other women is the only way to feel comfort. These girls mature and grow to believe that they were lesbians their whole life. They begin only having sexual desires towards other women. This teaches them to "walk" a homosexual lifestyle. Many of these girls believe that they were born this way because it is the only way that they can remember thinking. Boys who have had a gentle man abuser may take the same route to be gay as well. Just like we don't remember learning to walk, we don't remember these thoughts that we had to form this new identity either.

So, our brains may have a faulty thinking pattern that has caused us to "walk" differently. These thinking patterns are strongholds in our life. They are like braces on our legs that teach us to walk differently than others. As we learned to walk with these "braces", we believe that we are doing it the right way. We have no idea that we are truly different and that these "braces" aren't supposed to be on us. These "braces" aren't visible to us but they are to those around us who are truly in Christ. They are spiritual braces.

The Bible says that faith comes through hearing the message and the message through the Word of Jesus Christ. (Romans 10:17) We can get faith through the Word. When we apply the Word of God to our lives, we will begin to see through the eyes of Jesus. We will then have faith that the Word is true and powerful. John 1:1 tells us that the Word is God. If we allow Him to, Jesus Christ, or Lord and Savior, will allow us to see those invisible "braces" or strongholds that are on us.

Once we allow God to have complete control in our life, He will remove those "braces" off us. With this, we need to understand that those braces were on us when we learned to "walk" through this life. Without them, we have to learn to walk again. We have to train our minds and relearn things. We have to redo our entire thinking process. We must allow God to teach us how to walk without them. We have to let go of all the thoughts and ideas that we once had about walking. We must learn to "walk" with God. We must allow Him to renew our lives.

As you can imagine, wearing these braces your whole life and then suddenly having them removed without warning would be very difficult. Even normal situations might be hard to deal with without those braces. Many times, you may want the braces back. It is also known by doctors everywhere that your legs won't be strong enough at first to do the things that you might want to do. A person would need therapy for a while to build strength. These braces were spiritual so it takes a spiritual therapy to help you build strength. This therapy is prayer meetings, church services, personal prayer times, fasting, counseling with a minister, and more. This will ensure that your strength is restored to the way that God intended. This will allow you to "walk" correctly. This new walk will be hard without those braces but we will not be alone; God will be right there with us.

We must also learn to follow Philippians 4:8: "Finally, brethren, whatsoever things are true, whatsoever things *are* honest, whatsoever things *are* just, whatsoever things *are* pure, whatsoever things *are* lovely, whatsoever things *are* of good report; if *there be* any virtue, and if *there be* any praise, think on these things."

When we allow our thoughts to line up with the Word of God, it will strengthen those leg muscles.

2 Corinthians 10:4-5 gives us an insight that those braces or strongholds are not something of this world. They are spiritual. This is why so many of us can't see them. This scripture says that the weapons we fight with are not of this world but have the power to demolish strongholds. These weapons that we have are found in Ephesians 6:10-18. These include: the Sword of the Spirit (Word of God), Belt of Truth, Breastplate of Righteousness, Peace from the Gospel, Shield of Faith, and the Helmet of Salvation.

Because we have to remove these "braces" or strongholds that are not of the world, we must use weapons not of this world as well. Those weapons can only come from God, Jesus Christ. It took me a long time to realize that those "braces" I had were formed by a faulty thinking pattern. The enemy placed that stronghold in my life. Ephesians 6:12 explains to us that we aren't fighting against flesh and blood but against authorities, powers, and rulers of this dark world and against the spiritual forces of evil in the heavenly places.

So, to allow God to renew our minds and walk with Him the right way, we must be fully aware of this and know the things we think are not always true but the Word of God is. We are to retrain our minds to allow God to take control and teach us to walk again. The Bible says living a homosexual lifestyle is wrong. Therefore, it must be from Satan, our enemy. James 1:17 states that every good and perfect thing comes from God. If we have strong holds or "Braces", they are not from God!

Because we are human, and our brains try to help us learn for events, sometimes things get mixed up in our heads and in our hearts. Many times, we try to find a way to alleviate some pain. We are unaware, sometimes our entire life, that our minds have come up with these coping strategies. We must allow God to show these "braces" to us and allow Him complete control to take them off of us. We will be able to understand these things when we use the weapons that God gives us to apply in our life. God can teach us to walk again. If we will allow it, He will relieve us by removing the braces, breaking the strongholds, and renewing our minds. He will then give us a new mind, the mind of Christ.

I knew now that the feelings that I had felt my whole life were actually strongholds that were attached to me. Being a homosexual wasn't a choice. No one would choose that lifestyle for themselves. Being a homosexual was not who God had created me to be either. This stronghold was placed there by the enemy to take me out. Once those "braces" were gone, I felt free to run with the Lord.

Before the wedding, Billy and I sat down to discuss what we thought would be important in our new marriage. I explained to him that I needed my husband to be the head of my household, put God first, and put our children next. I also told him that I found it important that he knows who God is. I sat down with him and showed him what God had revealed to be about who is was. I started with God is one and ended with the necessity of baptism in Jesus' name. Billy told me that he had always believed this way. I never knew that Billy thought that way. We called a Pentecostal minister and He took Billy down to the same river that I had went to. Billy was baptized in that very same river in the mighty name of Jesus. We then asked that pastor to officiate the wedding.

The Perfect Day

Just days later, on a bright and warm Saturday morning, I woke up with excitement. Finally, May 7th had come. This day was going to be the happiest day of my life. I woke up early and spent time with God. I spent most of my early morning thanking God for the huge miracle that He was doing for us this day. Laney went out for a walk and to pray before my big day. After she left, Billy came over. I was in bed when he opened the door. I have no idea what took over me at this point. It was like I heard someone else speak through me. I patted the bed and said, "Come snuggle me". Now, I believe that was probably the first time that I had ever said that to him. Before this day, I NEVER remember wanting him to touch me. God had been changing my desires and the last couple weeks had been so different than any other time in my life. For 2 weeks now, I had loved kissing this man and sitting next to him. The thought that I wanted him to hold me was new to me. Billy seemed a little shocked by words as well. He came over to me and slowly took his shoes off and laid ever so carefully on the bed. He looked at me as if I were going to play a prank on him or something. I don't think that I had ever seen him that nervous before. As I laid there in his arms, he began praying over me, our children, and our marriage. As I listened, my heart melted. I felt the hands of my potter pouring melted gold into my cracks. Some cracks are smoothed out by the potter but others are filled with gold and are left to show that the crack was once there. As the gold was melted and poured into the cracks, it was painful. This pain was good. It was like a pain that breaks your heart yet makes you feel better all at the same time. He continued to pray as the tears began to run down my cheeks. My broken vessel was beginning to be formed into something beautiful. Billy finished praying and I had a new respect for this man. I looked into his beautiful blue eyes and I saw something I had never saw before. I looked and saw......... my future. I saw everything I ever wanted. I wanted to be his wife for the rest of eternity. I wanted to grow old with him. I saw myself walking through life with him. I even saw us sitting by a river and watching our grandchildren play in the shallow water. This man truly was the man I always needed. Billy was the one I was supposed to be with my whole life. I had finally found the person that was created for me and he had been there the whole time. Billy wasn't the man I would marry and make a life with. He was my husband that God had given to me on August 25th, 2003. It took me almost 13 years to accept this gift that the Lord gave me. I did NOT want one more minute to go by without us together as husband and wife. I was ready to be with him. I was ready to be his wife in every area!

This moment was truly one of the most beautiful and precious moments I have ever experienced. Then, in just a few minutes, it hit me. I had a thought that stopped me in my tracks. You see, I had never wanted to be intimate with a man before. Besides the one time with my uncle while being abused, my body had never felt like it was right that moment. What if I married this man and couldn't be him intimately? What if what I was feeling went away? What was going on with me? I closed my eyes and prayed, "God, can I really want to be with this man? Is this normal? Is this okay?" I don't have a scripture what I felt the Lord told me. I have never heard a preacher teach what I felt. All I can tell you is what I felt God said to me. I felt like God said that Billy was my husband and I was supposed to want him. I felt that in God's eyes, Billy never stopped being my husband. I opened my eyes and looked again at that man's handsome smile. He was staring at me with the sweetest grin. I smiled back and said, "Make love to me, please." I think I shocked him because the smile left and a straight face took its place. He held his breath, he then asked, "Are you sure?" I kind of laughed a little and told him that I had never been so sure in my whole life. That morning, in the house I had been living in with a woman, in the bed I had committed sin in, God created something beautiful. He took what has always been a dirty and nasty thing and molded us together in perfect unity to create something amazing. This morning, we were husband and wife just as God had intended. There wasn't anything between us. I gave my heart and soul and allowed God to bind us together; we became ONE.

The experience with Billy was a little awkward but worth it. I couldn't let myself "fully enjoy" it but I did like it. I knew that I could let go more and more after we were living together again. It was more of an emotional intimacy for me than physical. I was thankful that I didn't have any flashbacks. I just enjoyed giving myself to him. I knew that intimacy was truly more emotional and spiritual than physically anyway. Being with him excited me because I knew now that I truly wanted to be with him in every way possible. After we held each other for a moment, we began getting ready for the day. This would be the day we would give our hearts to each other in front of our chosen few family and friends.

All of Laney's children and mine were part of the wedding. We got our children ready and headed out to the lake where the ceremony would be performed. The more hair I prepared, dresses I tied, and collars I straightened, the more excited I became. My hands began to shake and my stomach felt as if butterflies were swarming inside. Our first marriage was just something that felt like a formality but this one, this day, this was something great. This day meant more to me than just about any other day in my entire life. The wedding party was lining up for the ceremony but I waited behind. I took a moment with Laney. As we stood there, just the two of us, I began to fall apart. This woman was my Maid of Honor. God had taken us on an amazing journey. I had thought for a long time that if I ever remarried, it would be to her. We stood there in silence with tears running down our faces. Part of us were excited for this day and to see what God had for us but the flesh part of us was slightly scared. We were letting go of everything that we had been through and allowing God to have His perfect will for our lives. I have very few moments were I am truly speechless but this moment I couldn't speak at all. I just stared at her. I thought of everything I had done, everything we had done. I couldn't believe the transformation that had taken place. I didn't deserve anything good from God but He had put this amazing life together for me. I had no idea where life would take me but I knew that that I wanted it. I wanted this marriage, and I wanted this life. I wasn't the same woman I was just 3 months prior. I was a different woman with different desires altogether. Laney reached out for my hand and smiled with tears still flowing, "Let me pray over you" she said. She then prayed the most precious prayer over me, my marriage, and my babies. It was almost if God himself spoke through her. With a quiet "Amen", we froze again. Laney took a deep breath and said, "Love bug, your husband is waiting." This was the most beautiful thing that

she had ever said to me. Her words broke down everything
inside of me. I felt as though everything we had been
through together was meant for this very moment. I felt as
though the whole journey was for this destination. She
leaned down and kissed my forehead. "You make a
gorgeous bride," she said, "I am so proud of you." Then,
she wrapped me in a huge hug as I told her that I was
ready.

Laney sang for us as we walked down the aisle. The
bridesmaids and groomsmen went first, then, the flower girl
with the ring barrier. At last, it was my turn. Liz's husband
took my arm and asked me if I was ready. I looked up to
the front and saw Billy. He looked so handsome. I saw
Laney, and all of our children watching me too. They were
all smiling with tears in their eyes. I looked at my dad and
told him that I had NEVER been more ready in my life.

As we approached the front, words can't express
what I felt. I have never experienced that much joy and
peace before. I felt my entire world come together in
perfect harmony. The preacher looked at me and asked me
if I had anything to say. I had told him that I did before the
wedding started but now, I could not remember any of what
I had rehearsed. I decided very quickly to just let my heart
speak. I had not ever just opened my heart to him before
but this day. I opened my mouth and just let it rush out,
"Billy John Hudson, I stand here today to give myself to
you. I want to spend the rest of my life with you. I love and
adore you as a man of God and the father of our children. I
submit my heart and my body to you and you alone. As we
stand before these people and God, I ask you to forgive me
for not doing this sooner. I am so sorry that I was not the
woman that you deserve. On this day, I promise to be the
wife that God intended me to be. I promise to love you,

honor you, and grow old with you until the day we leave this world. I promise to serve God with you all the days of my life. I promise to raise our children to love and fear the Lord. In everything I do and say, I promise to put God first, then you, my husband, and next our amazing children. This day, I give everything I am to you."

After I finished, and we both stopped crying, the preacher led us in our vows. When he finished and said "You may now kiss the bride", my whole world changed! From that moment on, I knew that I was no longer the abused girl, the lesbian, the divorced woman, or anything else. From that moment on, I was the wife of Billy Hudson. I was so proud to be his wife. We left that ceremony with a bright future ahead of us. God had taken this day and orchestrated such a beautiful creation. I knew that this vessel was still being formed but I now could see that I was beginning to take shape into something that God, the potter, could use. I could finally see that God had a plan the whole time. I didn't know the rest of the plan but I knew He did. I would allow God to keep molding me, until I could glorify Him. I now didn't need a plan, I just wanted to love God, my husband, my children and my life. I wanted to enjoy Him having me in His hands.

Learning to be a Wife

To say that my life changed, the day I married Billy, would be understatement. I had been legally married before but in all honesty, it wasn't a marriage. What Billy and I had before was more like a roommate agreement with benefits. I had never really been in a marriage before. I was a 31 year old woman with 5 children and just now entering into a marriage. I had never wanted to be married to a man until now. The feelings that I had towards Billy and being his wife were very new to me. I really had no clue what was acceptable to feel, want, or do as a wife. I began seeking the Lord for him to show me what marriage was and wasn't. I had no idea what to think anymore. I could be intimate with Billy but I couldn't let myself fully enjoy it. I felt as though it was still weird for me to want him. Although I was attracted to him in every possible way, I didn't know what to do with it. I decided that I needed God to teach me. Many times in my life, I thought that I understood things but sincerely I knew nothing. I truly got to the realization that Paul had in 1 Corinthians 2:2 when he said that he was determined to know nothing except Christ and him crucified. With the exception of the last 3 months, everything I had ever known was a wrong. I truly had to rely on God to teach me how to live for him. I needed God to mold my mind, body, and soul. I needed Him to redo my whole thinking process. I needed the Lord to teach me how to be the wife and mother that He created me to be. The first thing I needed to understand was marriage. What was God's purpose for marriage and why did Satan want to attack it?

I could not help but wonder... "Why do we have gender issues? Why is Satan blinding so many with this? Why is he even attacking our young children with this?" I prayed and began seeking God's Word for the answers:

Genesis 1:27-28- So God created man in his own image, in the image of God created he him; male and female created he them. And God blessed them, and God said unto them, Be fruitful, and multiply, and replenish the earth, and subdue it: and have dominion over the fish of the sea, and over the fowl of the air, and over every living thing that moveth upon the earth.

Both males and females were made in the image of God. The very first command ever given by God was to be fruitful and to multiply. They were made in the image of God and then were expected to reproduce and increase in humans (males and females) that were in His image. After the serpent tricked Eve, God hands down the punishments and in the midst of this.

Genesis 3:15- And I will put enmity between thee and the woman, and between thy seed and her seed; it shall bruise thy head, and thou shalt bruise his heel.

Satan would be against her "seed".

Satan wanted to be like God. He wanted His position in heaven and now, these humans were not only made in God's image but would multiply.

Isaiah 14:12-17- How art thou fallen from heaven, O Lucifer, son of the morning! How art thou cut down to the ground, which didst weaken the nations! For thou hast said in thine heart, I will ascend into heaven, I will exalt my throne above the stars of God: I will sit also upon the mount of the congregation, in the sides of the north: I will ascend above the heights of the clouds; I will be like the most High. Yet thou shalt be brought down to hell, to the sides of the pit. They that see thee shall narrowly look upon thee, and consider thee, saying, Is this the man that made the earth to tremble, that did shake kingdoms; That made the world as a wilderness, and destroyed the cities thereof; that opened not the house of his prisoners?

Ezekiel 28:12-18- Son of man, take up a lamentation upon the king of Tyre, and say unto him, Thus saith the Lord God ; Thou sealest up the sum, full of wisdom, and perfect in beauty. Thou hast been in Eden the garden of God; every precious stone was thy covering, the sardius, topaz, and the diamond, the beryl, the onyx, and the jasper, the sapphire, the emerald, and the carbuncle, and gold: the workmanship of thy tabrets and of thy pipes was prepared in thee in the day that thou wast created. Thou art the anointed cherub that covereth; and I have set thee so: thou wast upon the holy mountain of God; thou hast walked up and down in the midst of the stones of fire. Thou wast perfect in thy ways from the day that thou wast created, till iniquity was found in thee. By the multitude of thy merchandise they have filled the midst of thee with violence, and thou hast sinned: therefore I will cast thee as profane out of the mountain of God: and I will destroy thee, O covering cherub, from the midst of the stones of fire. Thine heart was lifted up because of thy beauty, thou hast corrupted thy wisdom by reason of thy brightness: I will cast thee to the ground, I will lay thee before kings, that they may behold thee. Thou hast defiled thy sanctuaries by the multitude of thine iniquities, by the iniquity of thy traffick; therefore will I bring forth a fire from the midst of thee, it shall devour thee, and I will bring thee to ashes upon the earth in the sight of all them that behold thee.

Satan doesn't want anyone in heaven because he can't be there. If Satan can get people to believe they are homosexuals, they can NOT reproduce. This means that there will be less people who are made in His image; the image of God. This also means there will be not as many people to inherit the kingdom of God.

Satan also can attack marriage with homosexuality. Marriage is defined by God as one man and one woman. Marriage between husband and wife will reflect the image of God. Satan wants to destroy marriages because he is attempting to destroy the image of God.

Genesis 1:27 says he made "them" in his image. Man and woman completes the image of God when they are in one flesh.

Genesis 2:24 says that when two are married that they become one flesh.

John speaks about sexual sin in 1 Cor. 6:15-20. He explains that this sin not just a sin against God but the body. We were created to be connected to a member of the opposite sex to complete the image of God. This sin is terrible because we are cutting out the purpose of our lives: to reproduce and be the image of God. He created us like Him to be able to be in unity with Him and have companionship with him.

When someone engages in homosexuality, they destroy the natural order that God ordained.

Ephesians 5:22-23- Wives, submit yourselves unto your own husbands, as unto the Lord. For the husband is the head of the wife, even as Christ is the head of the church: and he is the savior of the body. Therefore as the church is subject unto Christ, so let the wives be to their own husbands in everything. Husbands, love your wives, even as Christ also loved the church, and gave himself for it; That he might sanctify and cleanse it with the washing of water by the word, That he might present it to himself a glorious church, not having spot, or wrinkle, or any such thing; but that it should be holy and without blemish. So ought men to love their wives as their own bodies. He that loveth his wife loveth himself. For no man ever yet hated his own flesh; but nourisheth and cherisheth it, even as the Lord the church: For we are members of his body, of his flesh, and of his bones. For this cause shall a man leave his father and mother, and shall be joined unto his wife, and they two shall be one flesh. This is a great mystery: but I speak concerning Christ and the church. Nevertheless let every one of you in particular so love his wife even as himself; and the wife see that she reverence her husband.

This compares marriage to the church. Our marriages on earth should reflect Christ in us. When we try to "re-identify" the meaning of marriage, we are essentially trying to change the image of God. Satan is trying to use this to his advantage. Satan isn't concerned about people "being who you are". He wants to destroy the kingdom of God and is using the people God created to do it.

Revelation 19:7-9- Let us be glad and rejoice, and give honour to him: for the marriage of the Lamb is come, and his wife hath made herself ready. And to her was granted that she should be arrayed in fine linen, clean and white: for the fine linen is the righteousness of saints. And he saith unto me, Write, Blessed *are* they which are called unto the marriage supper of the Lamb. And he saith unto me, These are the true sayings of God.

Revelation 21:1-2- And I saw a new heaven and a new earth: for the first heaven and the first earth were passed away; and there was no more sea. And I John saw the holy city, new Jerusalem, coming down from God out of heaven, prepared as a bride adorned for her husband.

In the end, the church will be united with Christ at the wedding ceremony. This marriage will be the ultimate marriage celebration of all time!! Satan is attempting to deface the sanctity of marriage now and most importantly the marriage between the Bridegroom and His church.

In Rev. 2:20-23, I believe that this shows us that those who are "accepting" the homosexual lifestyle will have to answer to God as well. Those who tolerate that spirit will be punished. He has given everyone time to repent though.

I can see "gay marriage" is an agenda straight from Satan himself? He can not only stop people from reproducing but can get people to destroy marriage which ultimately destroys the image of God!!

I knew God had ordained marriage but I never understood why Satan wanted to destroy it until now. The Bible talked so much about marriage. I wondered what else it could teach me. I began to search for what a Godly marriage would look like. I needed God to tell me what was acceptable in my marriage. I needed Him to show me what was allowed sexually in a marriage. If homosexuality was in the Bible, it had to show the ways that God intended a sexual relationship to be as well.

The first thing I did was look up sexual relationships and Christianity to find scriptures. I found that many religions had different theories on sex. Many cults and religions actually have sex as part of worship in their temples. The Greek and Roman culture, from which many areas are mentioned in the Bible, had heterosexual, bisexual, and homosexual prostitutes in the temple. These were at the worshiper's disposal while at the temple. This even included the church in Corinth that Paul preached to in the New Testament. They didn't even see how sinful this lifestyle was. Sexual acts were not just performed in buildings though, sex was such an open event that it wasn't uncommon to see people openly having sex outside. The churches began to notice that the people were out of control and began putting restrictions on sexual acts. They first began restricting the days which having sex was acceptable. At one point in time, if you had sex on Sunday, you could be put to death. The church also began to regulate the positions that were allowed as well. Eventually, priests and nuns were not allowed to even engage in sexual pleasures therefore, there weren't allowed to be married. Throughout history, sex has went from a very popular topic that was open to the whole world to something that is rarely talked about. Many of us nowadays have so much guilt and shame associated with sex that we don't want to talk about it. I know that I can't be the only one who has no idea what a Godly healthy sex life within marriage should look like.

I began my search in the "Book of Love" AKA the Song of Solomon. I have always heard that this book of the Bible was the one that was all about love so I thought that it must contain answers. I knew that somewhere in the Bible, I had to find what I was looking for. This book was written by a man who was known as the wisest man in the Bible. Solomon was the son David, a man after God's own heart. Song of Solomon is conversations written between Solomon and his lover. These conversations were written in poems or songs. At first, the woman speaks to Solomon who is about to be married to her. Since this book is written as a poem, we have to evaluate it and break it down as poetry.

Song of Solomon 1:2-4

(2) Let him kiss me with the kisses of his mouth: for thy love is better than wine.

(3) Because of the savour of thy good ointments thy name is as ointment poured forth, therefore do the virgins love thee.

(4) Draw me, we will run after thee: the king hath brought me into his chambers: we will be glad and rejoice in thee, we will remember thy love more than wine: the upright love thee.

She is telling her fiancé that she wants him to kiss her. She can't wait until they are married and he can make "love" to her. Many times, the woman is not the one to initiate conversations about the bedroom. This woman was opening heart unto the man of her dreams. She was very open to letting her lover know that he was wanted. She was asking him to take her in and make love to her. This shows me that I should not only want my husband, but I should tell him as this woman told Solomon. I can only think of a couple of times where I actually thought this way let alone said anything to him. When the thought would come to my mind, I would dismiss it. I didn't think that it was right for me to think that way. This is exactly what I had been searching for. I needed the Word of God to teach me what was appropriate and inappropriate between two lovers. I wanted God to teach me to be Billy's wife.

Song of Solomon 1:8-17
(8) If thou know not, O thou fairest among women, go thy way forth by the footsteps of the flock, and feed thy kids beside the shepherds' tents.
(9) I have compared thee, O my love, to a company of horses in Pharaoh's chariots.
(10) Thy cheeks are comely with rows of jewels, thy neck with chains of gold.
(11) We will make thee borders of gold with studs of silver.
(12) While the king sitteth at his table, my spikenard sendeth forth the smell thereof.
(13) A bundle of myrrh is my wellbeloved unto me; he shall lie all night betwixt my breasts.
(14) My beloved is unto me as a cluster of camphire in the vineyards of Engedi.
(15) Behold, thou art fair, my love; behold, thou art fair; thou hast doves' eyes.
(16) Behold, thou art fair, my beloved, yea, pleasant: also our bed is green.
(17) The beams of our house are cedar, and our rafters of fir.

Solomon tells her of her beauty and brags about what an amazing woman she is and she delights in this. Not a day has gone by since I met Billy that he didn't ravish in my beauty and yet somehow I believed that it was not only annoying but unacceptable. I am already understanding that I am doing two things wrong. What else could there be? I pressed on, in chapter 2 they are now married. What did they do then?

Song of Solomon 2:1-3
(1) I am the rose of Sharon, and the lily of the valleys.
(2) As the lily among thorns, so is my love among the daughters.
(3) As the apple tree among the trees of the wood, so is my beloved among the sons. I sat down under his shadow with great delight, and his fruit was sweet to my taste.

Wow! If he is her apple tree, and she sat down beneath it, that means he must have been standing. She then "taste" of his fruit. We have to understand that this is poetry. Poets and song writers do not just come out and say the underlining meanings to their work. You have to read between the lines, so to speak. This is two lovers who just became husband and wife. I believe that this is referring to oral sex on her husband. He is standing and she is beneath him. She tries his "fruit" and she likes it. Wow!! This is a subject that I don't hear preached from the pulpit. I have always felt that oral sex was wrong and gross in a sense. I imagine that some of you reading this right now may have the same thoughts as I once did. I believed that oral sex was simply for the man and that it was a selfish act on the man's part. Here, in the Bible, this woman enjoyed pleasing her husband. When this is done inside marriage, it is acceptable. This was also to be enjoyed by both parties. I need to be okay to perform oral sex on my husband. Honestly, I should allow myself to enjoy it as well. I should enjoy bringing him pleasure. I added this to my list entitled "What a Godly wife looks like in the bedroom". I wanted to be taught but this was much deeper than I had expected. I must admit I was reluctant to move forward but I did.

Song of Solomon 2:4-5
(4) He brought me to the banqueting house, and his banner over me was love.
(5) Stay me with flagons, comfort me with apples: for I am sick of love.

When I go to a banquet, it is usually very fancy and "All I can eat" but here she has a banquet of "love", or should we say "love making", instead of food. Now, I know that this scripture is used in hymns in the church and that Song of Solomon also reflects the love of God over us but right now I want to address the intimate meaning here with her husband. Here, the "love" is better translated as "love making". This means that they had sex. Actually, they had all the sex they wanted and then she asks him to wait with her while she eats. They must have worked up quite the appetite. Many times, we tend to believe that we should just perform our "wifely duties" and quickly get them done and over with. This woman felt differently. This woman made a "feast" of it. This lasted so long that she had to stop and eat. I believe that this is telling us to take our time with our spouses and enjoy them. There is no need to quickly do what is needed and "get it over with". Now, I am not saying that having a "quickie" isn't okay; it's fun sometimes. What I am saying is that making love is more than that. We should make it a banquet for our spouse. When we enjoy them, and allow them to enjoy us, it builds our marriage. I must learn to slow life down in the bedroom and allow God to use it to bring us closer.

Song of Solomon 2:6
(6) His left hand is under my head, and his right hand doth embrace me.

Next, the man holds her with one arm and "embraces" her with the other. Here is where I was shocked. In the bedroom, when one arm is holding the woman and the other is pleasing her, it is usually a manual stimulation from the man. Here is also where I bring another "taboo" subject among Christians but common among worldly people. He is satisfying her with his hand or fingers. Now, I know that this is hard to hear especially if your view on sexual relationships are already a mess in your mind but this is not wrong between husband and wife. Satan uses things that God has given to us against us. He took something so amazing and altered it so that we couldn't fully enjoy it. I have to be able to enjoy my husband touching me sexually. I should give myself fully to him so that I feel comfortable in this area. Sex should not just be to repopulate the earth. God intended it for pleasure for us as well. I need to allow Billy full access to my body. This is acceptable in marriage and I should accept it too. I am sure Billy would love me to trust him this much to grant him the ability to touch me in such an intimate way. Not only is it acceptable for him to this this for me, I should even be able to ask for it.

Song of Solomon 2:7
(7) I charge you, O ye daughters of Jerusalem, by the roes, and by the hinds of the field, that ye stir not up, nor awake my love, till he please.

I love this verse. So far, the poem/song was about love making and now this verse is put here to inform us of one important detail. We all need to know that these things mentioned is ONLY for marriage. God gave us a beautiful gift to enjoy with our spouses but it is NEVER acceptable outside of marriage. Many people want to know, when is the right time to engage in a sexual act? We should wait until He (God) is pleased with it. There ONLY time that is acceptable is after the "time" of your marriage. After you say your vows, then and only then is it okay to "awaken love".

Song of Solomon 4:5
(5) Thy two breasts are like two young roes that are twins, which feed among the lilies.

Well, I must say that men have not changed! Here he was telling the woman how beautiful her breasts were. I have yet to meet a man that wasn't obsessed. I have often found myself annoyed with my husband. No matter what I am doing, he can somehow manage to grab me. I am certain that most men believe that our breast are there for their pleasure alone. As I read this, and thought of my husband, another verse came to my mind. Mark 10:8: the two shall become one flesh. If I took this scripture literally, then my body belongs to him and I shouldn't get offended when he wants to touch it. There are so many things that this world has "taught" me that wasn't right. Many women hold their heart, emotions, and even their bodies from their husbands. This isn't the way God intended it to be. It is perfectly acceptable for our husbands to want to touch us. The husband and wife are to be one flesh. In order for this to happen, everything we have should be for our spouse.

Song of Solomon 4:12-15
(12) A garden inclosed is my sister, my spouse; a spring shut up, a fountain sealed.
(13) Thy plants are an orchard of pomegranates, with pleasant fruits; camphire, with spikenard,
(14) Spikenard and saffron; calamus and cinnamon, with all trees of frankincense; myrrh and aloes, with all the chief spices:
(15) A fountain of gardens, a well of living waters, and streams from Lebanon.

He is referring to her vagina here. We can see this when we look at the following verse. She responds back in verse 16.

Song of Solomon 4:16
(16) Awake, O north wind; and come, thou south; blow upon my garden, that the spices thereof may flow out. Let my beloved come into his garden, and eat his pleasant fruits.

She is literally offering her body to him. She is telling him to come and perform oral sex on her. She is so open to her husband that she feels confident in telling him exactly what she wants and allows him to give her those desires. It is very hard for me to see that this is acceptable with God. This thought I have isn't because I don't think that God wants us to enjoy it but because of everything that I have experience in my life. You see, I always believe that if I liked this then I was a lesbian. I never understood that it was perfectly acceptable to allow my husband to do this. I have always had the thought that sex for the man only and it's not! I can enjoy it too. My God gave us, both us and our husbands, this amazing wedding gift. Not only did this woman want it but she asked him for it; I should be more like this woman. I need let down my walls and allow my husband to fulfill my desires. I began praying that God would help me do this. I wanted to be like this woman.

Song of Solomon 5:1
(7) I am come into my garden, my sister, my spouse: I have gathered my myrrh with my spice; I have eaten my honeycomb with my honey; I have drunk my wine with my milk: eat, O friends; drink, yea, drink abundantly, O beloved.

After he pleases his wife, he tells her how excited it made him and that he enjoyed it. If I allow my husband to please me, it will bring him pleasure too. Too often, after sex, we tend to just be done. I love how this verse shows that even afterwards, there should be communication. We should talk about what we liked or even disliked. Intimacy should not stop after we have "finished". In my mind, what I liked shouldn't even be talked about and yet, they talked about it after they were done. This is such a hard thing for me to do. I have to allow God to help me. I have to be open with my husband. I have to be completely transparent is all areas with him. I began to pray, "Lord, help me open up to him…"

After they are married for a while, another poem/song was written. This is written by Solomon. Song of Solomon 7:1-9

(1) How beautiful are thy feet with shoes, O prince's daughter! The joints of thy thighs are like jewels, the work of the hands of a cunning workman.

(2) Thy navel is like a round goblet, which wanteth not liquor: thy belly is like an heap of wheat set about with lilies.

(3) Thy two breasts are like two young roes that are twins.

(4) Thy neck is as a tower of ivory; thine eyes like the fishpools in Heshbon, by the gate of Bathrabbim: thy nose is as the tower of Lebanon which looketh toward Damascus.

(5) Thine head upon thee is like Carmel, and the hair of thine head like purple; the king is held in the galleries.

(6) How fair and how pleasant art thou, O love, for delights!

(7) This thy stature is like to a palm tree, and thy breasts to clusters of grapes.

(8) I said, I will go up to the palm tree, I will take hold of
the boughs thereof: now also thy breasts shall be as clusters
of the vine, and the smell of thy nose like apples;
(9) And the roof of thy mouth like the best wine for my
beloved, that goeth down sweetly, causing the lips of those
that are asleep to speak.

When I read this, the very first thing I noticed was
that she is naked! He is talking about every part of her from
the soles of her feet to the top of her head. She has stripped
for her husband and he is gazing upon her beauty. Satan did
not invent stripping and within marriage, this is completely
acceptable! I can't even tell you how many times I have
screamed at my husband, "Don't look at me!" As I read
this, I can see how this woman was so open to her husband
that she could be naked before him. I shouldn't be so
insecure that my husband can't look at me. Most of the
time, I have to have the lights OFF while being intimate. I
am sure this woman left her lights ON. I am sure that she
didn't see herself as having the perfect body because no
woman does. Let's face the fact that every woman alive
thinks there are parts of her body that is ugly. This woman
sets aside her insecurities to give her husband some "eye
candy". She has found a secret to life, I believe. She knows
that setting aside her insecurities will enhance her marriage
and place a protection around it. Why would her husband
want to look elsewhere when she gives him everything a
man could desire? Let me pause to say that this is true for
most men but not all. Sometimes, it doesn't matter what the
woman does, the man can still step away and have an
affair. We as women can't control our spouses. Sometimes
men have an affair not because of what is wrong with us
but what is wrong within them. We should, as women, try
to protect our marriages to the best of our ability. I want to
not only protect my marriage but to fulfill every desire my
husband has. I want to be able to please him in all areas. I

want to let go of my insecurities and allow him to see all of me. I want to be able to strip for my husband. I want to be the woman he dreams of.

Song of Solomon 7:10-13
(10) I am my beloved's, and his desire is toward me.
(11) Come, my beloved, let us go forth into the field; let us lodge in the villages.
(12) Let us get up early to the vineyards; let us see if the vine flourish, whether the tender grape appear, and the pomegranates bud forth: there will I give thee my loves.
(13) The mandrakes give a smell, and at our gates are all manner of pleasant fruits, new and old, which I have laid up for thee, O my beloved.

This woman delights in knowing that she belongs to him. She also brags because her husband desires her. Wow! I have had such a hard time allowing people to know how much my husband loves me. It is almost as though I don't want people to know that I belong to him. I have always considered this a weakness yet, it makes this woman strong. I can see now, allowing your heart to show isn't a weakness at all but, a true strength. This takes effort to allow your heart to be so open. She also wants him to take her away. She wants to go away, just him and her, and be together. She is saying that if he will take her away and spend time with her she will give him her "love". She is asking him to take her and make love to her once again. She wants them to be together like they once were. She wants to be with him away from their daily lives. She also explains that she wants to do the things they usually do but try new things as well. I need to allow my husband to take me away from our daily lives and rekindle what we once had as well as build new memories. We shouldn't do the same things each and every day. We should look for new things to do with our husbands. I need to improve in this area too. All too often, when I do get comfortable with something, I don't want to move forward. I want to stay right where I am. I also get to where I don't want to leave my daily life to make time for him. I want to go through life as "scheduled". I need to make God my first priority, of course, and then my husband. I need to make time for us. I need to allow him to take me away for a weekend so that we can be intimate without distractions. I need to build the intimacy in my marriage. I pray God keeps molding me. I want to keep moving forward and allowing God to mold me into a good wife for Billy. I want to be who God intended me to be for Him and my husband.

Song of Solomon 8:6-7
(6) Set me as a seal upon thine heart, as a seal upon thine arm: for love is strong as death; jealousy is cruel as the grave: the coals thereof are coals of fire, which hath a most vehement flame.
(7) Many waters cannot quench love, neither can the floods drown it: if a man would give all the substance of his house for love, it would utterly be contemned.

This verse sums up the entire book. This is the woman speaking to her husband. A signet ring was either worn on the right hand or on a necklace that would hang over the heart. This ring was referred to as a seal. This was like an emblem of authority. This was the bride's way of saying that she wanted to be her husband's most valuable and treasured possession. She wanted to be his only love. This love she has for him is so powerful that nothing can destroy it. She is also saying that the love she has for him cannot be bought with money. Nothing can compare to her love for her husband. Even with all his wealth, he couldn't afford her but she gives it to him freely. I need to fully give my love to my husband. I need to freely give him all authority over me. I need Billy to have full authority in the bedroom too. The love I have for him should be so strong that nothing and no one can pull me away. I pray that God continues to build this love. I pray that I can learn that is not only acceptable but necessary to allow my husband to fully be one with me. We need to be one in spirit and in body. I need to let down the walls I have placed around my heart, mind, and body and submit them humbly to the man to which God blessed me with. I need to fully comprehend and access the best wedding gift of all; true intimacy between husband and wife.

Life Was Too Perfect

I began trying the things that I had learned in the Songs of Solomon and praying that God would help me to let my walls down. I loved Billy with all my heart and I enjoyed being with me but I couldn't let go fully. I wanted so badly to but I was so afraid. Part of me was afraid that I would love him and things wouldn't work out and I would be crushed. The other part of me was still not use to having life so perfect and it was scaring me. I believed that I didn't deserve to have life perfect. I knew that God loved me but I just still didn't feel worthy enough to be loved by such a man. Laney and I were closer friends than ever. She would keep me on track. She sent me scriptures daily and completed Bible studies with me. God took everything terrible that we had done and made it beautiful.

Just a few months after Billy and I were married, Laney spoke at church. She taught a message on the true meaning of love. She spoke on the meaning behind Jesus washing the disciple's feet. What she did next still shocks me to this day. She call Billy and me up to the front of the church and brought out the tubs of water and clean towels. She first started with Billy. As she began washing his feet, the tears started falling. She had asked Billy to forgive her before but this time was different. She told him she was so sorry that she had an affair with his wife. She apologized for tearing apart our marriage and the plans that God had for us. She explained that now, she would forever put our family above her and her family. She said that she loved us and was our biggest fan. After him, she moved on to me. I immediately began to weep too. She washed my feet while apologizing to me. She asked me to forgive her for not loving me the way that God intended. She was so embarrassed that we had done the things that we had done. She promised to always put God first, her children and then me and my family. I have seen a foot washing before but this one was different. This woman humbled herself and opened her heart and soul to the world. That day, I knew that God had gave me a special friend. He gave me someone who would pray for me, lead me, and serve the Lord with me all the days of our life. I knew that I could depend on her to keep me on the narrow path. Laney wasn't my ex-girlfriend anymore. She was now my prayer partner, my accountability partner, and my best friend. God redeemed us. She washed our feet but God washed away our past.

Just a few weeks later, God moved us 700 miles away to a place where we only knew two people from church camp. I talked to Laney and Amie on the phone but for the most part, I just had Billy and our children. We found a church but didn't get involved with the people there. We would go to church and come home. We focused on God and our family. While at church, we would all worship together in unity. It was so beautiful. Many times during church, I would open my eyes and look down the row to see my husband and children all standing with their hands lifted to the Lord. We also went on picnics, hiking trails, and playing in parks. We spent every moment that we could together. While Billy was at work, the children worked on their school work and I studied God's word. When Billy came home, he would sit and talk with us or play with the kids until bedtime. It was almost like we were in a constant counseling session with God. He was teaching us daily how to be a family again. God began tearing my walls down too. The more I begged God to teach me, the more He did. I began enjoying being with Billy more and more. Instead of trying to be with him, I began trying not to because the more we were intimate, the more I wanted to be. It was so hard not to let him have all of me. I wanted to but it was scary.

One night after the kids were asleep, I prayed and asked God to make me brave. I wanted Him to help me give myself to my husband. That night, something happened. As we began making love, it was different than before. I didn't have to hold back. I was open and told Billy what I wanted and I also wanted to please him as well. I was nervous and scared but I wanted it. The best way I can describe it is it was almost like we both lost our virginity that night. It was calm yet scary. It was intense but beautiful. I felt God take our hearts and mold them together. I felt my heart open up and places of my heart began to feel his love where I had never felt before. My body felt as though I was in a cloud. I couldn't even think about anything except how much I loved him. That night, I made love to my husband the way that God intended. We were husband and wife with NOTHING standing between us. We had no worries, no cares, and the whole world fell to the side. The only thing that matter was Billy, me, and the love God gave us. I had never experience such euphoria with a man before. I truly understood what I had been missing all those years. Nothing, I mean nothing, compared to truly giving my heart to him and making love to him. As we fell asleep, I laid my head on his chest and wept. I had allowed myself to fully enjoy him and my whole heart was open. I fell asleep thanking God for giving me such an amazing man.

I woke the next morning to Billy gone. He had left for work and left me a message on my journal that said that he loved me. What happened next is still the most embarrassing thing that I have ever done. As I laid there that morning, I realized something; my life was perfect. I never wanted anything else. I couldn't think of one thing I would change. I missed Laney and her children but I loved the therapy God had us in. I knew that I had the life that I always wanted. Every dream that I had for a marriage was complete. The thought of these sacred me more than anything I had ever been through. I could handle chaos. I could take the heartaches, flashbacks, and disappointments but this was different. This was true happiness and the newness was intimidating. It was just days before the anniversary I was put in care and the anniversary of my father being released. I thought back to all the things I had been through. I thought that life wouldn't stay perfect too long so I better get out while it was going good. I truly thought that if I didn't break the streak of happiness, something else would and since my whole heart was now involved, I would be crushed. Amie messaged me and asked me to drive down for a fall festival. I didn't even think about it. I told her that I would be there. I had to get away. I told myself that I didn't deserve a good life. I just knew that Billy would soon realize that too and leave me. I figured the best thing to do was for me to destroy our marriage by myself and then at least I was in control. This is the DUMBEST thing I have EVER done. I was head over heels for this man and scared to death. I didn't know how to handle it. I didn't know how to allow my heart to stay open. I built walls as high as I could and packed a few outfits. As soon as I was could, I left for Amie's house.

I wasn't at her house more than a couple hours when my heart became heavy. I was scared for my marriage, the anniversary of being placed in foster care, and the anniversary of the release of my father from jail. The worse part of all was that I missed my husband. I missed his voice. I missed his smile. The thing I missed the most though was his arms around me. I wanted to go back home. I told myself that I needed to "toughen up". How dare I let all my walls down? I had let people in my life before and they hurt me and yet I was going to open my heart to a man, fully? What was I thinking? I asked Amie to go to Walmart with me. I told her how much I hated my marriage and wanted out. I didn't lie, I did hate my marriage. I just hated it for a different reason than I manipulated her to think. I hated my marriage because it was perfect. My marriage was absolutely perfect. I bought a bottle and vodka and began trying to "drown" my thoughts. I drank almost the entire bottle and have no idea how I didn't die. The more I drank, the worse I felt. Then, I told her that I wanted to "mess up my marriage". I tried to go back to the way it was before. I tried to be with Amie. This time was different though. I had been delivered. It didn't feel like it once did. I didn't want it anymore. It was like two friends trying to do the same things they once did but there was no emotional or sexual connection. It didn't mean anything to me anymore. This scared me even more! Everything I had ever wanted truly had changed. I talked to her about getting a divorce. I had to get out of my marriage. I loved him. I truly loved him. I made a plan to leave Billy the following January. Even if I never wanted to be with anyone else, I didn't want to have my heart open like that again. I spent a few days with Amie and then drove to see Laney. I will NEVER forget what happened next.

As I walked into Laney's house, she was pale. She spoke very calmly and quietly. She told me that she needed to talk to me. Our children went outside for a picnic and Laney and I stayed inside. Laney told me that while she was praying for me, God showed her what I had done and the plans I had made. She told me almost word for word the things I had said. She asked me to be honest and tell her if she had truly heard from God. As a sat there speechless, tears rolling down my face, I just nodded. She jumped up off the couch and ran out the door. I ran after her to find her puking beside the house. The thought of me going back or even trying to go back to the lifestyle made her physically ill. She grabbed me after she finished and she began screaming and crying, "After all God did for us, why would you do that?" I didn't know how to respond. I couldn't tell her the truth. I couldn't really lie to her either. We went inside and I just wept. I knew that I was delivered. I knew that I couldn't go back to the things I had done before. I asked for forgiveness and decided that I had to allow God to once again tear down my walls for Billy. I couldn't be scared of the future. I had to trust God.

Rebuilding Trust

I went home from Laney's and had to tell Billy
what I had done. I begged him to forgive me for running
away AGAIN. He thought that we were okay when I left.
He thought that I was just going to see a friend. He was
heartbroken when I told him. It destroyed our marriage.
The way he looked at me was now different. He didn't
smile like he once did. He didn't even want to be intimate
with me much at all. I had the perfect life and I threw it
away because I was scared. God have delivered me from
so much and yet I tried to go back to it. I thought back to
the "braces" that God showed me. I remember that God
told me that many times I might want those "braces" back
on but I hadn't believed Him. I wanted the "braces" back
because I was use to them and thought it could help me
"walk" easier. I realized I could no longer could use those
"braces". I had to "walk" without them despite the
discomfort. Although Billy forgave me, this put a strain on
our marriage. It was almost as if I had to start all over with
allowing Billy in again and vice versa. I began seeking God
to help me see why I ran. I had to have the potter mold me
once again. There was something about my vessel that was
still cracked. There was something that I had missed. As I
began to seek God, I kept coming across the word
"thankful". It seemed to pop up in Bible studies, daily

scriptures, and even common conversations. So, I began studying being thankful.

Romans 1:21-32

(21) Because that, when they knew God, they glorified him not as God, neither were thankful; but became vain in their imaginations, and their foolish heart was darkened.

(22) Professing themselves to be wise, they became fools,

(23) And changed the glory of the uncorruptible God into an image made like to corruptible man, and to birds, and fourfooted beasts, and creeping things.

(24) Wherefore God also gave them up to uncleanness through the lusts of their own hearts, to dishonour their own bodies between themselves:

(25) Who changed the truth of God into a lie, and worshipped and served the creature more than the Creator, who is blessed for ever. Amen.

(26) For this cause God gave them up unto vile affections: for even their women did change the natural use into that which is against nature:

(27) And likewise also the men, leaving the natural use of the woman, burned in their lust one toward another; men with men working that which is unseemly, and receiving in themselves that recompence of their error which was meet.

(28) And even as they did not like to retain God in their knowledge, God gave them over to a reprobate mind, to do those things which are not convenient;

(29) Being filled with all unrighteousness, fornication, wickedness, covetousness, maliciousness; full of envy, murder, debate, deceit, malignity; whisperers,

(30) Backbiters, haters of God, despiteful, proud, boasters, inventors of evil things, disobedient to parents,

(31) Without understanding, covenant breakers, without natural affection, implacable, unmerciful:
(32) Who knowing the judgment of God, that they which commit such things are worthy of death, not only do the same, but have pleasure in them that do them.

Wow! Everything that I had ever struggled with was on this list. I was struggling because I was NOT thankful. If I had been truly thankful for what God had done for me, I wouldn't have tried to go back. If I had been truly thankful for my marriage, I would have never cheated on him. I had played "church" so long that God handed me over to a reprobate mind. He had delivered me, yes, but if I didn't get ahold of things, I was headed backwards. When I first got married, I was so thankful for Billy. After we moved to South Carolina, I began slipping back. I had so much to be thankful for. I had to repent and start truly being thankful for God, my husband, and my children. I had to stop being so selfish. I had to learn to put God first and then my family.

I knew that there was more of me that God needed to mold besides the unthankful spirit that I had. I prayed and sought God for healing. I didn't even know the area in which I was struggling but I knew there was a crack in me that was not visible to the naked eye. Many days went by and I felt like I was on a roller coaster of emotions. One day I was happy, next sad, and the following day I was numb. It was crazy. Why couldn't I find some sort of homeostasis with my emotions? I still talked to Amie and Laney but our friendship was not the same. Their words use to comfort me, but now nothing seem to break down the walls around my heart. I began listening to sermons on YouTube throughout the day. I kept asking God to just show me why I was struggling. I was following the directions of Song of Solomon but something was different. It wasn't the same as that one night. There was a wall around my heart that I couldn't penetrate. Something was holding me back. While homeschooling, I came across a sermon by Paula White. I had listened to sermon before but this day it affected me differently. I started taking notes on her sermon and studied it out for myself as well. The title of her message is called, "Breaking Ungodly Soul Ties". Here is what I got out of it...

Genesis 29:31-35

(31) And when the LORD saw that Leah was hated, he opened her womb: but Rachel was barren.

(32) And Leah conceived, and bare a son, and she called his name Reuben: for she said, Surely the LORD hath looked upon my affliction; now therefore my husband will love me.

(33) And she conceived again, and bare a son; and said, Because the LORD hath heard that I was hated, he hath therefore given me this son also: and she called his name Simeon.

(34) And she conceived again, and bare a son; and said, Now this time will my husband be joined unto me, because I have born him three sons: therefore was his name called Levi.

(35) And she conceived again, and bare a son: and she said, Now will I praise the LORD: therefore she called his name Judah; and left bearing.

You see, Leah wasn't the favorite. She didn't even feel as though she was anything special. Her father basically sold her for 7 years of work to a man who thought he was getting her sister. Imagine how this would make a young girl feel. She probably felt unloved, betrayed, and rejected. Today, we would say, "She had Daddy issues". She didn't get the love she expected from her father, so she tried to do whatever she could to get that love from her husband. She had an ungodly soul tie. Jacob was her idol. She wanted to have Jacob's love above anything else. An idol isn't necessarily a big statue that you bow down to. An idol is anything that you yield yourself to. It is the thing that you put above all else. You can worship something or someone by paying too much attention to it. When we have unfulfilled needs or cracks per say, this is an open door to idols or ungodly soul ties. These "needs" will make you do things that you never thought you would do. When you allow someone's opinion to give you value over what God says or does, they become an ungodly soul tie. Through it all, God tried to show her His love. He tried to fill that gap in her heart. God kept giving her children to show His love, but she only wanted to use that gift to win favor and love from her husband. At the very end, she finally realized that God is trying to show her love and praises Him.

In today's society, most of us have some sort of emotional damage. Many of us don't even realize that those damaged parts of us dictate the things we do. We have teenagers seeking relationships too early with boys much older than them because of "Daddy issues". We have people on drugs because they are trying to cover up the pain of their past that they don't even know how to deal with. We have married men and women having affairs because they are seeking a "love" that only God can give.

Exodus 20:3-5
(3) Thou shalt have no other gods before me.
(4) Thou shalt not make unto thee any graven image, or any likeness of any thing that is in heaven above, or that is in the earth beneath, or that is in the water under the earth:
(5) Thou shalt not bow down thyself to them, nor serve them: for I the LORD thy God am a jealous God, visiting

the iniquity of the fathers upon the children unto the third and fourth generation of them that hate me;

God should be the source of our joy, peace, validation, and more. God should guide our will and emotions. When we get into an ungodly soul tie, their emotions become ours. When they are having a bad day, so are we. When they are doing well and thriving, so are we. It is almost like you are on a roller coaster and they are the track. You can't help but follow where they go. When Satan wants to side track you, he will send you someone to pull you away.

Leah was birthing blessings and using them for the wrong things. When you have an ungodly soul tie, you misread the blessings that God gives you. Everything seems to be wrapped around that idol instead of where your focus should be. You begin to care more about what that person thinks than anyone else. Leah just wanted her husband to want her. She didn't understand the blessings that God was laying on her. We can't look for validation from anyone but God!

We are all made to cleave to one another but there are Godly and ungodly soul ties. A soul ties is where two souls are knitted together and in a sense they become one! We need Godly soul ties in our lives. They are Biblical too. The Bible says that where two or more are bound together in His name it shall be done. There is power when we bind together for the Lord. It also says that one can put a 1,000 demons to flight but two can put 10,000. (Deut. 32:30) Soul ties are not just in marriage. The soul of David was knitted to Jonathon. God created soul ties for His kingdom. Satan has misused this against us. We are going to have different ties with people. A soul tie is when you are tied or closely joined to one another. A soul tie is an emotional glue to someone. This relationship ties you spiritually to them as well. When you have sex with someone, you can transfer spirits. You don't have to have sex though, it can be an emotional connection that makes this a soul tie. Soul ties will draw two people's emotions and spirituality together like magnets.

Paula White said that there were 6 signs of an ungodly soul tie:

- An ungodly soul tie produces irrational thinking. Irrational means not capable of reasoning, having lost mental clarity, illogical.
- An ungodly soul tie causes a person to evaluate themselves and others according to previous context. They can't see outside of that relationship or mental paradigm.
- An ungodly soul tie causes a person to shut down emotionally.
- An ungodly soul tie produces an unhealthy, unnatural desire or attraction to people, places and things, even to the person's detriment.
- An ungodly soul tie will cause a lack of judgment and discernment.
- An ungodly soul tie produces the inability to establish and maintain proper adult relationships.

As I listen to her message, I realized that I was still tied to Laney and Amie. Laney's marriage wasn't restored like mine was so I felt like my marriage was terrible. I began feeling towards Billy the way she was feeling towards her ex-husband. Amie was basically just married to a friend. She loved him but not as a spouse. When they were "up", I was "up". When they were struggling, guess who else was struggling. Somehow, I also felt as though everything they did in their life impacted me even though it didn't. The scariest thing though, my emotions were uncontrollable. I had shut them down and couldn't find a way to turn them back on. I loved them as my friends but I knew that God needed to sever the soul ties between us. I realized this problem of an ungodly soul tie and prayed, "Lord Jesus, I need these soul ties broken off of me in Jesus' name. I ask that you forgive me for the positions that I have put myself in that allowed these to form. Lord, please take me and bind me to my husband and him alone. Let us become one flesh. I cancel the attack from the enemy on my life and the life of my family. I rebuke the trick of this ungodly soul tie in Jesus' name. Please, do whatever you need to do to set me free. Take me and make me your vessel. Mold me into something beautiful for you."

Within 24 hours after this, I received a phone call from Laney. I was actually listen to Paula White again about Godly soul ties when the phone rang. I was thanking God for giving me a Ruth and Naomi relationship with her. I answered the phone and Laney asked me to talk to her for a moment. She told me that she had something to say but that I wasn't going to like it. I had all the confidence in the world that our friendship would be stronger than ever now. I smiled and said, "Whatever it is… we will be okay. I will always be your best friend and love you in the most pure and Godly way." Laney began to weep. I hadn't heard her cry like this very often; it scared me. "We have to separate our lives for a while. We need to separate so that God can re-establish us. I don't know how long or what will happen but I know that I heard from God and I must obey Him." she sobbed. My heart was crushed. She was my best friend, my kindred spirit, and my "Naomi". How could God do this to me, I thought? I was doing the right things. I was praying and studying for the right reasons and yet God took her from me. I was hurt, angry, and felt alone. I didn't want to, but I knew the reason. He was separating the soul ties until he could heal us emotionally. The Potter was molding me. I have gone through many things, but this was one of the most painful things that I endured. When we pray and sincerely believe, God will answer our prayers. He was helping me. He was molding me just as I had asked. I just didn't like the way that this felt. This hurt. This cut parts of me out that I didn't know was still there. This wasn't fun.

I thought of the potter, looking at this vessel that He was creating. I saw that it was molding me into something beautiful, but there was not enough room inside the vessel. I felt as though to make room, he took out his loop tool. For those who haven't done pottery or worked with clay, a loop tool is designed to cut out a controlled amount of clay from a sculpture or vessel. The shaped cutting heads are made from heavy stainless steel ribbon with sharpened edges. These can cut out ½ inch thick chunks. Sometimes, the potter molds us gently but other times, it is painful. This time, I felt the sharp edges of His tool deep inside me. This event didn't just happen in a split second and be done either. He began cutting and removing clay from me for months; maybe over a year. He had to remove anything within me that hindered my full submission to Him and my husband. He had to cut out the ungodly soul ties. The relationship that Laney and I was a Godly relationship but our souls where still very much an ungodly soul tie. They were entangled and weaved together so tightly that we couldn't allow God to heal us to our full potential. We had not allowed God to take us and separate us. I knew that I relied too much on her to give me value. I relied on her far too often for my joy and peace. Many times, we would even run things by each other that God spoke to us before obeying Him. It was almost like we put each other above everything. We had unintentionally made idols out of one another. God knew what He was doing. Even though it was painful, God still did what was best for us. He was answering my deepest desire, to be fully formed by the potter into the vessel that He desired. I didn't want to be who I wanted for myself. I wanted to please Him and Him alone.

I still occasionally spoke to Amie, but I felt God telling me to let go of her too. I couldn't fully let her go yet though. I had so many changes going on that I thought I would lose my mind. With Laney out of my life, I had to rely on Billy. I noticed that I began telling him things that I would have normally told Laney. When I was sad, I prayed first and then went to Billy. He would sit and hold me and listen to me. Looking back, I see that God was healing Billy and me at the same time. I needed a best friend, Billy needed me to confide solely in him and just to be needed. God needed to open my heart to make room for Billy. I loved Billy but still not as deep as I knew I should. It was almost like I was too scared to give him my all again. My love for him was so deep that it terrified me already and I knew that God wanted me to go deeper.

God soon moved us back to our hometown and we awaited God to tell us where to go from there. I poured my entire life into being a mom and wife at home but not out and about. I felt as though God was molding me still and that I needed to not have contact with people who would bring up Laney. I also didn't want to run into her at a store or park so I stayed home. It was still hard on me. I still missed my friend. Billy did all the errands to keep me from it. I began visiting with Amie more again and becoming close with her again. The more I became close to Amie though, the weaker Jynna became.

Jynna began to be so tired after about half a day that she couldn't walk. She cried of her legs hurting often.

When we would take a family trip to the zoo, we would have to take turns holding Jynna. She loved playing outside but fell all the time. I took her to the Orthopedics to have her checked out. They told me that her legs were bent or bowed and that was the problem. They told me that Jynna's muscles were not strong enough to hold the bones in place correctly. They recommended a muscle biopsy to find the cause of the problem. The issue with a muscle biopsy is that with many muscle disorders, the biopsy would never heal back. I took Jynna home and just catered to her. As a family, we took turns taking care of her. I thought back to the day the doctors said that Jynna wouldn't live. I thought that if this was her only problem in life, it was better than her not living at all.

At the end of the summer, God opened a door for us in Illinois. He moved us to a small little church that had great involved pastors. I knew that God called us to be there because as I sat in the front row of the church, I heard the Lord tell me, "Welcome Home!" This church was not like any other that I had ever been too. This church was called "Second Chance Ministries" and they stood on that thought process. They fully believed that everyone needed a second chance. They truly believed that everyone makes mistakes and God uses those mistakes for His glory if we will allow it. This church quickly became not just a church that we attended but a lifestyle and family. The people at Second Chance taught me what being part of a family really meant.

The pastors of this church were the type who get to the root of the problems in their congregation. They aren't afraid of dealing with things or helping others fix the issues in their life. As they saw Billy and me together, they could tell that I was still not allowing myself to be fully open up to him. The pastor's wife kept telling me that I couldn't fully open my heart to the Lord if I couldn't open up to my husband. Once, she asked me, "What is God telling you to do that you won't just do?" I knew that it was the soul tie with Amie but I didn't know how to let go. We had been friends so long. I couldn't figure out if I wasn't sinning why God would make me give her up. I didn't understand why I had to let go?

Jynna began not only struggling with her legs but her facial muscles. When she would talk, her face would look like she was struggling. It was almost as if all the muscles in her body were weakening. Just a few months after moving to Illinois, she began also have heart palpitations. The doctors told me it may be a muscle problem. No matter how much I prayed over her, she wasn't getting better. She got so bad that many mornings, she couldn't even get out of bed. Many times, she would try to sit up and would fall out of bed. It was so terrible that on several days a week, she couldn't even dress herself. It wasn't uncommon for me to see her crawling down the hallway to get to the bathroom. We just limited her activities and carried her a lot. We were waiting on God to heal her and I didn't know what He was waiting for.

Letting go of it All

I was searching for answers to tell me what to do. God had told me to disconnect from Amie, so I talked to her on the phone but wouldn't visit her. Little did I know, partial obedience is still disobedience. Many times in our lives, God shows us what He wants us to do. He teaches us through people, experiences, and His Word. We have the choice to obey or disobey. Obedience brings blessings but disobedience brings destruction.

There are many examples of this in the Bible. Genesis 2:15-3:24
Adam and Eve ate from the forbidden tree and not only were they punished but so were their offspring. Destruction came to all of man-kind.

Genesis 19:12-26
Lot's family were being saved from the destruction of Sodom and Gomorrah and to help them, God told them not to look back at the city as they left. Lot's wife disobeyed and was turned into a pillar of salt. I am sure that this caused destruction to her family's lives. They had to now live without her.

Numbers 14
The Israelites were told to take possession of the promise land but instead were too afraid and didn't obey. This brought destruction to all of them who refused to obey. Only Joshua and Caleb wanted to obey so, their families were the only ones to enter the promise land. Destruction hit the rest of the Israelites and they died in the wilderness. Each of these people were given instructions yet choose to disobey what the Lord instructed them to do. As a consequence, destruction came into their lives. This destruction not only effects the person who disobeys but also those around them.

Let's look at the book of Daniel.
Belshazzar was the grandson of Nebuchadnezzar. Nebuchadnezzar was the king who was responsible for Shadrach, Meshach, and Abednego being thrown into the furnace.

Daniel 3
After Nebuchadnezzar saw the image of the Son of God in the furnace and the 3 men saved, he made a decree that no one could speak against their God. Although he made this decree, Nebuchadnezzar didn't have change of heart.

Daniel 4
Nebuchadnezzar has a dream and no one can interpret it. They bring in Daniel. Daniel basically tells the king that if he doesn't surrender to God that he will lose everything. Nebuchadnezzar doesn't believe he needs God's help therefore, the dream comes true and Nebuchadnezzar loses his mind and ends up in a field like a beast. He surrenders his life to God and soon after, historians say he was killed and his son takes the throne.

The Bible doesn't tell much about the new king. He was only king for a few short years and then is killed and his brother becomes king. He is known as Evil Merodach. Historians back up the fact that he was evil and didn't last too long as king. He is mentioned though in 2 Kings 25:27-30.

This brings us to Daniel 5.

The grandson of Nebuchadnezzar is king, Belshazzar is his name.

Belshazzar has a huge party and even uses the golden vessels that Nebuchadnezzar had taken from the temples in Jerusalem to serve his wine in. They began praising false gods and became drunk. The king was having a great party when he sees a finger writing words on the wall. Out of fear, he calls in everyone to try to interpret the writing; no one was successful. The queen (probably his grandmother who was Nebuchadnezzar's wife) comes in and recommends Daniel. Daniel comes in and reminds Belshazzar about the history of his family and how God had given his family chance after chance. Daniel reminds him that everything they have was from the Lord. He even reminds him of Nebuchadnezzar and what had happened to him when pride came in. He advises him to turn to God.

After this, he interprets the writing.

Daniel 5:25-28

[25]"This is the message that was written: mene, mene, tekel, and Peres.

[26]This is what these words mean: Mene means 'numbered'—God has numbered the days of your reign and has brought it to an end.

[27]Tekel means 'weighed'—you have been weighed on the balances and have not measured up.

[28]Peres means 'divided'—your kingdom has been

divided and given to the Medes and Persians."--NLT version

Belshazzar then thanks Daniel and makes him 3rd highest in authority in the kingdom. This is probably because His grandmother was still 1st and he was 2nd and so Daniel was made 3rd. Belshazzar praised Daniel for the information yet still doesn't repent. That night he lost his kingdom just as Daniel said would happen. Destruction came to his whole kingdom because he didn't obey. He knew the experiences of his family yet refused to surrender to the Lord.

Many times, God gives us many chances before full destruction comes but disobedience always brings destruction. As we look around us, we see the warning signs everywhere. You can't drive down the interstate very far without seeing a billboard that says, "Jesus" or "God loves you. Repent." We are just like Belshazzar! We see everything God has done around us. We all see the consequences of disobedience. We all know the stories. We all know what is expected of us but we simply ignore it. We are all seeing the "Handwriting on wall". We have the same choice that Belshazzar had: repent and serve God or simply praise the messenger and ignore the message.

After studying all this, I still didn't understand. I look back and think, "Donna, were you really that blind?" Unfortunately, the answer to that question is a solid, "Yes." I truly thought that I could just live my life and "try hard" to obey and I would be okay. I had disconnected myself from Amie. I had not seen her in a very long time but still talked to her often on the phone or through text. Looking back, I can see now that I was still disobeying God. God wasn't answering my prayers because I was living in sin. I was not breaking the 10 commandments but God had given me a direct order and I was refusing to obey.

I was such an emotional mess. I had so much on my mind. I was trying to be a good wife and mother but honestly, I was just going through the motions. I was still hurt from losing Laney's friendship and also messing up my marriage. I didn't know what to do. I didn't know how to allow God to heal me. I had been healed from so much and yet these last couple things seemed almost impossible. I decided to go to a Joyce Meyer women's conference with my sister and her friends from church. The worship was amazing. I began to get lost in His presence. God began tearing my walls down. I felt as though the walls that I had built back were crumbling. I felt a tear run down the side of my cheek. I didn't want anyone to know that I had built walls after God had brought me through so much. To escape the presence of God, I went to the bathroom. When I came back, I felt as though the Lord told me that I had to be broken. I had to be like the woman with the Alabaster box. I had to break something so precious and dear to me to be used. As I stood there, my sister's friend told me that she had something to tell me after the session. When we took our lunch break, my sister's friend told me that she felt as though God told her that I had to allow Him to break me. Wow! That is exactly what God showed me. I knew that I had heard from God. When I got home, I had to research that woman. I had to know what was in her box.

The story is in Luke 7:37-46
"And, behold, a woman in the city, which was a sinner, when she knew that Jesus sat at meat in the Pharisee's house, brought an alabaster box of ointment, And stood at his feet behind him weeping, and began to wash his feet with tears, and did wipe them with the hairs of her head, and kissed his feet, and anointed them with the ointment.

Now when the Pharisee which had bidden him saw it, he spake within himself, saying, This man, if he were a prophet, would have known who and what manner of woman this is that toucheth him: for she is a sinner. And Jesus answering said unto him, Simon, I have somewhat to say unto thee. And he saith, Master, say on. There was a certain creditor which had two debtors: the one owed five hundred pence, and the other fifty. And when they had nothing to pay, he frankly forgave them both. Tell me therefore, which of them will love him most? Simon answered and said, I suppose that he, to whom he forgave most. And he said unto him, Thou hast rightly judged. And he turned to the woman, and said unto Simon, Seest thou this woman? I entered into thine house, thou gavest me no water for my feet: but she hath washed my feet with tears, and wiped them with the hairs of her head. Thou gavest me no kiss: but this woman since the time I came in hath not ceased to kiss my feet. My head with oil thou didst not anoint: but this woman hath anointed my feet with ointment."☐☐☐☐

To understand the importance of this passage, we must first understand the alabaster box. This box would have contained her most precious ointment. Many historians believe that she may have been saving it for the man that she would marry. It literally was all she had to her name. It was her most valued possession. It was everything she could give and she gave it to Jesus.

This woman was a sinner. Jesus tells the disciples that her sins were many but she loved the Lord and was forgiven. The love God had for her meant so much to her that she wanted to give Jesus everything she had. She gave him her most precious item.

My question to myself was this: What's in my alabaster box? What is my most prized possession? What is the one thing I am holding on to? What is it that I don't want to give to anyone? What would happen if I gave that precious ointment to Jesus? What would happen to my life if I poured my love completely on Jesus?

There are so many things that I keep to myself. There are things that I don't want to give up. There are parts of my heart that I really don't want anyone to have. I keep parts of me secluded in my Alabaster box where they are safe. This challenged me to give it all. I wanted to pour out my alabaster box at the feet of Jesus. My past, depression, insecurities, fears, anxiety, and failures are all His. I have to give him my whole heart, every broken piece. I also wanted to give him all my love, my desires, my possessions, and everything else within me. I wanted Him to know that I love Him with everything I have. He has forgiven me for so much and I can't give him enough. This day, I vowed to give my all. He is so worthy and He deserves more than I can give Him but I will give everything I have. (Luke 14:33 KJV So likewise, whosoever he be of you that forsaketh not all that he hath, he cannot be my disciple.)

I knew that I had to find a way to let God have me. I wanted to do whatever He wanted. I came home and began focusing on giving God everything that I could. I can't even begin to tell you how painful it was to allow God to break me again. I would spend hours crying out in the shower until the cold water would run over my body. I would get on my knees in the tub and just scream in pain. My heart ached. I missed Laney. I felt so alone. Billy would try to comfort me but it didn't seem to help. I guess that I just had to let myself grieve. I had to grieve my friends, family, and the feelings they brought. I would give God one emotion at a time. I would ask him to heal one specific feeling at a time. I would spend as much time as I could in my Bible. If I couldn't be reading, I would have sermons playing on YouTube as I worked. I wanted God to continue to do a work in me. I wouldn't stop until every area of my life was broken open for the Lord.

Within a few weeks, I had a dream. This dream was very vivid. In this dream, my pastors, Billy and I took my 5 kids camping. Pastor took the kids to the right side of the lake to swim and play in the water while the adults were setting up camp. The pastor's wife was setting up the inside of their pop up camper and Billy was leveling a R.V. I saw that I had a free minute to myself so I grabbed my fishing pole and headed to the left side of the lake. I love to fish! Within just a few minutes, I caught a huge catfish! I took it off the hook, picked up my pole, and headed up the campsite. I was so excited that I began yelling for Billy to come meet me so that I could show him. The pastor's wife, Becky, heard me and thought that something was wrong so she ran to me as well. I held up the fish to Billy. He took it from my right hand to see how much he thought it weighed. After he took it, I looked around to see where a safe place would be to set my pole. As I looked around, I saw a scrape on my left forearm. It captured my attention and I froze. It was dirty so I took my right hand and proceeded to brush away the dirt. As I did this, tiny drops of water fell off my fingertips into the scrape on my arm. Although it was tiny droplets, I could see inside it. What I saw terrified me. I saw tiny, almost microscopic, clear ghost-like fish swimming out of the droplet and into the scrape. They were all alike and looked like the shape of an Angel fish. I felt like time slowed down and everything was in slow motion as the droplets fell. Those tiny things began eating my flesh. I began screaming that they were eating away at my good. My arm was tingling and burning. Billy stood in shock while Becky grabbed my right hand and told me to stop screaming and that I had to pray. She said, "This is spiritual! We have to pray!" I held up my arm and said, "This is NOT SPIRITUAL! I can see this. I can feel this. It is NOT spiritual."

I begged Becky and Billy to take me to the hospital but she kept repeating the same thing, "Pray because it's spiritual". Billy took my fishing pole from my left hand and set it down. I was still crying and telling them that those things were eating away at all my good. I tried to get my left hand out Becky's hands. In the process of this, I noticed a cut in the palm of my hand between my middle finger and my pointer finger. I pointed at it to show Becky and Billy and something happened AGAIN!! Small water droplets filled with those tiny things fell and began eating my flesh again. I started screaming that it was eating away at my good. Then Becky started screaming at me. She said, "Do you trust me? This is spiritual! We need to pray now!" I told her, "I trust you but this is REAL!! It is eating away at my good! I can feel this! (I held up my arms) I can see this!! I need to go to the hospital! This is real and it's eating at all my good!!"

As Becky was grabbing my hands and screaming to pray, I was pulling away and screaming that it was eating away at my good. At that moment, in real life, my alarm went off and I woke up. I hit the snooze button on my phone and sat up. My arm and hand were still tingling as though something was crawling inside my skin. I prayed, "Lord, if this is spiritual, please show me."

Within a few minutes, I knew the answer... It was SPIRITUAL!

The Lord reminded me that in the dream I kept saying that it was eating away at my good. I felt the Lord say that it was a parasite! I took my phone and looked up the definition of parasite.

I felt the Lord say that we all have parasites that are eating away at our good and we are allowing it!

par·a·site
(noun)
an organism that lives in or on another organism (its host) and benefits by deriving nutrients at the host's expense

So, the Lord began leading me. Animals who have parasites usually don't even realize that they have them. They are so completely comfortable with it. Most of the time, they never even know about it unless it is removed. We have parasites that are eating away our good but we have become so comfortable with it that we no longer even know that they are there. We can't even see them.

First thing I noticed, the word parasite is a noun. This means it is a person, place, thing, or idea! What parasites did I have? Is it a place I go, people I hang out with, things in my life, thoughts or ideas that I allow my mind to meditate on. What about thoughts I have about myself or others? Do I have something that eats away at my good? Am I so comfortable with it that I don't want to get rid of it?

You see, when parasites are removed, it is painful. Sometimes, removing these parasites will leave an open wound that takes time to heal. But, if not removed, the parasite will continue to eat away at all the good until the host dies. It will weaken the host until it has depleted all the good and the host dies. Parasites in your life will weaken you until you die spiritually!

So, what am I doing to get rid of such parasites?

Romans 12:1-2
I beseech you therefore, brethren, by the mercies of God,
that you present your bodies a living sacrifice, holy,
acceptable to God, which is your reasonable service. And
do not be conformed to this world, but be transformed by
the renewing of your mind, that you may prove what is that
good and acceptable and perfect will of God.

James 4:7-10
Therefore submit to God. Resist the devil and he will flee
from you. Draw near to God and He will draw near to you.
Cleanse your hands, you sinners; and purify your hearts,
you double-minded. Lament and mourn and weep! Let your
laughter be turned to mourning and your joy to gloom.
Humble yourselves in the sight of the Lord, and He will lift
you up.

1 Peter 2: 11-12
Beloved, I beg you as sojourners and pilgrims, abstain from
fleshly lusts which war against the soul, having your
conduct honorable among the Gentiles, that when they
speak against you as evildoers, they may, by your good
works which they observe, glorify God in the day of
visitation.

1 Thessalonians 5:22-23
Abstain from every form of evil. Now may the God of
peace Himself sanctify you completely; and may your
whole spirit, soul, and body be preserved blameless at the
coming of our Lord Jesus Christ.

James 1:21-25
Therefore lay aside all filthiness and overflow of
wickedness, and receive with meekness the implanted
word, which is able to save your souls. But be doers of the
word, and not hearers only, deceiving yourselves. For if

anyone is a hearer of the word and not a doer, he is like a man observing his natural face in a mirror; for he observes himself, goes away, and immediately forgets what kind of man he was. But he who looks into the perfect law of liberty and continues in it, and is not a forgetful hearer but a doer of the work, this one will be blessed in what he does.

James 4:17
Therefore, to him who knows to do good and does not do it, to him it is sin.

2 Timothy 2: 19-22
Nevertheless the solid foundation of God stands, having this seal: "The Lord knows those who are His," and, "Let everyone who names the name of Christ depart from iniquity." But in a great house there are not only vessels of gold and silver, but also of wood and clay, some for honor and some for dishonor. Therefore if anyone cleanses himself from the latter, he will be a vessel for honor, sanctified and useful for the Master, prepared for every good work. Flee also youthful lusts; but pursue righteousness, faith, love, peace with those who call on the Lord out of a pure heart.

After reading these scriptures, they all have one thing in common: they tell us to do something! They tell us to get rid of the parasites. I feel as the Lord impressed upon me that we all have had parasites. I thought, "Gross! Jesus, please remove it!" Instead of feeling those parasites leaving, I felt the Lord say, "Do it yourself..."

Many times, we sit around asking God to remove things in our lives but we can do it ourselves. Now, I can already here some religious person saying, "Wait! We can't do that. We have to allow God to do it for us. We can't do it."

Matthew 16:19
"And I will give you the keys (or authority) of the kingdom of heaven, and whatever you bind on earth will be bound in heaven, and whatever you loose on earth will be loosed in heaven."

Those are RED in my Bible. They are straight from the mouth of Jesus as He was walking on the earth.

Luke 9:1-2
Then He called His twelve disciples together and gave them power and authority over all demons, and to cure diseases. He sent them to preach the kingdom of God and to heal the sick.

Luke 10:19
"Behold, I give you the authority to trample on serpents and scorpions, and over all the power of the enemy, and nothing shall by any means hurt you."

He give us authority over EVERYTHING that comes against us! Through Jesus Christ, we do have the authority to do it! Also, we cannot base our decisions to remove parasites by what we feel. We can't allow our heart to lead us.

Jeremiah 17:9
"The heart is deceitful above all things, And desperately wicked; Who can know it?"

You cannot follow your heart! It is also okay to be uncomfortable. Look at Joseph, Sarah, Moses, Samson, Esther, Paul, and even Jesus. Everything was uncomfortable or painful that God did in/or through them. Nothing in the Bible is comfortable but those things had to happen or parasites would have come in, death would have won, and God's perfect will could not be completed. God was telling me that I had a parasite and I needed to remove it myself! My friendship with Amie was my parasite. Now, Amie wasn't trying to get me to sin. She wasn't even being a bad influence but something about her in my life was stopping God from having complete control. She was just being a good friend, but God told me to let go of her. God knows what that was doing to me spiritually; I didn't have a clue. I had to tell her that I couldn't have her in my life. I had to allow God to re-establish me without her. I had to fully rely on God and my husband for every need that I had.

Letting go of her was very difficult. I would have something come up in life and I would want to call her but couldn't. She had been my safe place for so long, that I had to learn to live life over. The hardest thing though was knowing that I had nowhere to run to anymore. If my marriage got hard now, I had to stay and work it out. I had no other options. I had no back up plan. By letting go of Amie, I see now that I was declaring that I was going to make my marriage work. My marriage was the only plan that I had.

Restoration

Just a couple months later, I woke up on a Sunday morning. I heard Jynna crying in the bedroom. I asked Joyanna to pick her out an outfit and Jeremyah to carry her to my room while I got dressed for church. As I got dressed, Jynna laid on my pillow crying. She was trying to get herself dressed before I had to help her. Her legs were bent and she was in the fetal position. She told me she couldn't stretch out her legs. The pain was too intense for her to handle so she just waited for me. I began getting her dressed very carefully. Inside, I was screaming. God had healed me from so much and yet here was my precious baby unable to even dress herself. I hadn't even been able to tell our friends and family how bad it truly was. I felt like I had no one that knew the struggle we were enduring. For anyone with an undiagnosed sick child, you would understand. It is so hard when no one understands the battle. I put my shoes on and then Jynna's while Billy helped the other kids. As I picked her up, she couldn't even wrap her legs around me. I had to carry her like a baby. My 9 year old had to be carried like a newborn. We went into church and sat down. Many church members saw my face and could see the pain that I was so desperately trying to hide. I had to stay strong for Jynna but inside I was falling apart. The people who were at church early got around Jynna and prayed over her but still nothing changed. I sat her on Billy's lap and went to the restroom to calm myself down. The pastor's wife, Becky, asked me if I was okay. I told her that I wasn't okay but I couldn't talk about it. I just told her that it was really bad now. I simply said that Jynna was getting much worse and went back to my seat. At the end of service, the pastor asked if we could bring Jynna up front. By this time, Jynna's legs muscles had relaxed and she could stand for a moment. She was weak but was standing. We brought her to the front and people began walking up to help us pray. As people came forward, I heard the Lord speak to me. He told me to repent. Repent for what, I thought? Then, I felt the Lord speak to my heart again. I had to repent for letting spirits around Jynna. Through my sins, I had opened the door for Satan to bring spirits into my home. As parents, we are to protect them physically, mentally, and spiritually. I had failed. Throughout the last few years, I had let many unclean spirits get to my children. Until this point, I don't really believe that I actually understood that I was responsible for the spiritual atmosphere of my house. I repented and asked God to take away anything that was an oppression on my daughter. The people around me had no idea what I was praying. About the time I finished, they all laid hands on my precious Jynna. We anointed her with oil and prayed over her. I asked that the chains of infirmity be broken in Jesus' name. After we finished praying over her, Jynna stood up tall. She walked away with a big smile on her face. She walked over to me and told me that her legs didn't hurt anymore and that they felt good. When church was over, Jynna began running around inside the church. She was flipping in the front. God healed my little girl that day. Our pastor said she could run and flip in the church whenever she wanted. We wanted everyone to see the amazing miracle that God had done.

We may never know what sin does in our life. When we sin, it doesn't just affect us but everyone around us. Many things that we deal with may be a direct result from spirits that have entered our homes though sin or disobedience. We need to make sure that we get healing and deliverance from emotional situations so that they do not influence us in the future. I want to state that Amie wasn't doing anything wrong. She wasn't trying to get me to backslide. Actually, I felt that she was getting closer to God at the time. It doesn't matter how we see the situation though, disobedience is still sin. The fact I wouldn't let go of her shows that there was some form of a soul tie that I didn't want to break. I truly understood now what God meant when He said that disobedience always leads to destruction.

Seeing Jynna healed and knowing that it was my fault was very hard. I had spent my life being so selfish that I never considered the damage I was doing to my children. Although it would be hard, I could not see or talk to Amie again unless God told me to. I also know that God will not only tell me that it is okay but my pastors too. I vowed not to contact her again unless we all agree that it is the appropriate time. Sometimes, we really have to trust God and our pastors with our heart. Too often, we go on feelings and not on the Lord. I had proven that I wasn't ready yet to make some decisions for life. I am leaving that part of my life in the hands of my trusted potter.

Just a few weeks later, Billy worked out of town for a few weeks. I was so lonely. I missed the friendship that Laney and I had. I missed my friend Amie too. I went into the bath tub and began to pray. I wish that I could say that when I asked to feel God, He was quick to respond but that isn't the case. I sat there for a long time and could not feel Him at all. Finally I thought, "I am going to email Laney. I miss my friendship. I am struggling and would love a friend to comfort me." I didn't feel God say it was okay but I also didn't feel Him say it wasn't okay. Actually, to be honest, I didn't feel anything at all. I sat there in the tub and just wondered what I should do. I thought about King David in the Bible. The Bible says that David encouraged himself. I sat there and began to rub my legs. I am a "touchy" person. My love language, although I don't like people to know, has always been physical touch. As I rubbed my legs, back and forth, back and forth, I started speaking to myself, aloud. I said, "Jesus loves you, Donna. You are called according to His purpose. You are the head and not the tail. You are above and you shall not be beneath. You are chosen. You are one of God's favorite. If you love Him, keep His commandments. If you love Him, prove it." I told myself these things over and over. Then, I said, aloud, "Lord Jesus, all I need is you! I don't even need to feel you. I know you are here and you are enough for me." All of a sudden, I felt the presence of the Lord in that tub. I felt a hand on the left side of my face. It was a huge hand. It was warm and made my face tingle. I closed my eyes and leaned back into the tub. I placed my head at the back, just out of the water. Within a few seconds, I saw a vision. It was of a potter holding a vessel. It had a handle on it. It was thicker at the bottom but got thinner as it went up. I saw a hand hold a tool with a very sharp point on it. The potter was etching out a design on the outside of the vessel. It was a simple, yet elegant design. In a sweet voice, the potter spoke, "Every time that you choose my will over yours, you allow me to embellish you as my vessel."

Many times, I have made decisions based on how I felt. This day, I found out that love is not a feeling. It isn't what makes you feel good or gives you a sense of accomplishment. Love is a choice. Love is an action. I loved the Lord so much that I wanted to please Him. It didn't really matter what I felt like. If I trusted that God had the best intentions for my life, feelings shouldn't guide me. I found out that day to go by what God says and not by what I feel like at the time. We are human, we have emotions, but shouldn't allow them to dictate our life. If we truly want to live for the Lord, we must obey Him.

Billy came back from working out of town. I sat on our bed thinking of my past. I was miserable and fighting the demon of memories. I missed my mother so much but when I thought of her it really just brought back the memories of pain. Not a physical pain but an emotional wound. I couldn't let go of the fact that she still didn't want me. We were approaching the anniversary of the day I was put into care. It was coming up soon and I had to speak at church on that very night. I was trying to wrap my mind around what I would speak about. As I sat beside Billy, body memories that hadn't surfaced in a long time were in full swing. He doesn't know much about what I have endure except the very basics; I was sexually abused. He had no idea I was struggling. I thought I would just want him to leave me alone. He is just another man. This time was different. I wanted something I had never wanted while dealing with my past. I wanted him. I wanted him to kiss me from head to toe, hold me close and tell me he loved me. I wanted him to take me and make love to me. Sex was still such a messed up concept in my head. Most of the time I was okay but some days I felt disgusting. I enjoyed being with him but there wasn't much of an emotional connection during it. I hadn't really fully connected with him like I should since we were in South Carolina. This night, I just wanted him. It made me so angry that with everything that I had been though that this is the thing that would make me feel better. I realized that God didn't just make us sexual human beings to reproduce; it was for comfort too. I put away the message I was working on. I wanted to snuggle up to him. I thought about all the times he was so good to me but I pushed him away. I thought back to our wedding day when I was 18, the day I told him about my affair, and even the day of our divorce. He loved me. He truly loved me. I had such a rollercoaster of emotions come over me. I didn't even deserve such an amazing man in my life but God loved me enough to put him there. I began kissing his neck, and the most beautiful thing happened. We weren't having sex. I was making love to my best friend. We both were lost in pleasing each other and that was okay. It was completely okay. Afterwards, I just snuggled up to him with my head his chest. I needed that. I needed to know there was a difference between sex and making love. I had finally given my whole heart to him and he didn't hurt me. God had taken something so dirty and gross and made something so beautiful. He took my broken vessel and filled it with pure gold. This was the most beautiful and priceless thing I ever known; my love for a man and his unconditional love for me.

That night changed my life. I began seeing our world together different. My mind had lied to me. He didn't want to just use me. He never wanted to hurt me. He loved me. This love is something no other male had shown me. Billy's love for me was pure, unconditional, and beautiful; just as God intended it to be.

The following Sunday, during worship, I went to the front and knelt down. I began thanking God for my marriage, my kids, and my life. I thanked him for creating something so beautiful between husband and wife. I lifted my hands to the Lord and prayed, "Lord, I truly give everything to you. Lord, break me open daily and allow your anointing to flow for your glory. This day, I vow to use my past to bring you honor. I will no longer sit back and be ashamed. I want to be used." Very few times have I heard the voice of God, but this day I heard it audibly. It felt as though the power from it shook my whole body. I heard the Lord say, "It's time to come out of the furnace, the kiln, and allow me to use the vessel I have created."

That Wednesday, on the anniversary of the night I was placed into care, instead of running away, I took the platform. Below is the exact message that I gave:
Today, I want to speak on celebrating what God has done for you. Many celebrations that the Jewish community have were because of what God had done for them. They celebrate what God did so that they remember who their God is.

Exodus 12:21-30

21 Then Moses called for all the elders of Israel and said to them, "Pick out and take lambs for yourselves according to your families, and kill the Passover lamb. 22 And you shall take a bunch of hyssop, dip it in the blood that is in the basin, and strike the lintel and the two doorposts with the blood that is in the basin. And none of you shall go out of the door of his house until morning. 23 For the Lord will pass through to strike the Egyptians; and when He sees the blood on the lintel and on the two doorposts, the Lord will pass over the door and not allow the destroyer to come into your houses to strike you. 24 And you shall observe this thing as an ordinance for you and your sons forever. 25 It will come to pass when you come to the land which the Lord will give you, just as He promised, that you shall keep this service. 26 And it shall be, when your children say to you, 'What do you mean by this service?' 27 that you shall say, 'It is the Passover sacrifice of the Lord, who passed over the houses of the children of Israel in Egypt when He struck the Egyptians and delivered our households.'" So the people bowed their heads and worshiped. 28 Then the

children of Israel went away and did so; just as the Lord had commanded Moses and Aaron, so they did.

29 And it came to pass at midnight that the Lord struck all the firstborn in the land of Egypt, from the firstborn of Pharaoh who sat on his throne to the firstborn of the captive who was in the dungeon, and all the firstborn of livestock. 30 So Pharaoh rose in the night, he, all his servants, and all the Egyptians; and there was a great cry in Egypt, for there was not a house where there was not one dead.

The Lord told them to remember this event and to celebrate it forever. God wanted them to remember that He saved them that day from all of the destruction that was surrounding them. He wanted every generation to remember therefore; we know the holiday Passover.

Esther 3:7-13

7 In the first month, which is the month of Nisan, in the twelfth year of King Ahasuerus, they cast Pur (that is, the lot), before Haman to determine the day and the month, until it fell on the twelfth month, which is the month of Adar. 8 Then Haman said to King Ahasuerus, "There is a certain people scattered and dispersed among the people in all the provinces of your kingdom; their laws are different from all other people's, and they do not keep the king's laws. Therefore it is not fitting for the king to let them remain. 9 If it pleases the king, let a decree be written that they be destroyed, and I will pay ten thousand talents of silver into the hands of those who do the work, to bring it into the king's treasuries."10 So the king took his signet

ring from his hand and gave it to Haman, the son of Hammedatha the Agagite, the enemy of the Jews. 11 And the king said to Haman, "The money and the people are given to you, to do with them as seems good to you." 12 Then the king's scribes were called on the thirteenth day of the first month, and a decree was written according to all that Haman commanded—to the king's satraps, to the governors who were over each province, to the officials of all people, to every province according to its script, and to every people in their language. In the name of King Ahasuerus it was written, and sealed with the king's signet ring. 13 And the letters were sent by couriers into all the king's provinces, to destroy, to kill, and to annihilate all the Jews, both young and old, little children and women, in one day, on the thirteenth day of the twelfth month, which is the month of Adar, and to plunder their possessions.

In Chapter 9, after much fight from the Lord for the Jews, God has Esther go before the king on the behalf of the Jews. The king makes a decree that allows the Jews to be saved.

Let's look at what happened after they were saved.

Esther 9:26-28

26 So they called these days Purim, after the name Pur. Therefore, because of all the words of this letter, what they had seen concerning this matter, and what had happened to them, 27 the Jews established and imposed it upon themselves and their descendants and all who would join them, that without fail they should celebrate these two days every year, according to the written instructions and according to the prescribed time, 28 that these days should be remembered and kept throughout every generation,

every family, every province, and every city, that these days of Purim should not fail to be observed among the Jews, and that the memory of them should not perish among their descendants.

This is now the Jewish holiday Purim.

It is found throughout the Word of God it is very important to remember the days that God has moved in your life. When we understand God has brought us out of so many situations and has fought so hard for us in the past, we begin to have faith and expect God to see us through on a daily basis.

We are now going to take a look at a young man who encouraged himself with what God had done.

1 Samuel 17:32-37

32 Then David said to Saul, "Let no man's heart fail because of him; your servant will go and fight with this Philistine."33 And Saul said to David, "You are not able to go against this Philistine to fight with him; for you are a youth, and he a man of war from his youth."34 But David said to Saul, "Your servant used to keep his father's sheep, and when a lion or a bear came and took a lamb out of the flock, 35 I went out after it and struck it, and delivered the lamb from its mouth; and when it arose against me, I caught it by its beard, and struck and killed it. 36 Your servant has killed both lion and bear; and this uncircumcised Philistine will be like one of them, seeing he has defied the armies of the living God." 37 Moreover

David said, "The Lord, who delivered me from the paw of the lion and from the paw of the bear, He will deliver me from the hand of this Philistine.

"And Saul said to David, "Go, and the Lord be with you!"

And who can tell me how the story ends??

David slays Goliath!

David reminded himself that God had already helped him kill a lion and a bear. In verse 37, He makes it clear it was completely God. Let's read that one verse again:

1 Sam. 17:37

Moreover David said, "The Lord, who delivered me from the paw of the lion and from the paw of the bear, He will deliver me from the hand of this Philistine.

See, David understood if God had saved Him before, He was capable of doing it again. He encouraged himself by remembering what God had brought him though.

Many of you may be thinking, "Okay, Donna, I can see celebrating the great things that God has done in our lives but God hasn't really done great things in my life like He did in those stories. He hasn't physically saved me from bondage or a situation that has impacted my life like those stories."

Well, I also want us to think about celebrating those "bad" things we have gone through that God has used for our good and His glory.

I want us to think about Joseph. In Genesis 30:22-24, God opened Rachel's womb and allowed her to give birth to a handsome boy named Joseph. Being born to Rachel, the favorite wife of Jacob, this quickly made Joseph the favorite child. The problem with this though is that the favorite child is seldom the favorite among siblings. In Genesis 37, Joseph starts having dreams. 37:2 says he was about 17 years old.

Genesis 37:5-11

5 Now Joseph had a dream, and he told it to his brothers; and they hated him even more. 6 So he said to them, "Please hear this dream which I have dreamed: 7 There we were, binding sheaves in the field. Then behold, my sheaf arose and also stood upright; and indeed your sheaves stood all around and bowed down to my sheaf." 8 And his brothers said to him, "Shall you indeed reign over us? Or shall you indeed have dominion over us?" So they hated him even more for his dreams and for his words. 9 Then he dreamed still another dream and told it to his brothers, and said, "Look, I have dreamed another dream. And this time, the sun, the moon, and the eleven stars bowed down to me." 10 So he told it to his father and his brothers; and his father rebuked him and said to him, "What is this dream that you have dreamed? Shall your mother and I and your brothers indeed come to bow down to the earth before you?" 11 And his brothers envied him, but his father kept the matter in mind.

God gave Joseph these dreams. These dreams made his brothers envy him even more. By the end of chapter 37, His brothers sell him into slavery. I can completely understand what he must have felt. It is hard when your family gives you away. Although Joseph was emotionally damaged and didn't understand why this was happening to him, he still committed his life to doing what was right unto the Lord. He continued to serve God with a broken heart but his life gets worse. Genesis 39 comes around and a woman tries to convince him to have an affair with her. He refuses so the woman gets even by accusing him of rape and he is thrown into prison. With everything this young man has gone through, he continues to serve the Lord. While in prison, God uses him to interpret dreams. He also uses him to interpret the Pharaoh's dream that no one else could interpret. This dream warns the Pharaoh a great famine is coming and his kingdom needs to prepare for it. The Pharaoh places Joseph as second in command and the head of the "Food bank" project. In Chapter 42, Jacob sends his other sons to buy food from Egypt during the great famine. Joseph ends up being able to save his family and be reunited with them.

I am sure that Joseph never understood why God allowed all of those bad things to happen to him but he continued to do what was right. God didn't save Joseph from the terrible events in his life but what God did do was use those events. Joseph and his family benefitted from those terrible things. God used all of those situations for God's glory.

Let's go to the very end of the story, where Jacob, Joseph's father, dies in Genesis 50:14-21

Genesis 50:14-21

14 And after he had buried his father, Joseph returned to Egypt, he and his brothers and all who went up with him to bury his father. 15 When Joseph's brothers saw that their father was dead, they said, "Perhaps Joseph will hate us, and may actually repay us for all the evil which we did to him." 16 So they sent messengers to Joseph, saying, "Before your father died he commanded, saying, 17 'Thus you shall say to Joseph: "I beg you, please forgive the trespass of your brothers and their sin; for they did evil to you."' Now, please, forgive the trespass of the servants of the God of your father." And Joseph wept when they spoke to him. 18 Then his brothers also went and fell down before his face, and they said, "Behold, we are your servants." 19 Joseph said to them, "Do not be afraid, for am I in the place of God? 20 But as for you, you meant evil against me; but God meant it for good, in order to bring it about as it is this day, to save many people alive. 21 Now therefore, do not be afraid; I will provide for you and your little ones." And he comforted them and spoke kindly to them.

Joseph's brothers thought he would surely kill them because their father was no longer alive to protect them. Joseph realized that something that his brothers didn't understand. Joseph knew even though evil had been done to him, God turned it around. He used what was done to Joseph to save many people including his family. God had a plan! What Satan meant for evil God made it good.

I have one more story I would like to read you…

17 years ago, to this exact date, in a Wednesday service, just like this one, a woman was given a Word from God. She took the microphone from the platform and spoke these words, "Sisters stick up for each. They do whatever it takes to protect one another."

Those simple words from the Lord struck a scared 15 year old's heart like a sledge hammer. All the walls that she had built over the last 15 years began to creek and slowly crumble. You see, no one in that church knew it but she was living in home where she was being physically, emotionally, and sexually abused by her mother and father and many other people in her family. Her father had been telling her she was longer good enough. When her baby sister turned 12 that upcoming month, he would leave her alone and begin raping the younger sister. Her sister didn't even have knowledge the abuse that was occurring. As she sat in that church, that young girl tried to compose herself. As she tried to hold it together, her sister who sat two rows in front of her, turned around and whispered 3 simple words. Those words delivered the final blows to bring down the walls around her heart.... "I love you".

The girl had enough; she couldn't keep it in anymore. She had to tell someone. She had to get help and protect her sister. She couldn't bring herself to admit to all of the abuse so, she figured if she simply told about her father, he would be out of the picture and it may stop her mother. She also could stand the thought of removing both parents from her siblings.

October 25, 2000, became the night that she would never forget. It started a process that couldn't be reversed. She opened up to an adult who helped out the youth at the church during the service. After a trip to the police station and the local hospital, the authorities gave the mother 2 options: 1. Place a restraining order against the girl's father and take the girls home or 2. Give the girls to the state to be placed in foster care.

That mother didn't even take a moment to think it through. She knew immediately what she wanted to do. The mother leaned over to the younger girl, kissed her forehead, and told her she loved her. She didn't even look at the eldest girl. She then turned to the social worker and said, "Take them."

That night that 15 year old lost her whole family. Not one of her family members believed what she said. Even her sister believed that she had purposely destroyed their family. Deep inside her broken heart, she knew that God had a plan for her. Although she struggled and failed greatly sometimes, she tried her best to follow the Lord and to serve him.

As that girl stands before you today and tells you her story, she can now celebrate that night. I know this because that girl is me…

After many years of hating this day, October 25th, I have decided to celebrate it. You see, what Satan meant for evil, God has made good. God has used that night to start a series of events that has placed me where I am today. God sent me a spiritual momma (the adult I told) that taught me what a real mom is. My children now have a mother who knows how to love, respect, and lead them. I now love my babies the way I was never loved as a child. God also uses my past to teach others about the unconditional love of a true father, our Lord. He allows me to help them to heal from their past.

I have come to realize just like when Joseph's brothers meant evil towards him and God used him to save his family, one day my biological parents and my brother will be saved by what God has done in my life. When they gave Joseph away, they actually did the best thing for him. Like Joseph, when my mother gave me up, without knowing it, she gave me the best life possible.

This might sound crazy but today, I celebrate my past. Although God allowed the abuse and my mother to give me away, He knew that was the best thing for me. He never left me. He also had my best interest at heart. Without my past, I would not be who I am today. God wouldn't be able to use me in the ways He does now. I am grateful for my life because it formed me into who I am today.

I recommend that you examine your life, the blessings and the trials and learn to celebrate them. God only allowed them to happen for your benefit and his glory. He carried through so much and is continuing to do so. What the devil meant for evil, God will make good. So many times we sit around and complain about what is going on in our lives. We complain about the hard times, the trials, and even all the changes. God has a plan! Everything you went through and/or are currently going through will teach you something and benefit you.

I want to close with one more scripture:

2 Corinthians 12:7-10

7 And lest I should be exalted above measure by the abundance of the revelations, a thorn in the flesh was given to me, a messenger of Satan to buffet me, lest I be exalted above measure. 8 Concerning this thing I pleaded with the Lord three times that it might depart from me. 9 And He said to me, "My grace is sufficient for you, for My strength is made perfect in weakness." Therefore most gladly I will rather boast in my infirmities, that the power of Christ may rest upon me. 10 Therefore I take pleasure in infirmities, in reproaches, in needs, in persecutions, in distresses, for Christ's sake. For when I am weak, then I am strong.

I closed in prayer and walked off the stage.

That night when I walked off the platform, I was a new creation. I was no longer the little girl who hid her story. I was now bold! I was now a vessel for the Lord. God can take anything in our lives and use it for Him. We just have to allow Him to do it. He will mold you just as He molded me.

God truly had healed me in many areas. My marriage changed after that night. I began wanting Billy to hold me more and more. I began wanting to spend more and more time with him. Things were still a little awkward sometimes but that can be expected with the healing process. The Lord began using me as a vessel to reach out to many women that had been abused. The questions that I received the most were about my intimate relationship with my own husband. I wanted to find a way that would help my marriage in that area and others. As I was folding laundry one day and praying about this situation, I turned on YouTube. I am unsure of who I listened to but it was a sermon on spirits. This sermon was talking about how spirits can be transferred from one person to another. I thought about how the people in cults actually have intercourse to share the spirits between them. I remember how hard it is to break a bond between to people after a sexual act had been committed. Within just a few moments I had a plan. I wanted to do a fast. A normal fast didn't seem like the right thing to do for this situation. I thought about the things that I enjoyed. I loved spending time watching T.V. before bed and my own quiet time after Billy and the kids were asleep. I came up with a different type of fast. I decided that for 30 days I would make love to my husband daily. I thought that it would unite us closer in many ways. I would give up my time, comfort, and much more. I knew that this would help us physically and spiritually. I made a plan of ways that I could be in bed early enough each night. We had to plan dinner and clean up earlier than usual. The kids had to be settled down and ready for bed on time as well. The planning took me a little while to figure out. When Billy came home that night, I popped the question. He looked scared when I told him what I wanted to do. I didn't go into details of my reasons why I wanted to do it but I did tell him it was important to me. He explained to me that he would do this with me but I had to do a few things. I had to make sure we were in bed earlier because he had to work extremely early in the mornings. I decided to call this adventure, "The 30 Day Challenge". I thought it wouldn't be that big of a deal but it impacted us more than I could have ever imagined. Before this challenge, we were only intimate a couple times a month. We were usually pretty regular at once every couple weeks. This challenged changed those stats forever. The first night of the challenge, I put on soft music and lit candles before bed. I didn't really know what to do to make this not something that I felt was forced upon me. The kids were in bed and settled in by 8pm. As I snuggled up to him, I began telling him all the reasons that I loved him. This made things easy to move on from there. That first night wasn't very awkward. It had been while since we were together so it seemed ordinary. By day three though, things became awkward. I ran out of things to say and do to make it different. I felt as though I was "touched out". I was definitely tired of not fully enjoying myself. I liked being with him but the awkwardness was almost too much. The thought of prayer came to me. I began praying in my head for us during our time together each night. In my head, I would ask God to show me how to be a good wife to him. I would ask the Lord to show me what Billy liked or didn't like. I know that this is crazy but I also prayed for me to like everything Billy did for me. I am sure that this isn't a normal conversation between Christian wives but God wants us to enjoy our spouses. Billy and I began doing things we had never done. We also began talking more. The intimacy between us became more emotional and spiritual than physical. During the day, our interactions with each other began to change. Our conversations about our life became easier.

By day 15, people began to notice the change in us. I had people come up to me in church asking me what happened in our life. The women at our church began commenting on the way Billy and I looked at each other. People told me constantly about the way Billy never stopped smiling. My friends would also comment about the way I would smile at Billy when I saw him. The connection that we had was noticeable by everyone around us. Even our children started asking what was going on with us. During the bedtime prayers with the kids, I noticed that he was starting to pray like me. Many times, he would pray things over our children that I had silently prayed. This amazed me.

Our marriage was growing fast. I was becoming comfortable with him in ways that I never dreamed. By about day 20 though, I had ran out of things to do or say to him in the bedroom. I felt as though I had been repeating things over and over. One night, I was so tired and worn out from the day that I told him I just wanted to go to bed. I told him I was too exhausted to try to figure out what to do or say that night. Billy just told me that it was okay and that making love was more than the physical. He took me in his arms. I thought he was just ready to go to sleep. As I closed my eyes, I heard him begin to speak. He started praying over me and our children. He went into great detail about our future, our marriage, and our ministry. I heard this man thank God for all of the things in his life. He took his time and prayed again over me as a person. He didn't pray about me being a good mom or wife. He began praying over things I pray over myself. This touched my heart in a way that words can't adequately explain. This man was making love to me in a way that no one had ever done. When he finished praying, I had more love for him than ever before. I also wanted to make to love to him physically more than ever before. That prayer tore down the barriers between us. I no longer held back my thoughts or desires. From that moment on, I felt completely comfortable with him. Since that night, I can sincerely say that I am unashamed of anything in our bedroom.

We finished the 30 Day Challenge as a different couple. We were closer physically, of course, but also spiritually and emotionally. We now had a new perspective on life. We were no longer intimated by one another. We also had a new respect for each other and ourselves. Although it was completed, we still like to go back and do the challenge again and again to keep our marriage where it should be. I now have the intimate relationship with my husband that I can brag about. I pray that if you or a friend is struggling in this area that you will consider the 30 Day Challenge for yourself. I am so thankful that God used it to bind my husband and me tightly together. I will forever be grateful for the relationship that Billy and I have now. Every bit of the uncomfortable things we have gone through was worth it. I wouldn't change our marriage for anything in the world.

Our marriage, family, and home became almost perfect. I couldn't imagine how much better our lives could get. God had blessed me with an amazing family. My marriage was more than I had ever dreamed of. My children were happy and healthy. God gave us an amazing home right down the street from our pastors. My life had finally worked out. I struggled slightly with how perfect life was. God had given me so much but I was waiting for something to go wrong. My life hadn't stayed good this long before.

Going Backwards Moves Forward

The summer came and church camp was approaching. I found myself searching for something to go wrong. I waited patiently for life to resume back to the chaos. I began having thoughts and temptations that I had experienced before. I knew that I was under attack. God was giving me messages for the church. He was using me almost daily to minister those around me and yet I was almost depressed. The thoughts I began having didn't line up with the life I had. I had to constantly correct myself. It was almost as if I were sabotaging my own life.

I began having difficulty with my emotions and my thoughts. I felt as though the whole world was against me and my family. I was bombarded with thoughts of suicide. I couldn't understand why I was having thoughts of quitting life. I would sit and think of all the reasons that my children were better off without me. I would dismiss the thoughts but they seemed to come right back. I was also so exhausted that I would fall asleep many nights before my children. My life was going perfect and I couldn't understand why my mind seemed to be lying to me all the time. I would think or feel things that I knew wasn't truth. I would pray but I could seem to shake the constant battle between my mind and my heart.

I began seeking the things that could be affecting me. I searched my Bible for answers. I also searched many different pastors and books to find the answer. I believe now that a problem so deep doesn't start with a single event. It starts with a legacy of sins. When someone makes a mistake, that is one thing but when sins are made time and time again then this means there is a problem. This is a sign that we need to look at the root of the problem. We need to go back to the source; the beginning. God began showing me that I was dealing with an attack from the Spirit of Jezebel.
I read 1 Kings 12

Rehoboam displays rebellion by rejecting the advice of the elders. Many times, we ignore what God instructs us to do and we focus on others. We need to wait for His timing. God sent Jeroboam and the elders but Rehoboam didn't listen. He then went to his friends instead. God sometimes puts blocks in our way because we are going the wrong way.

I Read Genesis 9

Ham uncovered his father Noah. Some say that this is the same sexual spirit that homosexuality comes from. Either way, a spirit of sexual perversion was lurking. Ham's oldest son is Cush. The pagans called him "Bell". This means "the god of confusion".

Cush founded Babylon. He had a son named Nimrod. Nimrod encouraged the people to rebel against God. Nimrod is the one who had the "brilliant" idea to build the Tower of Babel. He didn't want a relationship with God but wanted to get to heaven on his own. Then, God confused the languages and destroyed the tower.

Side note: Sometimes, God will confuse our plans because He has given us power but many times we begin believing that we don't need a relationship with God. We start building our lives without Him.

When Nimrod started building the tower, God confused the languages and sent the people in all directions of the world. Then, Nimrod married his mother. Yes, his own mother. Nimrod and his mother then joined paganism. These series of events birthed a spirit of perversion. They began to worship many false gods. One of these were the god named Baal. Baal was the male spirit and his counter partner was a statue named Ashtoreth. Baal is a territorial spirit. It literally names and claims territories. Ashtoreth is a spirit that transposes itself as male or female. These two work together to "birth" demonic strongholds.

Jezebel was born in Baal worship. Ahab was the son of many generations of false worshipers. These women camouflage themselves to blend in and try to get righteousness. These demons can even speak in tongues but they can't have righteousness.

Jezebel and Ahab got married. Just as two become one, in a sense these demonic strongholds or spirits joined forces as well. This is what caused the idol worship in Samaria. When Jesus met the woman at the well, he came to break that same spirit.

Read John 4

To break the spirit of Jezebel, we must worship the one true God. We must worship in spirit and in truth because where the spirit of the Lord is, THERE IS FREEDOM.

The Jezebel spirit is originally from Baal which means it has a masculine form. That's why they stand up to men of God without fear. How many have heard women stand proudly to a man of God and say, "you aren't going to tell me what to do!"? This is that Jezebel spirit rising up.

Symptoms of Jezebel:
1.) Give them a task and they try to "over" do it.
2.) They always demand recognition.
3.) They take credit for everything.
4.) They want to be the star of the show.

These spirits will give people a "word" just so they can take credit for it. They also want to encourage those they are controlling that they should stay where they are. These demons jump from age to age. They don't care how old a person is. They convince you to go against the Word of God. When you refuse to do what God has instructed, you are operating in the spirit of Baal which is the spirit of Jezebel.

Jezebel didn't take over. She persuaded Ahab and he stepped down and gave power to Jezebel. If we are on an assignment and we don't do it, the spirit of Baal will give you a new assignment. This allows Jezebel to take over. If we aren't in the position that God puts us in, then we have allowed Jezebel to step in and take our positions. This is what she did with Ahab. This spirit loves to step up and fill positions in our churches. Before long, the spirit is in operation and they are a "one man band". They also make sure they get the credit for it. They mouth everyone and everything. This spirit disagrees with everyone. When this spirit picks up that you don't want to wait on God, it rushes in to alleviate the stress and gets the job done on its own. We must wait on Gods timing and move when He tells us to.

Read 1 Kings 16 - 2 kings

The spirit of Jezebel only wants part in what it can take over. It is a lying spirit. It lies to others and lies to you. It makes you believe that you are more than you are. People who know who they are don't make a big scene about it. Those drawing attention to themselves are trying to make everyone believe that they are more than they truly are. They want someone to glorify them instead of God using them to glorify Him.

Jezebel talks in gray and switches the truth with lies. The spirit quickly says, "That's not what I meant" when caught in a lie. It switches words and always makes excuses. It also targets those in authority. They want the best of everything. They hate: repentance, stability, and control. It brags on itself too.

We need to stop tolerating this spirit.

Read Rev. 2:18

God tells the church that he isn't happy with them because they tolerate the spirit of Jezebel. God gives them time to repent but they don't. It says that He will destroy her and her children.

The spirit of Jezebel cannot operate without the spirit of Ahab. Ahab conquered more land than everyone but Solomon. This shows that you can be conquering but still be under that spirit. Jezebel conquers by manipulation and fear.

Jezebel has many effects on people
.

1. Fear. 1 Kings 19

Elijah, a man of God, who just called fire down
from heaven was afraid of a woman. When someone causes
you to fear, it isn't the person who is intimating you, it is
the Jezebel spirit within them.

The spirit only has power if you allow it. It is a
controlling spirit through fear. It tries to attach itself to you
through someone else. Jezebel was rejected by her father
and had a controlling mother. This is a pattern. Most who
have this spirit, have had this life or one similar. These
people have been so wounded that the want to control
everything to keep from being wounded again. They even
control their family. They are known as "control freaks".

People gain access through "friendship". They
believe they are called to serve you and be your best friend.
Sometimes they believe they are to be your intercessor.
Many times, the spirit of Jezebel takes up residence through
the open door of rejection.

2. Isolation. 1 Kings 19

This is where you want to run away from everyone
and be by yourself. Not really even with God. Elijah leaves
everyone and makes himself completely alone. He just
wanted to be alone and withdraw for the world. He felt
completely alone and that no one understood him.

3. Exhaustion. 1 Kings 19:4

Elijah fell asleep until the angel of the Lord wants
him to rest. Then, he falls back asleep. This is where you

feel so completely exhausted you can't seem to get enough rest.

    4. Depression. 1 Kings 19:4

    Elijah wanted to die!
Jeremiah 20:14-15 He hated the day he was born.
Jonah 4:3 "Take my life"
Thoughts of suicide are from the spirit of Jezebel. Thoughts of quitting are also signs. This spirit finds ways to get you out of your passion.

    5. Impure sexual thoughts. Rev. 2

    Sexual immorality are taught by this spirit.
    This spirit also gives the thoughts, "You are rejecting me like everyone else."

    6. Prolonged sickness- Rev 2

    This is those people who are sick all the time and have near death accidents often. This is the spirit literally trying to kill you. This spirit is out to kill, steal, and destroy you! It tries to steal your peace, joy, and confidence.

    What's the answer? Jesus Christ!!

    After studying many different pastors and the Word of God, I found that I had been experiencing this spirit. I was so hurt when I was younger that I wanted to maintain control. This opened a door for the stronghold of this spirit. I was delivered. I loved the Lord. This was a spiritual attack. I had to be free.

There are steps to take if you are experiencing this:
-Get with God.
-Give Him your life. (Repent and receive salvation)
-Seek council from elders.
-Take action against the spirits attacking you!

Jesus Christ can free you from these spirits because He delivered me. As I was praying about these on the drive to church camp, I began to weep. I went through the list of things to do. I repented for allowing this spirit in my life. I asked God to forgive me for all the awful things that I had said to people around me the last couple of months. I rededicated my life to the Lord and then planned to seek council from the pastor of my church.

That night at the church service while at the altar, my pastor approached me. He told me that he felt that God had impressed him that I was dealing with something. He told me that he knew what the spirit was. I told him that I also knew. Pastor Jim asked me to tell him. I only said three words, "Spirit of Jezebel". Pastor Jim immediately put his hands on me and began praying. Pastor Becky soon joined him and began praying in the spirit over me. I felt the chains fall off of me. I could feel a weight leave me. In that moment, I knew that the things that I had believed were lies. I knew the truth. I knew that I was loved. I knew that people really weren't against me. I knew that life really could be perfect and I didn't have to control anything. I became free that day.

Filling In the Cracks

The Lord allowed me to do three weeks of church camps on that campground in the next few months. I saw the Lord deliver many young people. Young kids and adults were delivered of many strongholds in a short period of time. God began allowing me to lay hands on people and see deliverance in Jesus' name. On one of the last nights of the final camp, I heard the Lord speak to me. I was on my knees in the front of the church. There was just a handful of people still praying. Most of people were already gone for the night. As I was quiet before the God, I heard him say that Amie deserved deliverance too. I began to cry. I had seen so many people delivered in the last several weeks and Amie need God too. I began praying for her. I knew that she had been living with another woman but wasn't sure if she still was. I hadn't talked to her in a long time. As I prayed for her, the Lord impressed me to reach out to her and invite her to a women's conference that I host each July. I thought that I was crazy at first. I also worried that I might be trying to subconsciously destroy my life once again. I began to pray about what to do.

I knew that I couldn't make such a decision on my own. My heart could not be trusted in this area. I prayed about what to do. The Lord had given me the idea of the women's retreat 3 years prior. I had completed two retreats and the third was close. I had never had anyone come that I had been involved with. The retreat was so special to me and I didn't want to effect it. I messaged Pastor Becky and asked her to pray about it. Billy was also asked to pray about me inviting her. I wanted to be very sure that I had heard from God. Billy told me that I needed to obey the Lord. Pastor Becky told me that she had no idea what to do and that she felt it was a decision that only I could make.

After much prayer, I unblocked Amie. Amie was shocked that I had unblocked her. She immediately messaged me about my intentions. At first, I wouldn't tell her. I just told her that I wanted to check on her. A few days later, Amie message me and told me that God told her to do something. She asked me to pray for her. I knew that God had told her to come to the retreat that I hosted. I simply told her I would pray. Several days passed until I finally messaged her and told her to do what God had told her. I explained that I knew what it was that God had impressed upon her. She was so confused until I told her that she had to come to His Bride, the women's conference.

I was not afraid for Amie to come to the conference but many around me were. As soon as she arrived, someone got upset and decided to leave. Most people didn't know our past relationship but a few did. I totally gave the retreat over to the Lord. During the worship service, Amie began to weep. I could see that God was dealing with her. I felt as though God would not allow me to approach her. The Lord did not want me to pray with her at all. A few of the ladies began to pray with Amie. She fell to her knees and surrendered her life to Jesus Christ! Everyone around us could see the change in her face. I could hear a change in her voice too. God delivered Amie that day. Amie was completely set free of emotional, sexual, and physical strongholds. After service, Amie shared with me that she wanted to work out her marriage with her husband. She felt a love for him that she had never experienced.

On the second night of the retreat, during worship, something happened in me. I was worshipping the Lord when God told me to open my eyes. When I opened my eyes, I saw Amie at the altar in worship. I immediately dropped to my knees crying. God had answered my innermost prayer. My life was perfect and He fixed the last thing that held me bound. I had felt so guilty for being partially responsible for Amie's marriage failing. Many times, the enemy would make me feel ashamed that my life was good and her life was still in shambles. God was literally fixing my mistakes. I become so overwhelmed with the goodness of God, I couldn't even speak. I wept on my knees in reverence to the God of the universe. He was healing her. The Lord was also healing a part of my heart that I didn't even know was wounded until that moment. As the Lord healed her, it brought me a joy and peace that is unexplainable. God truly gave me gift that night that not many could understand.

As I lay on the floor at the altar, the Lord spoke to me and told me that Amie would want to be baptized before the end of the retreat. I spoke to Pastor Becky and asked her what to do. She said that if she asked that she would be there with me to perform the baptism. I had to be careful because I didn't want people to be thinking of our past and not see the miracle that God was doing.

The next day we had a baptism for women who had given their lives to Christ or rededicated their lives. We had several ladies who had never been baptized ask to be part of the ceremony. We also had a few people who wanted to be baptized again because they felt like they needed to because they had made a new commitment to the Lord. About an hour before the baptism, Amie said she wanted me to step outside and talk to her. Amie and I stood outside of the cafeteria and she asked me a question. She asked me to baptize her in Jesus' name. I told her that God told me that she was going to ask. She was shocked that God prepared me the day before. I told her that I would be honored to baptize her.

As we got to the river, I could feel the presence of God with us. A couple women went before Amie but it was soon her turn. She gave her testimony of how God had delivered her and then we baptized her. I will never forget the way I felt when she came up out of the water. I felt as every weight lifted. I felt light and free. I knew that she had sincerely surrendered her heart and soul to the Lord. After lifting her hands and thanking God, she hugged me tight. We stood in that river together clean and free. The shame was gone! We hugged each other as all the women around us clapped and thanked God for His love and mercy. I knew at that moment that God would forever get the praise for delivering us. Satan could no longer hold our past over our heads. The more people who knew about our past relationship, the more they glorified God. God would forever be glorified. We walked out of that river cleansed by the mighty power of Jesus.

The women's retreat changed my life. I left the campground that weekend excited to see what God had planned. I knew Amie was delivered. I knew she would go home and God would begin to rebuild her marriage like he did mine. My God is a God of restoration. There isn't a person that God can't deliver. There isn't a marriage that God can't restore. The Lord had put Amie on the potter's wheel and was beginning to mold her and her family.

As I returned home, my marriage seemed to be a mess. I could see that Satan was trying to pull me down. When God uses you, the enemy gets mad. I could see that everything that God had done had intimated the devil. Billy and I had many arguments. Every aspect of our marriage was attacked. I held on as the Lord came in and smooth out the chaos once again. I can see now that Satan was seeing if I would run to Amie or fight for Billy. I never told Amie what was going on. I took my broken heart to the Lord and to Pastor Becky only. After a short while, God dealt with Billy and healed his heart.

By September, God had laid it on Billy's heart and mine to meet with Amie and her family. Before we Amie and I committed adultery, our families did many things together. God was restoring everything that was stolen by sin. Billy and I decided to meet her family at the zoo on September 27th. The Lord was moving in my life again. I could feel the presence of God I everything that I was doing. I knew that God was up to something incredible.

Just days after we made the plan, something crazy happened. I was in the middle of grading papers for my students when my phone rang. My phone is always on silent and put away but at this time I had been using it for my calculator. As my phone rang, it vibrated on my desk. I looked down and saw a number I didn't know. I quickly ignored the call to stop the vibrating. While the phone was still in my hands, it rang again. It was my real mother's number. I was shocked it rang immediately after the unknown caller. I was worried it was an emergency so I answered the call. I became even more scared when I heard the voice on the other end. It was my father. "Whatcha doin" he asked. I asked him if everything was okay with my mother. He said she was just fine. I was dumbfounded. "Can you talk for a minute or are you busy? I have something I want to tell you." he said. I was still in shock. I rudely told him that I was at work and would be busy until 3:00. Calmly, he told me he would call back later. I hung up without a word.

Later?? Why would he call back later? Before that call, my life was perfect. Why would he be calling me now? Part of his probation was that he couldn't see me or even talk to me. I checked the date. It was September 13th. I knew that since he got out of jail in October that he might be calling me because he was off probation. I won't lie, my first reaction was fear. I instantly became sick to my stomach. If he was off probation, I had nothing to legally protect me. I couldn't believe that he had the nerve to call me. What could he possibly want to say me? Why did he want to talk to me? My head began spinning.

At 3:00 on the dot, the phone rang again. It was him again. I ignored it and several others. He began calling me every day. Call after call, I declined them. I did not want to talk to him. As I prayed for my father after each call, I felt the Lord speak to me the same thing. Almost every time I prayed, God would remind me of the promise He made to me. The Lord told me several times over the past few years that I would lead my father to Christ. I started praying constantly for my father.

The more I prayed for my father, the more I felt like I needed to speak to him. I couldn't shake the need to talk with him immediately. I spoke to my pastor and his wife about the way that I was feeling. They told me they would go with me to meet him if I wanted. I explained to them that it was important. I told them that I needed to speak with him before he died. I have no idea why I kept thinking I had only a little time left. I felt as though I was running out of time.

The phone calls continued. Several times a day he would call me. After a week or so, I answered the phone. Billy and I were watching a movie with our children when my phone rang. I still had no idea what to think about the situation but I answered his call. As soon I answered, I heard the same think he said before, "Whatcha doin'?" I wish that I could say that I was nice to him but I wasn't. I quickly responded, "I am busy watching TV with my babies. What do you want? Why do you keep calling me?" The man that I once knew would have yelled at me. The father I grew up with have been very angry with my rudeness. The voice on the other end wasn't angry. He spoke softly to me, "I wanted to check on you. I wanted to see how you are. I thought maybe there was a few things you might wanted to say to me." He told me that he was off parole now and he wanted to tell me something but he wanted to see if I wanted to say or ask anything first. I had nothing to say to him. I couldn't find words. I composed myself and said in the nastiest voice I could, "I don't have anything to say to you but when I do, I will call you. Stop calling me!" I could hear the hurt in his voice when he responded back, "I deserve that. I really deserve that. Well I will wait to tell you what I wanted to say until you are ready." I just hung up on him. I couldn't bring myself to say another word. I was so scared that hearing his voice or talking to him would bring back the hurt. I was afraid that I wasn't healed as much I thought I was. After I hung up, I told my husband that I had to meet with him in person. I knew that I couldn't allow fear to rule me again. I told Billy I would call him when I was ready and ask him to meet with me. I wanted to hear what he had to say to me in person.

My father was constantly on my mind. I couldn't stop thinking of the phone calls. I kept replaying the short conversations in my head. Even as I sat at work, I prayed for him. On Friday, the 26th, I had a small break at work. My students were in P.E. and I was all alone. I sat there doing what I seemed to constantly do. I sat there praying for my father. As I was praying, I started feeling like I had failed. I felt like I had ran out of time and not completed a mission I was to complete. I felt my heart begin to break. I knew that I was supposed to lead my father to Christ but I had been too afraid. I wanted him saved. I wanted him to know the Lord. I laid my head on my desk and began to weep. Through the tears, I began to pour my heart to the Lord. I wept and prayed, "Lord, I am so sorry that I was scared. Please forgive me, God, for not telling my father about you. Lord, I forgive him. I pray though that you would forgive him. I pray that you would take him and make him whole. I pray that you would not punish him for what he did to me but that you would wash his sins away with your amazing love. I pray that the blood you shed for us would wash him clean. Lord, speak him tonight as he lays down to sleep. Please save him. Please show yourself to him. I want you to show him your love. I pray that you would speak to him like you did me. Lord, save his soul tonight. God, lead him to you and help him give his life to you. And Lord, (long pause) once you save him, if he would ever turn his back on you in the future or change his mind, I pray that you would take his life."

My heart seemed to stop as I prayed that last part. I don't believe I have ever prayed that before about anyone. I knew my prayer was scary but I was desperate. I wanted my father to know God. I wanted him to know what love was. I also wanted my father to spend eternity with the Lord. I knew that I was probably never going to pray a prayer like that again. The tears were flowing down my cheeks and onto my desk as my students walked in. I composed myself and finished up the day.

The next day was the zoo trip. Amie messaged me that she was on the way and we left our house to meet them. My family was so excited to see the restoration that God was doing. My children had missed their friends very much. Our children were best friends and hadn't seen each other in a couple years. I was expecting Billy to be on edge and a little cranky but he wasn't. Billy was telling jokes with the kids and having fun on the trip. I was shocked by the peace that we had. As we drove, I began praying for my father. I decided that if he called again, I would ask him to meet with me. I wanted to allow God to use me. I would no longer ignore his calls. We entered the zoo and met with Amie and her family. Both of our families hugged each other and compared each other to see how much each of them had grown. This day would be the day that put our families back together the way that he intended. We began walking around the zoo and looking at the animals. We were walking for about 15 minutes when my phone rang. As I looked at my phone, my face lit up. It was my father calling. I looked at Billy and told him to say a quick prayer because I was going to be brave. I answered the phone the way he would. I answered and said. "Whatcha doin'?" The voice on the other end stopped me in my tracks. It was mother instead of my father and she sounded terrified. I froze as time seemed to stand still. It felt like several minutes past as I waited for her to say something.

"Donna. Donna. Are you sitting down?"

I felt my world rip apart. I knew. I knew it was about my father. I practically yelled, "What's wrong?"

My mother began crying, "It's your dad. He was just killed in an accident. I am on the way to him now. Donna, he is gone."

It seemed like someone else screamed out of me. A loud "No" bellowed out from deep in me. I couldn't believe this was happening. "This can't end like this!" I shouted. I couldn't seem to compose myself. I started shaking and screaming. I soon found myself gasping for air. I was supposed to meet with him. I was supposed to talk to him. I was answering the phone to tell him I was ready to hear what he wanted to tell me. I was ready but now my time was up. I was too late. I would never get to talk to him now.

Billy had our family and Amie's family pray over me. After praying, Billy told me that I needed to understand that God was fixing things in my life and I needed to be okay. He wanted us to stay at the zoo and allow our families to spend the day together. Our families were healed that day. Our friendship was restore. Billy's heart was soften and he enjoyed seeing God work in Amie and John. We could all see God was with us. God healed hearts that day. God answered my prayers. That day, He even answered the scary ones.

The next few days were hard. I couldn't understand why God told me that I would lead him to Christ but take him before I did. As I prayed, I felt that God told me that I did lead my father to Christ. I felt that God showed me that I led him to the father through my forgiveness and prayers. God showed me a vision of my father late at night looking at every post I ever made on Facebook. He reminded of my prayer the day before he died. God assured me that he answered my prayer. The Lord told me that my father was wanting to tell me that he was sorry. You see, my father didn't feel forgiven until he could ask forgiveness from me. The thing that he wanted to tell me was an apology. My father had found the Lord. My father was saved and that is why the Lord took him.

The next couple days, I searched through photos and talked to family. I saw pictures of my father at tea parties with his grandbabies. I saw this grown man with nail polish on and playing with baby dolls. My mother talked about how he had become a gentle man. She told me stories about late nights when he would brush her hair or rub her feet. I heard stories about a man that I couldn't imagine. This man was a good husband and an amazing grandpa after he got home from prison. My father had a different heart. He hadn't even drank an alcoholic beverage for years. Everyone around him spoke of what a different man he was. He truly had changed his life. After learning all of this, I knew that I had to speak at the funeral. I had spent many years afraid but that was all gone. God had changed him like he did me. I prayed about what I would stand and say. I knew that my family didn't believe what my father had done to me. They all knew that he was a very mean man when I was younger but couldn't imagine him being a child molester. My family would never want me to speak at the funeral. I would have to be bold.

The day before the funeral, my brother's wife called me. She explained to me that the funeral might have to be postponed. The family couldn't come up with the money for the funeral or even a down payment. I prayed and felt that I had to do it. I called the funeral home and set up the payment arrangements. We set up monthly payments and agreed upon the terms. I would pay every month until the service was pay for. This man was my father. I had to show that love trumped evil. I had to be like Jesus. I wanted to do what God would want. The thoughts my mind had were hard to control. I couldn't believe that I was allowing myself to go through with this. It hurt so bad and seemed to burn deep inside of me but I knew that I had to do it. I had to be love.

The next morning, I sat down and wrote what I would say. The more I wrote, the more my heart had peace. The more I wrote, the more love I had for this man. I had forgiven a long time ago but this was different. I found myself no longer being angry at the past. When I finished, I loved him. I loved the man I knew he had become. I knew that God had answered my prayers and saved him. I was confident that I would one day see him in heaven and that made me happy. I wanted to spend eternity worshipping the Lord with him.

On October 2, I walked into the funeral home for the service of my father. People starred, pointed, and rolled their eyes as I entered. I picked up a copy of the obituary and read over it. As I read, the reality of the day became more real. I turned the card over to see that I was listed last as his child. I was oldest yet listed last as if they wished I wasn't listed at all. My husband and children weren't even mentioned at all. I was standing in the midst of people who didn't want me. I walked to the front to find two large poster boards filled with memories. There were many of my brother and sister and their children. There was only 2 pictures of me and they were in the family pictures of all of us when I was about 8. There was not one picture of my children on their. It was almost as if I had died years ago or just no longer existed. I seriously wanted to just leave.

The service started and my Sister-in-law and sister spoke. I was the last one to speak. I was threatened not to mention God or anything of that sort or they would stop the service. My brother and his wife claim to be atheist. I prayed and took the microphone. I tried my best not to look at the people clinching their teeth or rolling their eyes at me. Some people just simply got up and walked out. I silently prayed God would speak though me and then I began my speech:

"I know that many of you are shocked to see me up here. Trust me when I say, so am I. Today day is the day that we say goodbye to my dad, Big Jim. It is no secret that I have not spent time with him in many years. But the last few weeks, my dad changed my life. Phone call after phone call my heart began to melt for him. He was no longer the man I grew up with. His voice was no longer mean and demanding but soft and kind. He only wanted to check on me and his grandkids. This new man was one that now brushed my mother's hair when she was tired after work. This man was just one of the princesses in the kingdom of his grand-daughters. He was now also the king of tea parties and played baby dolls. This man was now a soft snuggly teddy bear. This man loved his wife, children, grandchildren, and rest of his family. This man's heart was different from the man I once knew.

You see this man gave his heart to Jesus Christ. God gave him a sweet kind heart. I came here today to not say goodbye to my dad but just to say that I will see him later.

It is written...

"Let not your heart be troubled; you believe in God, believe also in Me. In My Father's house are many mansions; if it were not so, I would have told you. I go to prepare a place for you. And if I go and prepare a place for you, I will come again and receive you to Myself; that where I am, there you may be also. And where I go you know, and the way you know." Thomas said to Him, "Lord, we do not know where You are going, and how can we know the way?" Jesus said to him, "I am the way, the truth, and the life. No one comes to the Father except through Me."

John 14:1-6

Many of us here can tell stories of the younger years of my father verses the way he was now. There is no way to not see how different he was.

Allowing God to be your savior is not a crutch. It takes a strong person to put your life in the hands of the Lord but if Big Jim, my dad, can, so can we.

If you can't say that you know you will be in that mansion someday, repent. We all are sinners. Ask Jesus Christ to be your Lord and Savior. Allow Him to have a relationship with you and guide you through this life and into the next.

I hate religion but this isn't a religious thing. It is a relationship with a God who wants to know you and spend eternity with you. Allow God to change your life and your heart. He changed mine and my dad's and he can be there for you too.

So, now it is time to say what I have come to say. I love you Daddy. I will see you when I get there."

As I sat down, my life changed. I felt like I was a new person. I truly had been given a new heart. Forgiving him really was worth it. God had brought me through so much but I made it through. I walked out of there and people began to talk to me. They talked about what a changed man my father was. They spoke about how often my father spoke about me. Everyone close to him knew why he had been calling me. He wanted to make amends and schedule Thanksgiving dinner for our whole family. He wanted to tell me how he was different and how he wanted to be part of my life. He wanted to tell me how proud he was of the woman I became. He was calling because he wanted to be my dad. He loved me. He died loving me.

The Lord has filled in every crack now. My heart is happy and healed. I have finally found my "happily ever after". Every day has been one blessing after another. I love Billy more than I can ever explain. I love being his wife and the mother of his children. If you can keep a secret, I will tell you one more thing…. I also love making love to him. I can truly say I give all of me to him every time! My children are all happy and healthy and serving God with all their hearts. They are so thankful for the story we have and how we get to help others. Amie's family and mine are friends and they are serving the Lord. God answered ALL of my prayers. My father even got his final wishes. I spent Thanksgiving at my house with my mother, brother, sister and their families. My family was altogether like my father wanted. The Lord restored my family and allowed me to be whole. God truly has given me everything I could ever need and more than I ever wanted.

The Japanese people believe a vessel is more valuable if it has been cracked and filled with gold. They say that it makes the vessel beautiful because it has "scars" that tell a story. They believe that these cracks should be displayed instead of hidden. These vessels are said to be stronger because of the filled cracks. Vessels who have been cracks are used with honor. The Lord, my potter, took this vessel from broken to beautiful. Now, it's your turn! Hop up on the potter's wheel and let Him take you for a spin! If you trust Him, it may hurt for a moment but He will heal you everywhere you hurt. I promise, if you allow Him to, He will mold you and you will never be the same. With God as your potter...... you will go from BROKEN to BEAUTIFUL!

Made in the USA
Monee, IL
23 July 2022

10205967R00163